TRAINING STRATEGIES for DRESSAGE RIDERS

2nd Edition

CHARLES DE KUNFFY

HOWELL
BOOK
HOUSE

Howell Book House

Published by Wiley Publishing, Inc., New York, NY

No part of this publication may be reproduced, stored in a retrieval system or transmitted in any form or by any means, electronic, mechanical, photocopying, recording, scanning or otherwise, except as permitted under Sections 107 or 108 of the 1976 United States Copyright Act, without either the prior written permission of the Publisher, or authorization through payment of the appropriate per-copy fee to the Copyright Clearance Center, 222 Rosewood Drive, Danvers, MA 01923, (978) 750-8400, fax (978) 646-8700. Requests to the Publisher for permission should be addressed to the Legal Department, Wiley Publishing, Inc., 10475 Crosspoint Blvd., Indianapolis, IN 46256, (317) 572-3447, fax (317) 572-4447, E-Mail: permcoordinator@wiley.com.

Trademarks: Wiley, the Wiley Publishing logo, and Howell Book House are trademarks or registered trademarks of Wiley Publishing, Inc., in the United States and other countries, and may not be used without written permission. All other trademarks are the property of their respective owners. Wiley Publishing, Inc., is not associated with any product or vendor mentioned in this book.

Limit of Liability/Disclaimer of Warranty: While the publisher and author have used their best efforts in preparing this book, they make no representations or warranties with respect to the accuracy or completeness of the contents of this book and specifically disclaim any implied warranties of merchantability or fitness for a particular purpose. No warranty may be created or extended by sales representatives or written sales materials. The advice and strategies contained herein may not be suitable for your situation. You should consult with a professional where appropriate. Neither the publisher nor author shall be liable for any loss of profit or any other commercial damages, including but not limited to special, incidental, consequential, or other damages.

For general information on our other products and services or to obtain technical support please contact our Customer Care Department within the U.S. at 800-762-2974, outside the U.S. at 317-572-3993 or fax 317-572-4002.

Wiley also publishes its books in a variety of electronic formats. Some content that appears in print may not be available in electronic books.

Library of Congress Cataloging-in-Publication Data:

De Kunffy, Charles
    Training strategies for dressage riders / Charles de Kunffy.
      p. cm.
    Rev. ed. of: Dressage questions answered © 1984.
    Includes index.
    ISBN 0-7645-2637-5
    1. Dressage.   I. De Kunffy, Charles.   Dressage questions answered.
   II. Title.
   SF309.5.D443   1994
   798.2'3—dc20   94-1935
                                                                 CIP

Manufactured in the United States of America

10 9 8 7 6 5 4 3 2 1

2nd Edition

Diagrams by Barbara Leistico
Book design by Laura Hammond Hough
Cover design by Wendy Mount

Contents

ALSO BY CHARLES DE KUNFFY

Dressage Questions Answered
Creative Horsemanship
The Athletic Development of the Dressage Horse
The Ethics and Passions of Dressage

Acknowledgments

This volume represents my most comprehensive writing on horsemanship. It was written over a long period of time. Some parts of it are highly theoretical and even abstract, while others are detailed and highly specific. As always, I can thank my students, who inspired me to write it.

My gratitude to those who contributed photographs is enormous. Few readers may know how difficult it is to receive for publication good photographs, taken expertly by the finest photographers. Riders are also modest about displaying in a publication even their excellent, praiseworthy work. Aware of this, I am greatly indebted to all the riders and their photographers.

I am especially thankful to Herr Arthur Kottas-Heldenberg, Chief Rider of the Spanish Riding School in Vienna, for again making available to me his outstanding pictures. He is one of the finest riders in the world and certainly one of the few truly elegant ones. He is very famous, unbelievably hard working, much sought after and greatly admired, which is why having his pictures in this book is an exceptional privilege. My appreciation to him, for having spent his time and energy to produce so many pictures, is great. These pictures, therefore, show that

Herr Kottas-Heldenberg is not only an outstanding rider but also an unusually generous friend.

My greatest appreciation goes to two friends who selflessly have given much more of their time, energies and indispensable editorial insights than would be required.

Mrs. Madelyn Larsen, Senior Editor, made this volume possible by encouraging its publication, devotedly and knowledgeably editing its contents and giving it its final form. Her expert work was constantly amended by her sustained willingness to accommodate all my many wishes and to tolerate my frequent calling for advice. I remain in awe of her cheerfulness and caring.

Richard Williams contributed photographs he took and also expert editing. I find writing easy but regard editing as excruciating work. For one must, in editing, reread one's own words and respond to them critically. Because my mind created what is in the book, I cannot find fault with it and detect shortcomings. So when I edit, my eyes read, my mind blindly approves and nothing suffers from correction. Until Richard reads the text. His understanding of my ideas about riding is impeccable. He has studied horsemanship with me most extensively and most consistently among all my students. He can quote me verbatim. He knows what I "mean to say" even if it is poorly stated. His critical faculties and incisive understanding of riding theory made this book a finer one than it could ever have been without his diligence.

Both Mrs. Larsen and Mr. Williams helped to make this book worthy of attention. I am very thankful to them both. Their devotion to horsemanship and their friendship to this author made their important contributions special and very precious to me.

Foreword to the 2nd Edition

As time passes, the riding and training principles I was taught have not changed, and my teaching, training and judging experiences reinforce the thought that they never will. Animated by the desire to pass on to contemporaries and future generations the vast tradition of classical riding and schooling of horses in a succinct and understandable manner, I wrote this book.

This volume was meant to be read as a companion to one of my other books, *The Athletic Development of the Dressage Horse*. In many ways their contents are inseparable. I had not intended them to be volumes one and two of the same work; their contents are widely different. However, they make one another whole.

I have devoted much of my life to assisting riders to improve their equitational skills and to design strategies for training horses. My often-videotaped lessons have recorded that for decades these training and schooling principles have worked for riders and horses, even within the confines of thirty- or forty-five minute lessons.

I am relentless in the hope that I can inspire in my readers the "right spirit" toward horses and riding; that I can also add to their scholarship and foster their "right-mindedness" toward the art of riding and toward their beloved horses.

Horsemanship is a complex science and, when done well, a great art. As a science, it is a matter for the intellect, acquired by scholarship. When practiced on the level of art, it ennobles the spirit and elevates the character.

By writing succinctly, I hope to make the classical principles of riding and horse training eloquent. Without reading and conversing about a great science, we cannot maintain its purity, nor can we hope to display it on an artistically exquisite level.

And, as with all great art, good riding is based on perfecting the necessary skills for the performance of artistic excellence. The contents must determine the form of art. Perfection of skills is the vehicle for artistic display.

When pursued correctly, horsemanship is a great sport that athletically improves both the human and the equine body. Riding correctly enables two vastly different creatures of nature to blend into one, melding their minds, focusing their efforts and, by dissolving into unity, bring into existence a third entity. This entity thrives by the physical powers of the horse and the insights of his rider. Power guided by wisdom, speed tempered by efficiency—thus the great image of the mythological Pegasus is born.

I certainly hope my readers find inspiration and information, guiding them to great riding. But most of all, I want to contribute with these writings to the well-being of all beloved horses.

Charles de Kunffy
2003

Foreword to the 1st Edition

Training Strategies for Dressage Riders is a transmutation of *Dressage Questions Answered,* which I wrote many years ago. Most of its thoughts were written already in the early seventies. In my teachings and lectures these principles appeared even earlier. It took a long time for the contents of it to germinate and grow into book form. In that book, I responded to questions posed to me by my students. Many of these questions were highly specific. By answering them and then sharing these answers with a large number of readers, the original book was born.

With the passage of time, I realized that a more generalized and less specific approach would benefit the general public in understanding classical equitation. Animated by the desire to put something useful before my readers, I decided to prepare a revised edition of *Dressage Questions Answered.*

As soon as I set to work on the revisions, my imagination ran out of control and a flood of new thoughts invaded my mind. As a result, a virtually new book was born. The greatest resemblance this volume has to *Dressage Questions Answered* is the topic they both entertain.

In my mind, this book is a new book. Time and riding and teaching experience have reshaped my thoughts and my ways of conveying them. But the principles I believe in and advocate have not changed. They are not mine; I learned them from my teachers and committed my loyalties to them. However, this new volume dynamically altered my approach to the topics I discuss, the style in which I write, and the organizational arrangements. Most of the photographs are new and the charts and drawings are either new or refurbished. The format of this book makes the information readily accessible to the reader.

I have decided never to reprint *Dressage Questions Answered*. I remain grateful to its readers. It has been well received, quoted, and complimented. This new book is meant to be a companion volume to *The Athletic Development of the Dressage Horse*, which was published in 1992. In that book, I devoted my efforts to assisting riders with the gymnasticizing of their horses. Now, I hope to further those efforts by helping riders with strategies that can improve their equitation and enrich their training plans. Beyond that, and very important to me, is my effort here to inspire in the readers the "right spirit" toward horses and riding and to help foster "right-mindedness" toward the horse and toward equitation.

I believe that horsemanship is a complex science and when done well, a great art. By writing and lecturing about it, I hope to inspire in others an academic attitude toward horsemanship that the subject deserves. Without reading, discussing, thinking, analyzing, and introspection, riding cannot succeed if merely "done by the seat of the pants."

Horsemanship is a science and very much a matter of scholarship and intellect. It is an art, depending deeply on the spirit in which it is practiced and displayed. Practiced correctly, it is a sport that improves athletically both the human and the equine body.

I hope that readers will find meaningful ideas in this book. I hope also that it contributes to the well-being of horses, all of whom I love so much.

One

The Art of Classical Equitation

The number of riders interested in dressage has grown rapidly in recent years, and that is cause for celebration. But many are those who express a desire to know how many kinds of dressage there are. Rampant are the speculations about having at our disposal at least two major attitudes toward dressage from which to choose. This gives us cause to reflect.

CLASSICAL EQUITATION, DRESSAGE: A DEFINITION

Members of the dressage community have begun to notice two different tendencies in dressage, tendencies that seem to conflict with each other. Dressage as an art seems to conflict with dressage as a technique. Taking time to develop a horse seems to conflict with the urge to produce quickly whatever will suffice in a race to meet competition dates and obligations successfully. Elegant competitors with artistic appeal seem to contrast with mechanically obedient, submissive, and boring ones. Slowly progressing idealists seem to contradict the hurried results of competitive practitioners. And all this happens in the name of dressage.

Today many riders are concerned about the future developmental course of dressage.

For maximum results, there is only one correct way of gymnasticizing a horse and that is through a single correct system of strategies that can be practiced by only one kind of equitation, derived from one continuous tradition. The standards of gymnastic training embodied in the dressage tradition were not contrived arbitrarily, nor were they dreamed up by sentimental romantics. What has survived centuries of testing is the sum total of pragmatic equestrian knowledge. Everything was tried, contested, and experimented with. That which worked was retained and that which didn't was discarded.

Classical horsemanship—dressage—is called "classical" because it is enduring. Only that which survives epochs by remaining meaningful in the human experience becomes a classic, classical. Dressage has survived for centuries because it consistently produced desirable results in the development of the majority of horses. In classical dressage, only that which is correct in terms of the horse's development toward his full potential is considered beautiful. Out of the most effective horsemanship emerged the concept of beauty and artistry in dressage. That which functions properly in gymnastic terms, and which is attained without compulsion or force, is inherently awesome and beautiful. A horse moving with beautiful gaits, effortlessly covering ground and happily complying with his rider's inconspicuous aids, displays his own artistry. In short, effective horsemanship is an art!

The mischief is caused by the eternal pitting of man's pragmatic instincts against his moral inclinations. On the one hand are those who are concerned with things as they are, the sociologists; on the other hand are those whose primary concern is with things as they ought to be, the philosophers. Of course, there is always a de facto situation: reality/actuality as it exists without any moral consideration. However, there is always the possiblity of a de jure situation: an ideal possibility that reflects a preference for things as they ought to be rather than as they are.

Ideally, de facto riding should be identical to and representative of de jure dressage. In fact, everyday riding should aim at approximating the ideal as closely as possible. The entire motivational force behind classical horsemanship is to create the gymnastically ideal horse rather than one that maintains the status quo. Indeed, dressage has its own morality and that must be its motivational force, not competition.

Because dressage is a living tradition, it exists only as its current practitioners endorse and demonstrate its ideals. If riders do not emulate dressage ideals, then the art will cease to explain itself in terms of correct results and will ultimately disappear. There will be riding, and that riding may be called "dressage," but the name will not mean more than a semantic facsimile of the great classical tradition. For an art cannot be practiced in name only, rather it must be kept alive by deeds. Classical horsemanship is based on love for the horse; it is not practiced for the glorification of the rider. According to Erich Fromm, foremost among psychiatrist-philosophers, love is the active promotion of the well-being of the love object. In this case, the horse. Then, the equestrian should dedicate himself to the horse's best interests, an attitude that logically leads to a commitment to develop the horse to his full, natural potential. To do this painlessly, gradually, and naturally is to practice dressage, which then becomes an expression of loving devotion. That which falls short of such an expression is dressage in name only.

To be an equestrian in the classical sense is not just to be a rider. It is a position in life. It is a stance we take in relation to life. We must make a choice between self-love, the promotion of the well-being of our own ego, and love for the horse. That is the fundamental attitudinal decision that earned Xenophon the title Father of Classical Dressage: he dared to love a horse!

If riding that aims at the promotion of classical dressage principles fails to be victorious in competition, it is merely a temporary defeat. Eventually, that which is correct will be discovered to be good, and in the long run, it will succeed. After all, in riding, it is not the fleeting glory of the ribbon but the enduring thrill of a well-trained horse that yields the true reward. The ways of any art form are slow, but those of the equestrian art are slowest. But through its gradual pace comes enduring validity, and that which endures is, once again, classical and representative of the finest in our tradition.

The English philosopher Jeremy Bentham suggested that the society that produces the greatest good for the greatest number of people is the best society. This principle is analogous to classical horsemanship. Only the techniques and methods that endured consistently produced the greatest good for the greatest number of horses. Bentham also defined "good" on the minimum level as the absence of pain and on the maximum level as active happiness. This definition should suffice for us when we seek to know how we should treat and train our horses. Not only physically induced pain such as the pain caused by a rider's bad hands, but also mental anguish created by speedy "riding technology" can produce an unhappy horse. The horse that is happy is a giver. Unless you can tell stories about what your horse is doing for you, there is not much in the way of happiness to report.

Riders who are unsure of their art need the reassurance of a ribbon. Those riders who are secure in their art accept a ribbon on behalf of their horse occasionally as an honor rather than a proof. The rider who knows what is right because he feels it does not need a judge to verify it for him, nor a ribbon to show to posterity. His reward is in having achieved something that goes on between himself and the horse, something he feels and therefore knows. The improvement of the horse is its own reward. Secure riders would never exchange the thrill of improving a horse for a ribbon. For such riders are interested in more than scoring, they are primarily interested in "playing the game."

The difference between civilized and barbaric behavior is in the difference between compassion, a combination of empathy, forgiveness, and compulsion. Classical horsemanship is compassionate; classical horsemanship is civilized. Where there is brutal or barbaric riding, there is no representation of dressage. Historically, civilization evolves when there is a surplus of the mundane, when everyday needs are more than adequately met, they are well met. Analogously, proper riding is a civilized luxury that evolves only when the hunger for the "bread and butter" successes in terms of the rider's ego has been satisfied. The luxury of civilized riding in that success is measured in terms of the horse, not the rider. Is the horse happy?

Haste is the enemy of any art. Michelangelo took his time with his art until the Pope who commissioned it died and left the bills to his successor. An artist can only be told what he must accomplish; he cannot be given a deadline by which he must accomplish it. The street artist who promises a portrait in five minutes reveals a great deal about himself. So does the rider who quickly "makes" a third-level horse. Competition forces the meeting of deadlines and contesting involves the ego. Deadlines and ego involvement encourage haste, the enemy of quality. They also encourage forced rather than natural development. For centuries, multitudes found it important to travel long distances to marvel at Michelangelo's creations. They came away inspired. Today, we need equestrians to whom we might make pilgrimages in the hope of gaining inspiration.

It is known that of all the people who have lived during the last million years, more than half are alive right now. Thus, the total of the present human experience, that being experienced simultaneously by all of us now alive, is greater than the sum total of the life experiences of all our predecessors. Speculation about the equestrian implications of these statistics suggests that all current equestrian experience exceeds the equestrian experience of the entire past. It is wiser, however, to surrender to the speculation that in the past, the quantitative equestrian experience was far greater than it is today, when the horse is no longer a utilitarian animal. Horses are no longer the means of transportation and the substitute for muscle they once were. The half of humanity that has gone before us, however, produced a narrow stratum of practitioners with equestrian wisdom known to us as the classical heritage of dressage. It has endured by its virtue, not by compulsion; therefore, it is good. As the half of humanity that is now alive rides simply for the sake of riding rather than for any utilitarian purpose, we should hope to contribute to the wisdom of dressage at least as much as our predecessors did. If we are to live up to the heritage they left us, our simultaneous performance should at least equal their cumulative one.

Fortunately, a boom is on! However, as in all booms, there will be many losers and a few winners. Those who think there is more than one type of dressage will be the losers. They will lose out on knowing the intoxication of having been a part of an art both as its creator and as one created by it, both as a participant in it and as an inducer of it. For in classical riding, the unit of horse and rider is both maker and made, both subject and object of the art.

DRESSAGE AS AN ART

I am convinced that when practiced at the highest degree of expertise and inspiration, riding is an art. I do not necessarily expect agreement on this issue, for riding as art sounds terribly exclusive, unavailable, and therefore pretentious to some. Well, all art is, by definition, exclusive, as is all excellence. Thus, one ought merely to build up tolerance, even respect, for that which is better than average and therefore unattainable by the majority.

All art is based on the knowledge of its traditions and history, and a full mastery of its techniques as well as the use of its tools. Riding, as an art, is no different. Riding, even on the level of great mastery, is still just a skill. Art is based on, yet goes beyond, these skills. The rider who has only skills is a sportsman and might feel that calling riding an art is either pretentious or offensive.

Many outstanding competitors are well skilled sportsmen. Fewer are artists, and so it should be. The craftsmanship of riding, the equestrian sport, is infatuating and often irresistible. Its pursuit is often seen in the show rings and at competitions. The art of riding is sometimes resplendently displayed in the competition arena but, being sufficient unto itself, is more often part of the everyday existence of its masters.

Observe, if you will, a horse and his rider, combined into one harmonious unit, oblivious of their surroundings. Both horse and rider seem to be in a daze or in a state of meditation, attuned to something the spectator cannot detect. They are joined in a limitless harmony without being obviously aware of each other. They appear attuned solely to an outside third force, an inspiration, that brought them together. The pair has beauty, for its energy and force are greater than human, greater than equine.

There is the art of riding! When it is seen at a show, one can hear spectators comment on the horse doing the program by himself, as if by memory. The foundation of that art is total harmony. All skills, techniques, and knowledge of riding are useless unless they can be effectively employed for the creation of total harmony. All other riding goals are subsidiary to accomplishing harmony with the horse through balance. If one thinks of the elements of riding, whatever they may be—relaxation or impulsion or balance or responsiveness to the aids or attentiveness or engagement or whatever—each element is desirable for its contribution to the ultimate establishment of harmony. Nothing is recommended in riding that destroys harmony and all that promotes it is strongly urged.

The skills that contribute to and promote harmony are many. They can be taught to riders. However, the sensitivity to and awareness of harmony, and the desire for it, cannot be taught, merely inspired in others. To some people, the most natural state of existence is a quarrel. To others, the favored state may be a stupor of some sort, while for another it may be playful frivolity. But there are those who understand and seek harmony and live by its ethics, and they naturally gravitate toward those efforts in riding that lead to total harmony, and thus the art of horsemanship.

Harmony has its physical bases. Those riders who have "feel," that mysterious and oft-mentioned but seldom explained concept, are well on their way toward the art of riding. "Feel" is predominantly an ability to physically seek harmony through the most accommodating position of togetherness. That is why some riders with feel may not sit as properly or elegantly as a competitor in the Olympic Games but may certainly make the horse happy. With delight, one can often see talented young riders with improper skills: mushy abdomen, rounded shoulders, lacking style. In spite of this, they may be delightfully harmonious companions on their horses' backs. The "natural" rider always keeps his center of gravity together with that of the horse, enjoys the energy that carries that center boldly forward, enjoys obedience from the horse by cajoling it and keeping things smooth. That is why their horses appear very rhythmic, for wherever their balance may be, they do not lose rhythm. The rider's and horse's centers of gravity are merged in harmony.

Riding is a creative art to the extent that it creates and re-creates its own artistic subject, the gymnastic horse. But it is also a performing art, and when the human mind effortlessly animates the horse's body during a performance, the art creates its own moment of beauty. The artistic statement is made by harmony obvious even to the beholder, and anything disrupting it shatters the moment. That is why a performance of high quality is breathless and flows seamlessly. If it is well done, a dressage test does not appear laced together from different movements but rather one continuous statement consistent in philosophy, feeling, and existence.

No art is mindless. It has been said that the intelligent, the very bright, person is a "genius," an artist. No, not necessarily! Intelligence helps, for the skills on which art is based need intelligent application. Its acquisition is also based on intelligence. But, beyond that, sensitivity and insight are the more important determinants of an artistic effort.

There comes a day, and later on perhaps every day, when one feels that one loses the awareness of skills. We become unaware of ourselves, become oblivious to our aids and whatever the limbs, torso, and musculature are doing. We become absorbed in an effort that seems independent of the senses and so thoroughly effortless that it suggests a feeling of being in a dream where we can ride for the first time without awareness of effort. When we no longer feel busy, we have entered the artistic experience. And there we find the motion, the flight, the suspension that eluded us before but now begins to flow almost in spite of ourselves.

Often, insruction spoils the chance for the artistic experience of the rider. Instruction, indispensable for the teaching of riding skills, is no longer necessary during the artistic effort. As in painting, once the artist has learned to use the tools of the craft from his master, he no longer finds use for the overseer. Establishing his own "art studio," he seeks solitude and immersion in his own thoughts, inspirations, and feelings.

The artistic rider is often disturbed, annoyed, disrupted by instruction. Important things happen during silence. Thus, when a rider is tuned to the chattering of his coach, he is not fully attending to communication with his horse. Therefore, in artistic riding, silence is essential. When the rider succeeds in harmony, it is not done verbally but as a multidimensional effort.

I had to discuss all this, but not for those who do not understand what I am writing about, because they may not have had substantiating experiences. I am trying to reach those who felt lonesome with their artistic experiences. For them, let there be reassurance in knowing that in the art of riding resides the true meaning of the effort and that there is good company for them to seek.

This beautiful Hanoverian stallion is Wertherson by Werther out of St. Pr. St. Walesca. With both people and horses, facial expression reveals the inner nature. In this case, the expression is that of an alert, intelligent, and kind horse. For horses, function defines physical beauty. His splendid conformation makes him appear awesome and suggests the power and swiftness that have been part of the horse's age-old attraction to mankind.

Photo: Cappy Jackson.

THE HORSE AS OUR PARTNER,
NOT A BEAST OF BURDEN

By nature, the horse is an animal that should not and cannot carry anyone easily. He is not an animal of burden. Examination of the horse's musculature and skeleton reveals that he should not have anything on his back at all, presuming that we want to keep him healthy, happy, and moving beautifully. He is much more suited to pulling, because his motive force derives solely from the hindquarters. Most of the horse's weight is in front of, not on top of the hindquarters, so the forehand serves as a crutch to support the weight. Humans, whose legs support all their weight and provide all the locomotion, are capable of moving easily and gracefully. By pushing a heavy wheelbarrow or a hand plow one can simulate the horse's problem: pushing the greater part of his weight from behind. So the horse's natural tendency is to put his weight on the forehand and push it by a kicking motion against the ground, catapulting himself forward with as much speed as possible. The Thoroughbred on the racetrack most approximates the activity for which the horse was really made.

When one hitches a carriage or buggy behind a horse, he is not unhappy, because his weak joints are not taxed by any burden on top of him, and he can thrust his weight forward to pull a light and reasonably mobile item. The haunches, the source of locomotion, are then at the center of the entire moving system, making the horse's task easy. But a horse lacks structural strength to carry additional weight on his back. Yet, we make him do that every time we ride. We not only expect him to live happily ever after, but, in addition, optimistically expect him not to break down. We also expect him to move well, even better than nature would inspire him to move. This is a tremendous challenge for the rider. We must set about it properly, because if we make a mistake anywhere, we can damage the horse's musculature and joints. The horse's haunches include four joints: hip, stifle, hock, and fetlock. In order for the horse to propel himself with the foreign weight of a rider and equipment without damaging his joints, we must develop him gymnastically. This idea is analogous to the development of a human gymnast. What does a gymnast do to look so fabulously coordinated and so beautiful in motion? A gymnast has developed his joints and musculature properly, so that with minimum effort and strain and maximum efficiency, he can gracefully perform movements that depend on incredible power. Similarly, the goal of our equine gymnastics (dressage) is to develop the kind of gymnast that can maximize his floating suspension above the ground with minimum effort and utmost grace. This is the goal that we pursue.

In order to develop muscular strength and elasticity and supple joints, we must exercise the horse with very carefully designed, progressive, gymnastic exercises. If it is not appropriate and progressive, however, the "training" will break down part or all of the horse's locomotion system. A horse stressed by incompetent training might tie up or develop azoturia. A horse's muscle tissue can easily break down or be torn. In the human realm, look at a laborer. In the course of a day, he will work at least as hard as, if not more than, most athletes do in the course of heavy training. Yet, he seldom possesses the full, finely sculpted body of the gymnast, nor does he move with the gymnast's elegance and grace. Instead, he often appears broken down, even emaciated. Because a laborer does not develop his body properly and systematically, he does not have coordinated grace. But a trained gymnast who works out eight hours daily will look beautiful. His musculature will develop in the right places, and he will coordinate and move with elegant posture and brilliance. Both the gymnast and the laborer may work the same number of hours and sweat equally, yet one becomes a beautiful human, and the other can become a broken person.

The rider, as trainer, will determine which direction the horse's development will take. Working a horse the wrong way will ruin him and make him a prematurely aged, stiff, broken-down unhappy creature living in pain. For instance, this is why it is important to understand that the hock is a smaller joint than the human knee. The human knee carries only one hundred to two hundred pounds, yet it is a common site of arthritis, pain, and swelling. It is predisposed to injury. The horse's hock carries from one thousand to fifteen hundred pounds! And in the trot and canter, gaits with moments of suspension, the force absorbed is even greater than fifteen hundred pounds; added to it is the kinetic energy of descent and the considerable force exerted by the horse in his propulsive thrust. And if the hock absorbs the impact the wrong way and is not developed to carry the burden with elastic flexion, that hock will defend itself against pain and injury. The joint will build up tissue and cartilage that will be very painful and eventually, of course, thicken the inner tissues just like regular outer tissue. This is why we see horses with a "hitching hock." These horses move with unlevel strides, with one hind leg moving shorter than the other. Performing an impure gait does not mean that a horse is clinically lame, nor would a competition judge eliminate him. The problem is called "rein lameness" because it is induced by the rider using his hands rudely or unknowledgeably. If pressure on the horse's jaw is sustained for a long time, he must eventually oppose that pressure. Nature gave the horse neck muscles of a certain length and they need to be carried in a comfortable stretch in order to remain relaxed. If the rider, for any reason, tries to compress the neck, it will hurt the horse, like tight shoes hurt our feet. The horse will bid his entire, strong neck musculature against the rider's hands. Pulling on the bit will make the horse's jaw stiff. He will open it in an attempt to release the offending pressure. Since a bad hand pulls back even on a gaping jaw, the horse has no alternative but to bid his strong neck muscles against the pulling arm. It takes two to pull! The horse stiffens and pulls in an effort to save his hocks from the whiplash that results from the tug of war in front. If a rider engages in a pulling contest, the horse will stress his joints by kicking against the ground with defiant force as he fights the torturous pain in his mouth and neck. He eventually will break down either one or both hocks, depending on one- or two-handed pulling by the rider.

Other undesirable results can develop from work on the so-called "light hacking rein," or working with dropped, loose reins. One can be quite rude with the hands (intentionally or unintentionally) when riding with a dropped rein, on the buckle. For example, when riding this way during a transition or a turn, taking up the loose rein suddenly can give a strong yank or rip at the horse's jaw. At that moment, the horse becomes alarmed and whiplashes back on the hock, a painful jolt against which nature builds up arthritic tissue. So whether it is a perpetually pulling hand or an occasionally rough, abrupt hand, one must realize that every time one does so, the horse's useful life is shortened.

The requirement is to leave the horse's mouth unridden. A possible cause for overzealous hands is that human beings are a visually and manually oriented species. We always want to see what we are doing. And the only immediately visible and manually controllable area of the horse seems to be his neck and head. Riders are so mesmerized by the beauty, agility, and power of that neck that they are tempted to dominate it. This is one reason riders "move into" the horse's head and take up residence there. Heavy-handedness also results from the too-much, too-soon method: when the rider is allowed to handle the reins before he has an independent, relaxed, and balanced seat. Traditionally, the rider is lunged up to eighteen months until he has a perfectly independent, balanced seat without any gripping or slipping. Only deep-seated riders should be allowed to control the horse on their own. He who lacks this secure seat will find himself in a vicious circle of losing balance and being frightened of falling. Seeking support, like grabbing for the rail on a listing ship, one seeks a handle to grasp. What can the hand grasp when losing one's balance on horseback? The reins! With each attempt to regain balance through the hands, one only makes the horse move clumsily and out of balance, in pain and panic. Also ruining his joints and musculature, one prohibits any progress toward a more brilliant future. An educational effort should be made so that riders could understand how to start, to invest the time to learn to sit properly in the correct balance and the correct relaxation, so that their hands are independent of their seats. A deep seat should make riders' legs independent and available for aiding.

Equitation is a sport of slow development and it is rewarding because we can pursue it into old age. Once we have developed independent and skilled legs, we can address the control of the horse's hindquarters. From then on, there can be riding for the horse's sake.

Wertherson is ridden here by Fred Weber, training in Frederick, Maryland. This close-up reveals the horse's longtiudinal flexion combined with lateral bending to the left. The precision and correctness of this flexion combined with bending is at the heart of the ideal of utter straightness and the ability to load the two hind legs evenly. Anyone who can keep a horse this properly flexed to the bit and this continuously bent at the same time creates the conditions in which engagement fosters suppleness.

Notice the similarly meditative expressions of both horse and rider, whose expressions also share trust, thoughtful tranquillity, and a sense of contentment. The good things in this picture, incidentally, have a lot to do with important details, such as a steady, even, and light rein contact and the importance of bending the horse with the rider's outside leg back and thereby controlling the haunches. Photo: Cappy Jackson.

A BRIEF OVERVIEW OF DRESSAGE

"Dressage" is a French word we continue to use, for lack of a suitable English equivalent, in connection with the improvement of a horse. It is a word denoting more than training. Rather, a total improvement of the horse is implied, both mental and physical. It means something qualitatively different from education, for it is a more intimate and less formalized method. Increasing numbers of equestrians are now riding their horses according to classical dressage principles.

In the past, horses were the most useful of our partners and the knowledge of horses and their effective training have been an all-important aspect of human existence. Horses were beasts of burden, extensions and enlargements of our muscle power and energy. For centuries, horses were the fastest means of transportation, both civilian and military, which made them as important as jets are in our day.

Dressage has a written tradition, which can be traced back over two thousand years to the writings of Xenophon, a Greek general. Over the millennia, as a consequence of the importance of the horse, every conceivable training method has been tried and that which succeeded in improving the horse has been retained. Since neither the physique nor the mentality of either horse or rider has changed substantially throughout the ages, the traditional principles of dressage remain relevant today.

While the utilitarian value of the horse has declined, its value in sports has increased, as we find ourselves reluctant to give up contact with nature and abandon such fine companions. To accept traditional principles in the art of riding calls for a degree of wisdom and humility, because we are part of a culture that experiences technological changes so rapid and dazzling that we tend to think that our forefathers were primitives in most endeavors and that nothing endures. Also, we are constantly encouraged to believe that change is synonymous with improvement, for, indeed, in technology, only that which is an improvement warrants change. But when it comes to the art of riding, we must remain scrupulously relevant and not allow ourselves to believe that principles applicable to technology are also applicable to riding. No tradition that developed over millennia should be discarded.

I am not advocating rigidity, however. We all know that any art form relies heavily on innovation, ingenuity, resourcefulness, and creativity. Good dressage riders possess and use these attributes. However, they must be used within the general boundaries of the well-formulated classical principles of dressage, those principles that have ensured equestrian success in living practice for centuries.

THE THREE BASIC, INTERRELATED MEANINGS OF "DRESSAGE"

Dressage, in general, is horsemanship that is based on love and respect for horses. It is aimed at the improvement of the horse's natural abilities to fulfill his ultimate potential. It results in a happy horse that usually lives longer, stays healthier, and performs better and for a longer time than one not dressaged. The method of dressage includes only natural means for the development of the horse. It is based on commitment to the education of the horse. Therefore, it is based on mutual understanding, respect, and trust between horse and rider. It is based on kindness and reward rather than punishment, and it excludes the use of force.

More specifically, dressage refers also to the logical, natural, sequential exercising of the horse in order to improve his natural physical and mental abilities. When we use the concept of dressage in this way, we often call it "gymnasticizing." The systematic gymnasticizing of the horse will result in a development similar to that occurring in human gymnasts, figure skaters, or ballet dancers. While their muscles and joints are improving in strength and their abilities to use this energy with control also improve, they become supple. A supple body manifests itself as the harmonious, controlled use of an extremely strong and well-developed musculature. It enables the body to expend a great deal of energy with comfort. It makes possible maximum performance with minimum effort. As the joints and musculature are being used correctly for the performance of a task, exhaustion is eradicated, physical and mental stress is reduced.

Finally, dressage denotes a special kind of competition.

Dressage competition is simply based on the showing of a horse in a flat arena of prescribed size in which the horse is ridden through logical gymnastic exercises. Dressage competition movements are based on meaningful daily gymnastic exercises, the only difference being that these gymnastics are performed in a prescribed area and proceed according to a well-designed, logical program. Depending on the horse's advancement, he can be shown at different gymnastic levels.

Ideally, horses that are shown in dressage have been trained according to general dressage principles of the classical riding tradition. They show the results of daily gymnastic work.

THE GOALS OF DAILY GYMNASTIC DRESSAGE EXERCISES

Physically, the horse should be strengthened and balanced in order to increase his impulsion. As a result of impulsion, the horse should be able to carry himself and his rider forward with even strides of great expression and strength. The ultimate goal is to balance the horse so that he can carry the majority of the combined weight of himself and his rider as much on the hind legs as possible—in other words, collected and "seated."

The horse must improve his suppleness, his ability to bend his joints. The ultimate goal of suppleness is a horse that flexes his joints in greater strength and articulation in order to move on very small arcs in balance and carry himself above the ground in increased suspension. Suspension refers to the moments when all of the legs of the horse are in the air. A supple horse suspends so powerfully and easily that he seems to float and his feet touch the ground only for brief instances. Finally, the horse must move evenly and in good rhythm in all natural gaits.

Mentally, the horse should become obedient to his rider through trust based on cooperation and consistent communication of guidance. The rider must represent reason, logic, and kindness to his horse. The horse's attentiveness should improve with training. Without an increased attention span, as well as an improved sensitivity, a horse cannot accommodate the ever more refined communications of the rider's aids. Nor can he improve his facility in self-awareness, required by the more sophisticated gymnastic exercises that are based on coordination.

The horse's physical and mental development take place simultaneously. They reinforce each other and are achieved by systematic, logical, and consistent gymnastic exercises. The development must be gradual, and therefore it is usually slow.

The gymnastic exercises that are useful for a horse include two basic kinds: those that longitudinally flex and/or stretch the horse and those that laterally bend the horse. These will be discussed in detail in later chapters.

A SIMPLE AND LOGICAL OUTLINE FOR DRESSAGE TRAINING

Imagine dumping a huge box of puzzle pieces on the floor. The pieces will be hard to fit together without knowing the final picture. The picture printed on the lid of the box provides the guideline for fitting the pieces of the puzzle together in the most effective and efficient way. I will attempt to give a panoramic picture of dressage in brief, like the top of the puzzle box shows the completed picture. Later, we can look at some of the pieces in detail. By then we should know a little better where the pieces belong in the total picture.

The stages in the horse's development are sequential. One cannot work on a sophisticated movement without having prepared for it by previously accomplishing the "lower" stage preceding it. The horse's daily work as well as his development throughout the years, therefore, is sequential. The developmental stages in horse gymnastics—dressage—grow in sophistication by repetition. Fulfillment of goals satisfactorily met will come by maturation through gymnastic exercises. Consequently, each exercise has its own history, beginning with a rather hesitant, poor-quality performance and maturing toward perfection.

Dressage tests, in fact, are measuring instruments by which the horse's general gymnastic development is evaluated. Scoring of the various movements is done to reflect the developmental sophistication required at each specific testing level. Each movement in a dressage test is reflective of a training idea, which is evaluated by the test. While the entire gymnastic development of the horse is a harmonious, continuous effort, movements in dressage tests are designated to reveal specific details of the general development. Therefore, some movement might predominantly test balance (e.g., flying changes on every stride) while another might test engagement (e.g., pirouette at the canter). Now let us look at the sophisticated stages of development and what observable tendencies they create. The rider must recognize how and when gymnastic development takes place in the horse.

Here is an outline of how every day of riding might be built in a logical sequence and how the days of training, logically spent, will build into years of work based on the same sequence of activities. The following developmental concepts are interdependent and therefore not strictly sequential.

◆ *Relaxation* is the prerequisite of all gymnastic work. The horse should be relaxed in mind (trusting the rider and accepting his aids) and in body (muscles relaxed, joints rotating properly). When a relaxed horse is engaged, he produces longitudinal flexion, a condition often called being "on the bit." Instead, I think that relaxation will result in the horse accepting and therefore being "on the aids." Primarily, this means the acceptance of, or submission to, the forward driving aids of the legs. A horse that submits to the aids will react to the rider's driving leg aids by engaging more—in effect, shifting more weight toward the haunches and increasing flexion in his joints—rather than hurrying! A horse on the aids will maintain a steady tempo while being influenced by the rider's legs to create engagement or bending. A horse that jigs, hurries, and plunges forward when driven by the rider's legs is not relaxed and not "on the aids." Thus, relaxation is manifested most obviously in the longitudinal flexion of a horse that "rounds out" his topline when driven, elevating his back, stepping further under himself with his hind legs, rotating his joints more slowly and lowering his haunches, rather than rushing forward. By "bowing," or longitudinal flexion, the horse develops new kinetic energy for improved impulsion. Just as a bowed whip has stored energy in the form of a spring, the longitudinally flexed horse has "resident energy" that a strung-out, tense horse above the bit does not have. The movement vibrates through the entire body of a flexed horse, as if softly blanketing him, dispersing the impact of his contact with the ground. A horse that is just striding with his legs will be traumatized by his impact on the ground. The relaxed muscles of a flexed horse allow resiliency and liquidity throughout the horse's structure. Therefore, longitudinal flexion is the foundation of all suppling.

In its most primitive form, relaxation depends on the absence of tension and resistance. Over time, however, relaxation will become the substance of all of the more sophisticated developmental stages and will be renamed. In fact, these new, sophisticated manifestations of basic relaxation are the further stages of development. In other words, relaxation, as it becomes sophisticated, is the essence of all progressive stages of development. When the horse is relaxed, flexed, submitting to driving aids, and producing pure and energetic basic gaits, we may work on the next stage of sophistication, which is balance.

Balance of the horse must be cultivated and maintained by the rider because it is what, by placing oneself into the saddle, one most disturbs. Balancing a horse is an ongoing activity that must result in the rider's control of the horse's center of gravity. Just as a tightrope walker continuously adjusts his body to keep his center of gravity perfect and prevent falling, so will a talented rider reorganize himself with every step of the horse's action without making his effort obvious to the observer.

Control of the horse's balance is continuous in three different dimensions.

1. One must control the balance of the horse longitudinally. Preventing running and sluggish denial of activities in the haunches is necessary to keep horses off their forehand.
2. One must also control the horse's balance laterally. Preventing any drifting sideways and any evasions of balanced movement is achieved by shifting the center of gravity toward one or the other shoulder or either of the hips. Any violation of lateral balance will cause uneven strides with front or hind legs and crookedness in the posture of the horse's body.

3. Finally, balancing the horse in his perpendicular dimension addresses the key issue of asking perpetually for increased collection. As the rider succeeds in increasing the horse's ability to carry the composite weight vector of horse and rider more and more toward his haunches, the perpendicular lightness of stride and carriage increases with progress in collection. A taller carriage, lighter forehand, higher swinging strides will improve the balance for lifting the combined center of gravity higher off the ground. Balance in dependent on consistency of rhythm in each gait.

◆ *Balance* is most commonly manifested and achieved with the help of lateral bending throughout the horse's spine without causing a change in tempo. It also manifests itself in transitions with clear demarcation, purity, and grace. A balanced transition is easy to recognize because the last step of the original gait is as clear and balanced as the first step of the new gait. If the transition involves a deterioration of the original gait before awkwardly "falling" into a new one, balance is missing.

◆ *Rhythm* is the essence of sophisticating the original relaxation of the horse. Only with the rhythmically musical measures of the horse's footfalls can we work toward sophistication. For if rhythm changes, evasion occurs. Any change of rhythm is an evasion; increasing or decreasing the tempo, the horse can avoid engagement of the haunches as well as lateral flexion.

Rhythm is best cultivated and tested for achievement by riding lengthening and shortening strides within the same gait. It is reinforced by transition work in the same gait. Relative extension and collection of the horse's strides must be introduced at the beginning of his training to initiate longitudinal elasticity, which develops into increased collection. As a result of impeccable rhythm, horses can extend and collect their strides without any change in the frequency of footfall.

◆ *Impulsion* is based on the horse's genetically determined tendency for taking flight. Impulsion is born of the energy for flight being tamed by the rider. The rider's increased control of the horse's energies refines itself into impulsion. Speed, indeed, is the enemy of impulsion. While flight begets impulsion, it is born of the rider's ability to curtail speed. Impulsion develops commensurate with the increased activity, mobility, and flexibility of the joints in the horse's hindquarters. The gradually increasing articulation in the joints of the haunches allows the horse to move with increased animation, yet with decreasing haste. Ultimately, a horse in good impulsion progresses with athletically improved gaits, which by their lack of haste, yet increase of animation, appear majestic, effortless, and brilliant in progression while carrying the rider.

◆ *Suppleness* is the consequence of the compound effect of a horse that works with utterly fluent, longitudinally flexed musculature and well-exercised and bending joints. The fluency of locomotion that is born of elastic muscles and strongly engaged joints documents a supple horse. The movement of a supple horse permeates him entirely and blankets his body in soft absorption of each stride.

◆ *Engagement,* like the preceding stages of development, grows in stages. Only supple horses can engage. Engagement of the haunches can be recognized in its sophisticated stage by a more cadenced movement displayed by an increased period of suspension (flight above ground) relative to decreased, but supremely accurate touch-down periods. The lightness and harmony of a well-engaged horse are manifested in maximum suspension produced by minimum energy, the economy of perfect gymnastics. The haunches "engage" and accept the majority of weight, thereby liberating the forehand and improved consistent engagement produces maximum collection and extension at the natural gaits. The lightness of the forehand is demonstrated by the rising of the withers to a point higher than the haunches, never by a pulled-up neck with a tucked-up head, but rather by movement in which the shoulders are completely free, allowing the lifting of the knees high (cannon bone perpendicular to the ground). The forehand seems to hover and hesitate in dance as the withers rise upward, somewhat glorifying in elegance the truly brilliantly engaged horse. In extensions, the forearm will momentarily reach a near-horizontal position.

Guenter Seidel is succeeding in showing lightness of the forehand. The correct relationship between lifting the knees and reaching from the shoulders allows the horse to lighten the forehand by "bouncing" the withers up and raising the neck carriage. Perhaps the most important observation should be the visible, fully flexed "top neck muscle," which runs parallel to the crest. It is flexed the full length of the horse's neck and down to the shoulder blades, as it should be, with a shaded "gullet" below it delineating it. Soft, hanging lower neck muscles verify the wonders that fully stretched flexion in the upper muscle can produce. The horse's posture toward the bit is exemplary, the result of using the correct muscles.

The photo captures a moment that shows the supple pasterns supporting the forward springing of the strides. A relaxed, floating tail verifies an articulating back on which a perfectly balanced, elegant rider is carried.

I suggest turning the page upside down. It will help you visually appreciate how the "horse hangs down from a perpendicularly balanced rider's head." When viewed upside down, the rider's head hangs at the end of a perfect plumb line.   Photo: Cheryl Erpelding.

Remember that younger horses will need more time on exercises, primarily those fostering the first three stages. While a green horse might spend much of the lesson relaxing, a fully trained horse relaxes and submits often as soon as the rider is placed in the saddle, leaving much of the riding time for efforts of engagement. A truly green horse cannot and will not engage absolutely, he will go through a "relative engagement."

Relaxation is the underlying quality required for all developmental stages. Whether it is rhythm or engagement or anything else one might work on, it is only a sophistication of relaxation. Engagement is committed relaxation, as opposed to the absence of tension, as in the first stage. The horse's musculature and joints are supple and elastic because they are relaxed. That is why in the "pool of relaxation," balance, rhythm, impulsion, suppleness, collection, and engagement all figure. These are all developmental sophistications of relaxation and cultivated extensions of it.

Any time spent on a tense horse is detrimental to him. The horse learns, then habituates, all of his activities. Thus, doing any work with a tense horse will promote the learning of incorrect habits.

THE DIALECTICS OF SUCCESS IN SCHOOLING

The rider has to keep in mind that *means* (how we achieve) and *ends* (the final result or goal) should be clearly defined and not confused with each other. Several different means (methodical actions) may lead successfully to the same end (goal). In fact, a combination of methods may more successfully lead to the quicker attainment of certain goals. That is why I find it important to remember Hegel's dialectics. Hegel was a German historian who learned from history that man never learns from history.

In brief, this is what he proposes: There is always a *thesis,* that is, an action that immediately provokes an *antithesis,* or reaction. The two contest, and as a result a *synthesis,* or solution, will occur. But that synthesis is not static because it immediately appears as a challenge to which a new antithesis develops and with which it has to fight for the next possible synthesis. In short, nothing is permanent; instead, everything is dynamic. According to Hegel, the only reality is an ever-changing process with no permanent resolution. For as soon as a goal has been seemingly attained, it is newly challenged by an antithesis that seeks a new goal. A simplified version is presented below:

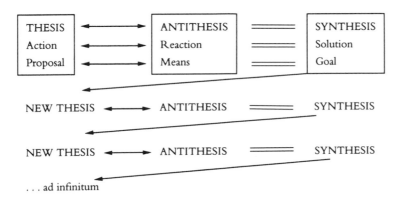

The importance of this philosophical theory to riders is that we are simply reminded that we start by recognizing a certain condition in the horse, which becomes our thesis. That could be a lack of impulsion. Immediately, we must propose our goal, or synthesis, to be the improvement of impulsion. Where we put the question mark in the formula is the antithesis. We must ask what means (methods) should be introduced to change the thesis and search out the proper antitheses that will predictably produce the desired synthesis, which is improved impulsion. Let us review lack of impulsion as an example.

The condition, or thesis, is a lack of impulsion. Good riding strategy ought to find the means best suited to achieve our goals. In this case, *relax* the horse to render him educable. Slow his tempo to develop the opportunity to drive. Follow the slightest impulse offered after the drive by traveling harmoniously on that minuscule amount of energy. Then drive again and harmonize again, until the horse becomes quite attentive to the aid and offers, beyond relaxation, a balanced and rhythmic movement that is sustained without perpetual prodding. Transitions within each gait (as described) and between the gaits increase impulsion by attracting the horse's attention to the rider's aids and facilitating increased energy.

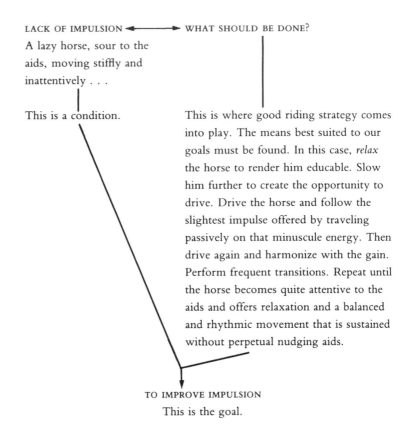

LACK OF IMPULSION ◄———► WHAT SHOULD BE DONE?
A lazy horse, sour to the
aids, moving stiffly and
inattentively . . .

This is a condition.

This is where good riding strategy comes into play. The means best suited to our goals must be found. In this case, *relax* the horse to render him educable. Slow him further to create the opportunity to drive. Drive the horse and follow the slightest impulse offered by traveling passively on that minuscule energy. Then drive again and harmonize with the gain. Perform frequent transitions. Repeat until the horse becomes quite attentive to the aids and offers relaxation and a balanced and rhythmic movement that is sustained without perpetual nudging aids.

TO IMPROVE IMPULSION
This is the goal.

Riders may go wrong in several places. Some cannot even identify the problem (thesis) correctly. Others, who may be aware of the possibility of the problem, do not necessarily notice the condition in their own horse until it has reached drastic proportions.

Let us examine the common case of those who usually can identify the problem, the thesis, but then proceed to propose an antithesis that ought to be the synthesis. In other words, they go wrong by trying to use the goal as their means. Consequently, they get an end result that is different from the one they wanted. Their desired end result is spent as a means and that produces unpredictable results! Let us review another example and the way it will go wrong:

- Thesis: Lack of impulsion.
- Antitheses: Incorrect means, which include poor driving with exaggerated posting; driving with banging legs and whipping; the rider with a torso slanted forward too much or even lifting elbows to urge the horse on.
- Synthesis: Plausibly, a tense, confused horse, dull to the aids, lazy and/or rushing above the bit.

LACK OF IMPULSION   INCORRECT MEANS

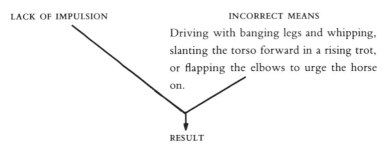

Driving with banging legs and whipping, slanting the torso forward in a rising trot, or flapping the elbows to urge the horse on.

RESULT

A tense, confused horse, dull to the aids, running around above the bit.

Remember that a rider who pursues his goals by riding his goals will never achieve them. But a rider who pursues various logical and proper means leading to a desirable goal will progress. When we define our goal as straightening a horse that moves evenly forward with good impulsion, we employ as a means bending. For it is through bending exercises that the horse becomes straight. That is why riders who just ride their green horses on straight lines will always have green horses that neither travel straight nor bend correctly. Through riding on a straight path, one reinforces crookedness, while through bending, one achieves supple straightness. In the same way, through stretching the young horse, we will eventually develop a collected horse in self-carriage. However, by elevating his neck early and artificially with the hands, we will achieve the opposite: a horse on the forehand, rushing "downhill" and/or pulling on the rider's hands. It is good for us to learn from Hegel's dialectics that those who confuse the means with the ends ultimately are unsuccessful.

MEANS/ENDS

All goals are achieved by suitable means. Check the steadiness of the torso by flexing the abdominal and upper back muscles. If someone else were to pull your arm forward, the torso should provide enough passive resistance to that horizontal pull to actually anchor the torso deeper down with a perpendicular weight vector toward the horse's spine. In fact, the rider should feel firmer down in the saddle as a consequence of the pull. This isometric realignment of muscle flexion should produce a firmer rider, yet one without any pull on his horse's mouth. Instead, there should appear an obvious feeling that the horse's space is well defined by the firm unity of the torso with the upper arms and elbows. The downward pressure of the seat passively resists any lengthening of the frame through the reins, yet it does not diminish it.

To develop the feeling for a deepening seat, a rider may lift the inside knee for a few strides during the canter and experience how that helps to put the seat firmly down into the movement of the saddle. Or a rider may experiment with riding some "sit-ups" while trotting, leaning the torso back behind the vertical and slowly returning it to the vertical position. These are the means to an end, not the way one ought to ride during a competition.

Only when the seat is deep and properly anchored does the rider feel that there is no need to ride the horse with effort, for the horse has been given a chance "to ride himself through the rider." This is analogous to a human gymnast using other items to create a gymnastic development and display. Without the floor mat, the parallel bars, or the rings, gymnasts can neither develop nor display their prowess.

The legs are the most important part of the aiding system. They both propel (provide the necessary aiding to inspire energy) and bend the horse. Legs cannot work effectively without an anchored seat. The influence of legs depends on their independence from any balancing functions. Balancing by gripping with the legs is necessary only for those who do not sit anchored. Useless, gripping legs always testify to an out–of–balance torso position. The rider's legs should hang, yet by their special po-

Elizabeth Ball demonstrates elegant equitation, which includes a deep heel and stretched calves. With this equitation she can inconspicuously influence the horse to step taller in collection (above) and to step longer in extenstion (below). It is important to note that both collecting and lengthening the strides must amplify the gaits as is the case here in the trot.   Photo: Richard Williams.

sition remain draped in contact around the horse's barrel. Such legs allow for a deep heel position, and pushing action on the horse's sides downward and forward. Riders should rest their toes on the stirrups, which makes for a longer foot, enabling the heels to sink. Only with well-flexed, supple ankles can a rider develop strength in his calves, which he must aid with.

To use the inner calves for driving rather than the heels, the ankles must be relaxed and capable of rotating. When the legs stay back under the rider's seat, where they belong, with toes behind the knees, then a rider can turn the toes inward, followed by lowering of the heels, which pushes the toes slightly outward, followed by turning the toes inward again, and so on. The feeling in the walk and canter is a slow, rhythmic pushing forward and down on the horse's sides. To build this skill and feeling, you should press toward the horse with the toes by circling the toes inward toward the horse's body. A rider does not actually touch the horse with his toes, of course. Yet, by pushing the toes inward, he succeeds simultaneously in supplying the ankles and actually driving with the calves! Ignoring calf aids, the only pushing aids possible, and insisting on aiding with the heels lead to the ruin of many riders.

Once the legs are capable of aiding, propel the horse by repetitious, rhythmically contracting aids, with adhesive legs. By good timing, the effect of the drive increases and the horse's motion is simultaneously and harmoniously accompanied. Just as we can break a glass by repeating the same note in proper intervals, so can we accumulate huge driving power effortlessly by repeating the same activity with the correct timing.

A good seat is an effective seat. Good aids are the consequence of it. Only through constant adjustment and honing can a rider acquire such a seat and aids. Therefore, we must constantly work toward an ideal seat and effortless aids. Heels don't stay down because we push them down. They stay there because we keep them there by small but persistently repeated readjustments during every stride. When it all comes together, we have the fantastic sensation of having the horse ride himself through our own effortless body, which is merely lent to him for his stability.

Two

The Development of the
Rider's Seat and Aids

Ideally, the beginning rider should have two instructors: a riding coach and a school horse. The rider must learn to harmonize with all the movements of his horse. In order to do so, he must acquire a balanced seat. Then he will be able to follow the horse's movements. He will sit correctly. A school horse can offer quiet tolerance and well-balanced, comfortable, pure movements without much need for activity by the rider. Lazy horses that need strenuous driving will always stiffen the novice rider. Untrained, unbalanced, or irregular horses with unpredictable movement will deny relaxation and good feeling to the rider and will cause anguish and anticipation in him.

This stage terminates, according to the rider's natural talents, when he acquires an independently balanced seat in which he can follow all of his horse's movements and, therefore, begin to feel free to influence him.

In the second stage, the rider learns the craftsmanship and skills of riding. He should diversify and build routine by repetition. In this stage, the rider is still taught by a coach and continues to learn from his horse. However, he becomes a partial instructor of his horse. A rider should ride as many different kinds of horses as possible. He should ride in as many modes as possible: go on trail rides, jump, and do gymnastic flatwork.

The rider learns the refined language of aids and how to use them effectively and consistently. Having attained a balanced seat, he has the ability to use any part of his body independently according to need, without the urgency to grip, hold on, or stiffen. Learning the use of aids also depends on natural talent. Some people will be able to coordinate aids consistently rather soon.

In the third stage, the rider becomes accomplished. Now he only needs a coach to guide him as he executes the work cooperatively, mostly through consultations and discussions. The rider now is the teacher of his horse. The horse emerges as the sole object of instruction for which the rider and his coach pool their knowledge and energies. The coach should make an effort to deny the rider any function as "crutch" or dictator.

Some riders will exhibit great skill and craftsmanship in teaching their own horses. They will improve throughout a lifetime as experience and routine increase their effectiveness. Few will emerge as artists. Through sensitivity, imagination, and creative approaches, they may add their new inspirations to the great body of classical riding knowledge. Dressage has absolutely no room for rudeness, intimidation, cajoling, cruelty, or trickery. The horse's abilities are just as varied and unique as those of human individuals. A dressage rider must proceed at the rate his horse offers; he must understand and respect the individuality of his partner.

At this stage, life is full of challenges. Competitions serve as educational experiences. Accomplished riders bid themselves against their own performances and seek to improve. They are totally dedicated to their horse's needs, having no more need to concentrate on their own skills. During this last stage, it is important for riders to be independent, to exercise their own judgment and base it on their perception of the horse. Coaching that is authoritarian or tyrannical has no place in dressage, for that would limit the rider's essential development.

Here are some concepts that riders in the middle of their progress in equitation should consider important:

◆ The horse's obedience is achieved by virtue of "conversation" that is going on continuously between horse and rider. The conversation is silent and eventually should become refined enough not to be apparent to an observer's eyes. At first, figuratively speaking, there may be some "shouting" going on, or "loud talk," but, later, as the horse's mentality and ability to concentrate are improved and as he becomes more capable of doing the required tasks, the "conversation" takes on the intimacy of a "whisper."

◆ These communications are always two-way. One cannot be an effective rider until one feels clearly and can discern the communications of his horse. He also ought to be able interpret these in order to react to them properly. Horses communicate through bodily attitudes. Riders feel these communications also with their bodies and reply to them bodily. The communications of the rider are called "the aids." That which communicates to the horse is "aiding." They are called aids because they should help (aid) the horse in understanding the desired change.

◆ The rider's aids must be clear, concise, and consistent. Without these attributes, no human could learn a foreign language, nor can the horse learn the language of the aids. As in all language studies, the teaching of the aids must involve frequent repetition and resemble vocabulary drills. Reinforcement by rewarding correct responses is indispensable. The language and its vocabulary are limited by the physical and mental attitudes of both horse and rider. The rider may communicate with his torso, seat, legs, and hands. Involuntary movements on the part of the rider should be eliminated because they create signals to the horse which can confuse or mask the aids and create undesirable or unpredictable results.

◆ A rider's contact areas, the seat and legs, convey the workings of his upper body, which does not contact the horse. Only in coordination with the rider's torso and in support of its actions can we meaningfully work with our legs and hands. The rider's body is mistakenly called "seat." A good rider sits on

three points. The back end of the pelvic bone, through the buttocks, anchors him on his seat bones. By adequately stretching
the upper legs back and down, the pelvis is laid down horizontally. The crotch should not be pressed into contact with the
saddle by forward-tilted hips and a hollow lumbar back with
the stomach pressed forward and down. Instead, with a straight
back and hips above the seat bones, the rider should slightly
raise the crotch off the saddle and feel no friction on it. The seat
bones are encased in the buttocks and should not grind down
to touch the saddle. Rather, sit with a supple lumbar back which
allows the human pelvis to remain adhesive to the horse's back.
The stomach should be flat, ribcage wide, shoulders back and
down. The aiding system of the rider depends for success on an
anchored seat. This guarantees the independent actions of the
limbs. Without it, the rider will anchor his balance in the horse's
mouth or on his sides by gripping with his legs and pinching
with his heels pulled up or on the stirrups.

THE AIDING SYSTEM

Specifically, the methods of classical riding are based on knowledgeable, patient, gradual yet systematic and consistent plans for
improvement. The instruments of communication for the rider
are:

- His weight and the position of his torso.
- The use of back and abdominal muscles (flex-relax), both of
  these communicated to the horse through the rider's seat,
  knees, and thighs. These communication areas must remain
  stable.
- His legs, always contacting but not gripping the horse's sides.
- His hands (only as an extension of the torso's activities) communicating with the horse's mouth.

All three contact areas—seat, legs, and hands—must affect
the horse all the time and be in harmonious coordination. They
must become more and more refined until the horse grows phys-

ically and mentally to understand their "whispering" rather than to expect their "shouting."

The results of classical horsemanship are manifested in consistent, enduring athletic achievements, near or at the top of the horse's natural potential.

This is a brief outline of the ideals, goals, methods, and results of classical horsemanship. Simultaneously, they are the ideals, goals, methods, and results of dressage. Classical horsemanship and dressage are synonymous and the terms are used interchangeably throughout the world. None of these principles contradict those involved in jumping! Furthermore, they can greatly improve the development and career of a jumping horse.

A great deal of attention must be paid to the correct development of each rider's seat and aiding system. I do not know the origin of the age-old adage that "Every horse knows how to be a horse; it is the rider who must learn to be an equestrian." Indeed, a horse can do no more than a rider's equitation allows him. Nature lives through its creatures. They are nature's vehicles for manifestation and cannot perform anything without a well-schooled rider making the performance possible.

A correctly seated rider always looks beautiful and usually elegant. The concept of a beautiful seat and elegant riding is based on the correctly placed riding positions, which allow the harmonious progression of horse and rider in unity of balance. In turn, this unity provides for the inconspicuous communications that a good rider uses to control his horse and renders these communications inconspicuous to outside observers.

An elegant rider will add to the beauty of his horse. A correctly sitting and inconspicuously communicating rider will allow observers to see the horse while the rider diminishes in visibility. The horse is to be on display. The beholder is interested in the beauty of the horse and only in the art of the rider insofar as he can control the horse's display without drawing attention to himself. The rider's art is to be inconspicuous while displaying a horse that is noteworthy for the beauty of his gaits and ease of carriage.

THE SEAT

The seat is the anchoring center of all communications in riding. With the help of the spine pointing perpendicularly down into the saddle, the seat should be kept straight and tall while riding dressage. The activities of the torso are communicated through a deep seat. The seat also serves to stabilize the legs and allow their independent aiding. A balanced, deep, independent seat is prerequisite to all successful riding.

The lumbar back should always be relaxed and supple. The rider should "sit tall," that is, have his rib cage elevated. The deep seat depends on the isometric unity of the torso. The torso's musculature should be in sufficient tone to hold itself and the upper arms in harmonious and steady posture. No parts of the torso should jolt, rock, or jostle. In spite of the horse's motion, the rider should remain motionless and appear at ease with the horse's progression. The rider's lumbar back should be relaxed and free to absorb the horse's back motion. In fact, the human and equine lumbar backs should synchronize their motion. Unless the rider's lower back can absorb the horse's movement, no pressure with the torso's weight can be applied.

The back, straight shoulders, and rib cage affect riding by their weight. In order to serve their useful purposes, the shoulder joints should be kept well back, shoulder blades flattened into the musculature, and chest elevated. The effect of the weight of the upper torso is often called the "seat aid." This is a misnomer. We must be aware that the seat merely anchors and transmits the aiding of the shoulders, and does not by itself aid by gyrating or shoving the saddle. The contract area of the buttocks should be evenly distributed over the saddle's surface. The seat also includes the draped thighs stretched well down toward a stabilizing deep knee.

The hands of the rider should be relaxed. The upper arms should hang naturally vertically downward without tension. The steady position of the elbows helps stabilize the hands. The lower arms should effortlessly reach forward toward the horse's mouth. The rider must close his fingers on the reins and ride with a closed fist with all his fingertips lined up touching the center of his palm. When the elbows and upper arms successfully stabilize and reflect the activities of the torso, the horse will feel the rider's seat and its influences through his elbows. The rider's buttocks are undeniably the contact surfaces with the saddle. But they convey to the horse merely the rider's weight. The weight is part of but not synonymous with the seat. The seat includes all the weight, plus the activities of the entire torso.

The seat of the rider is the anchor from which other communications may quietly issue. The seat is the center of all information both perceived from the horse and distributed to him. The unity and anchorage of the torso are required to make possible cohesive, consistent, and harmonious aiding.

The seat consists of several distinct areas, according to the functions they deliver. The buttocks contain the pelvis. The seat bones are part of the pelvis. The seat bones are appropriately protected by the buttocks muscles and are not in direct contact with the saddle. The three-point seat is a product of the rider hanging down on the horse's spine with not only fully seated seat bones but also by the stretching of his thighs back and down while turning his knees and thighs inward, toward the horse's body. The successful lowering of the knees, and the ability to remain stretched as well as adhesive to the saddle with the thighs and knees, produce the three-point contact support of the rider's seat. The support is as if on a pie-shaped wedge, the wide end of it containing the seat bones cushioned by the buttocks and the narrowing front pointing to the crotch, which is not to be pressed down to the saddle but float above it horizontally, as the deep-hanging knees place it naturally. The importance of closed, adhesive (not gripping) thighs and anchored knees, even in a sitting trot and collected canter, cannot be emphasized enough. Vertical or horizontal rocking of loose knees prevents the anchorage of the rider. The three-point seat should never be produced by hollowing the rider's lumbar back. On the contrary, a combination of lumbar tucking allows the horizontal progression of the pelvis with the horse's back movement. Without this rounding lumbar thrust, the rider's seat would dislodge, anchorage and contact unity would dissolve.

The rider's ability to sit erect, with a straight spine, demands a great deal of isometric awareness, training, and sheer strength. The misconception of the totally relaxed torso in which everything is slack, mushy, quivering, bouncing, jolting, and bobbing is the very annihilation of the classical position. In fact, a rider must sit absolutely quiet, erect with straight shoulders, utterly void of involuntary hand actions, carrying his head motionless on the top of a stretched neck. The monument to immobility is, indeed, the rider who can sit the first jarring and later softly swinging gaits of his horse without being bobbed around. The so-called relaxed rider, who looks like someone lacking a skeleton, is the antithesis of the classically schooled equestrian, whose skeletal structure is very apparent and whose body is immobilized in the face of the upheaval the horse's gaits created by impaction on the ground.

The rider's torso down to his lumbar back should be presented as his "cabinetry"; it includes the upper arms and elbows. By flattening the shoulder blades and rotating the shoulder joints back and down, the cabinetry is formed. From flat shoulder blades comes a straight upper back; from the shoulder joints the upper arms hang effortlessly vertically down to the motionless elbows and in front of the upper arms project the elevated collarbones and rib cage that facilitate deep breathing and the stability of an erect posture. In riding, the torso is held exactly as a soldier holds himself when standing at attention. To observe this, look at the Marines standing honor guard at the White House or any soldier standing at attention anywhere. Where are their heads, where do their eyes stare? How straight are those shoulders and where do they allow the arms to hang? How does the rib cage look and how can this wonderfully straight, tall torso maintain its tranquillity and immobility for hours if needed? Easily. For this is the balanced posture in which humans can relax. Isometric unity takes over from effort.

Once the rider "sits at attention" on his horse, he can feel that the horse's mouth is influenced by the seat, i.e., the torso. From the elbows issues the direct line to the muzzle that is the natural extension of a straight, tall seat's steadily perpendicular interception of the horse's horizontally traveling spine. This perpendicular interception designates the rider's elbow as the joint analogous with his seat. Indeed, we do not buttock or pelvis ride—that is, make use of our anchorage, our adhesive unity, our frictional consistency with the horse. But our seat's activities

TRAINING STRATEGIES FOR DRESSAGE RIDERS

are transferred to the horse's mouth through the elbow. The upper arm should form a plumb line from shoulder to elbow. The perpendicular (to the ground) upper arms are included in the "cabinetry" along with the torso. From elbow to hand, the lower arm, wrist, and fist all belong to the horse. The lower arm supports, sustains, and communicates to the horse's horizontal progression. Thus, the rider is anchored at the elbow, which effortlessly communicates the verticality of the rider's cabinetry and through a supple lower back unites the seat with the reins.

The horse's motion is delivered in three dimensions and riders can sit with ease and immobility only if they learn to understand and then follow the horse's motion inconspicuously. To be harmonious with the horse's motion, we must realize that it consists of three dimensions. His horizontal motion is his progression in space. By holding superb abdominal isometric firmness similar in tone to that of performing a sit-up, the rider must lean the torso to tilt slightly behind the pelvic structure in order for it to move adhesively ahead. The torso "pushes" the pelvis forward not by gyrating, abdominal dancing but by absolute abdominal silence that holds the cabinetry behind the pelvic structure and allows its weight to propel the pelvis forward with a loose lumbar back. The lumbar back is the "hinge" that makes proper pelvic thrust possible. This hinge must communicate the directional push of the cabinetry. By leaning back, it will push the pelvis forward. The straight spine, from the nape of the neck to the tailbone, is only straight if the rider's torso is "slanted" ever so slightly back, so as to facilitate the horizontal lumbar thrust.

The horse's verticality comes from his impact on the ground alternating with periods of suspension. As the horse travels and his legs, depending on the gaits, strike the ground, a shock travels upward and impacts on the rider's hanging pelvis. The upward hammering of the horse on the rider's pelvis is greater when the horse is not gymnasticized and his body is stiff. With training, the impact will soften, until the supple horse transmits very little vertical impact. Thus, the "sledgehammer" below us becomes "liquefied" through gradual suppling. The softly swinging back and supplely yielding joints of the horse will articulate more with correct training and act as shock absorbers. Some vertical movement remains, however. The rider's head will always move up and down relative to a constant architectural backdrop. This motion is absorbed primarily in the rider's lumbar back and secondarily in the cushioning of the soft and relaxed buttocks and inner thigh muscles. If the lower back is arched, hollowed, stiffened, and opposed to the motion of the rider's pelvis, vertical absorption becomes impossible and is replaced by concussion. This is harmful to the spine and to the entire riding structure and prevents any success in influencing the horse's gymnastic development by traditionally refined and effective classical training methods. In order to accommodate the verticality of the horse's movement (especially when that is still in its sledgehammer stage), many riders allow their heads to bob or their shoulders to jolt or their elbows to swing, or all three, and mistakenly think that if these motions are displayed as rhythmic shock absorbers, they are among the cognoscenti who know how to remain relaxed, hang loose, and look harmonious with the sledgehammer. Very often, these are symptoms of a rider with a stiff and hollow lower back. The vertical actions of the horse must be absorbed by the correctly placed and correctly moving lumbar back, and the elastic shock absorption functions of supple ankles.

The third dimension inherent to the horse's motion is its laterality. Horses do not hop on parallel legs like kangaroos or sparrows. They use their front and hind legs alternately. In that sense, their lateral actions are "double." Sensitive riders must feel the motions of both front and hind limbs and how they transmit through the horse's articulating back muscles. Like humans, horses progress by forwarding one side of their body at a time. Kangaroos and sparrows hop with both legs simultaneously, their bodies stiff and steady. Their motion lacks "laterality," (i.e., sidedness). Riders should always sit so as to parallel with their shoulder the horse's shoulder movement and with their hips parallel the horse's hip motion. Therefore, there is always a subtle lateral diversion of the rider's torso as his cabinetry walks, trots, or canters in total unity with the horse's corresponding limb movement beneath it. In addition to its exposed horizontal thrust and vertical floating, the rider's pelvis must add the alternately supple sinking and heaving accommodation to the horse's lateral alternation of his hind legs. To move as if one were born on horseback, to look as if part of the horse's motions as included in his lateral "undulations," is the distinction of a truly harmonious rider. It is not a task for a book to explain how one grows to acquire the classical seat and resulting indiscernible aids. Suffice it to say that without riding cross-country, over varied natural terrain, the laterality and undulations of the horse's movement are hard to conceptualize and discern. Riding in open country gives birth to good equitation feelings. Adding to that, regular riding under careful instruction on the lunge on a school horse is indispensable for the acquisition of riding skills and positions.

ACHIEVING UTTER UNITY WITH THE HORSE

The important thing to remember about the seat is that it must accompany the horse step for step in all three dimensional motions. The horizontal, vertical, and lateral direction of the motion as performed by the horse must naturally be accompanied by the same activities of the rider. Each stride contains all three of the directional components! A rider who sits motionless relative to the ground is rigid. Immobility while in locomotion and transgressing space is achieved by moving at the correct rate and in all three correct directions.

I caution against demonstrative bobbing, wiggling, and dangling activities as some sort of proof as to how well the rider handles the vertical punch. Likewise, to elevate the knees, hang the toes down, lean behind the vertical, and hang the head down to a hypnotic stare over the horse's head does not prove the easy horizontality of travel. Nor should the rocking of shoulders or hips and visibly alternating shimmying around be offered as proof of accompanying the lateral motion. All proper accompanying movement in the rider should stay so small that it remains hidden inside the riding coat, and certainly a good rider will remain seemingly motionless relative to the horse, erect, stretched tall, "at attention," and with an aloof look of concentration. I often ask my students to finish their properly tall and

quiet seat with an aloof facial expression of concentration without tension.

The rider's legs are the primary source of the all-important
impulsion aids. They are also responsible for bending. When the
torso hangs down correctly with perpendicular interception to
the horse's horizontal spine, the legs can hang down long and
deep. The rider must train the now-independent legs (no longer
gripping to balance) to stretch and drape around the horse's
barrel. The torso sits on a horse absolutely effortlessly, naturally,
when sitting correctly. Riders can, and did in wars, sleep while
sitting on a horse. However, the leg position of the rider is not
natural and must be learned. Gradually, with tutoring, perpetual
reminders, and repeated self-readjustments, the legs will take on
the learned but correct position that allows them to hang with
well-stretched calves, be powerful without tension or gripping,
and yet remain perpetually in contact with the horse's sides. Not
only must the legs remain draped onto the horse like a sticking
wet rag against his ribs but also in that intimacy the rider must
isometrically vary the pushing and bending aids. The horse has
a very sensitive area on each side, where, incidentally, the correctly placed riding legs happen to touch him. There he perceives
the activities of the rider's leg, which can deliver the impulsion
aids with rhythmic coordination, mindful of which hind leg is
ready to be engaged as it is leaving the ground. A horse's hind
leg cannot be urged to activity when anchored on the ground,
supporting the body weight at the moment of impact. However,
the leg can and must be influenced as to where to step and in
what fashion, at the time when it is leaving the ground. Only
adhesive, well-wrapped, and draped calves can perceive this timing and deliver the necessary muscular contractions that produce
the driving or bending aids.

The rider's skill in positioning his legs must include such
details as well-closed, adhesive thighs and knees and hanging
lower legs pressed down by the deep knee position and back
enough to allow the heels to hang under the seat bones and the
toes to remain behind the knees of the rider most of the time.
This is a difficult feat on account of the requisite unnatural positioning of the hip, knee, and ankle joints. Furthermore, while
bending the horse and while cantering the rider must keep his

outside leg stretched somewhat farther back than the position of his inside leg. It is around the inside leg that the horse bends, yet it is not the inside leg that does the bending! Instead, the inside leg is the leg responsible for propelling, for the impulsion and the rhythm of the gait. It is the outside leg that must stay stretched farther back (from two to six inches, depending on the conformation of the horse and the degree of bending required), with the heel still scrupulously the lowest point of the foot, and remain steadily leaning against the horse's outside to create bending. The outside leg is responsible for the horse's bending. It also displaces the horse during some two-track work and assists in all turning. It remains adhesive to the outside of the rib cage without any rhythmic bouncing. Rather than assuming the assignments of the inside leg, the outside leg presses more or less but always steadily, depending on the degree of bending needed.

One of the most important features of a deep, balanced, and therefore independent seat is that the rider is utterly capable of using each of his limbs according to necessity: no longer should the rider deliver accidental signals prompted by the horse's jolting or the rider's bad habits. Instead, all movements should be by design. Their strength should be by will! Seldom is the rider in need of identical actions of both hands and legs: that is, most riding consists of "diagonal aiding" and infrequently requires "parallel aiding." That is, riders seldom use their limbs as we use windshield wipers. Just because one side moves, the other is not obliged to parallel its actions. In fact, what a rider's inside leg does is vastly different from what his outside leg ought to do. The position of the legs is usually different and the strength and nature of their activities differ greatly. When a rider stretches his outside leg back adhesively, of course, he is automatically placed on his inside seat bone. One never sits on the inside seat bone by leaning in like a motorcycle rider or pressing and grinding on it. Instead, one simply places the outside leg back correctly and that elevates the outside seat bone higher up into the buttock muscle, leaving the surface of the saddle. Simultaneously, of course, the inside seat bone drops down and forward inside the relaxed inside buttock muscle and falls down toward the saddle.

The rider's feet must remain parallel to the horse's sides and the feeling is that the big toes are elevated off the stirrup irons and weight increases on the outside rims of the boots. The ankles fold outward and the toes can rock the stirrup irons toward the horse's belly if necessary or when exercising, in a free rhythmic, relaxed manner. However, the inward dabbing with the toe does amount to the pushing aids of the calf, and, in fact, any toe-out and/or toe-down with heels gripping the horse is utterly contrary to the production of impulsion and bending. The stretched inner calf muscles deliver the impulse that originates from motion at the ankles as the toes are rocked inward.

Classical equitation is based on all the influences that the seat and legs emit. The hands, which are effectively lengthened by the inclusion of the reins, remain mere extensions of the influences of the rider's seat. Disharmonious, strong, punitive use of the hands is permissible only in an emergency. When a horse is out of control, endangering his rider and even himself, a rider should do whatever is necessary to regain control—even through pain, shock, surprise, administered by strong use of the hands. Yet in such extreme circumstances, riders still strengthen the hands by anchoring the weight of the torso to them and by making the punitive emergency hand action as brief as possible. After such an episode, the rider must make peace with his horse expeditiously. Reassure him of your friendship and continued reliable guidance.

Excluding extreme circumstances and emergencies, the hands, as said before, remain mere extensions of the seat's influences. The most important concept in such unity is "passive resistance." Other than using the hands as participants in passive resistance, they can be used as active, yielding hands. This latter function should prevail and is an indispensable part of properly driving a horse.

"Passive resistance" is a result of the rider anchoring his lower arms to stillness by the increased strength of the vertically downward vector of his upper arms and elbows. The rider isometrically straightens and flattens his shoulder blades, increasing the straightness of his upper back, and emphasizes the shoulders' directional pressure back and down. The rider's upper arm and elbow, indeed, must act as if they are part of the rib cage. They belong to the rider's cabinetry. The lower arms extend almost horizontally. They belong to the horse, through their extension by the reins.

"Passive" means simply that the rider temporarily refuses, with an absence of motion, to follow the horse's movements with his seat-and-arms combination. "Resistance" means that if the horse were to contest this by suddenly jerking on the reins, hammering down or leaning forward against the hands, he should not succeed in dislodging the rider's fists, arms, or torso. The strength of the rider must come from the correct position of the vertical upper arms' relationship to the torso's identical vertical downward-pressing influences. Any attempt to dislodge the rider's hands should not only fail, but also the horse should feel that he pulled the rider down into himself. That is to say, instead of horizontally "unseating" his rider, as would be the case if the elbows were loose and subsequently dislodged, the horse's efforts "help" the rider add to the perpendicular downward pressure, increasing rather than decreasing the rider's seat.

Again, only by sitting properly and being isometrically well honed can a rider be in charge of himself, remaining "seated on his horse" and not "unseated" by his horse's head-tossing or jarring movement. A rider who cannot hold his upper arms and elbows absolutely still, and, consequently, fists, has no seat. Instead, he has only hands! Disturbing, disruptive, punitive, confusing, misguiding, uncontrollable, jolting hands. The hands are kept still by the isometric stillness of the upper arm and elbow relative to the rider's torso. All riding skills depend on the rider's training for, and ability to, retain isometric unity without stiffness.

POSITIONING THE SEAT, LEGS, AND HANDS

Riders should sit properly so that their hands never make any involuntary motion. The rider's hands must move only by design. Such independent hands (independent from the manipulations of equine motion and from the motion of the rest of his own body) can indeed flow with the horse's movement, as will the rider's entire seat flow with the horse's back motion.

Yielding hands appear quiet, even motionless. This virtue is an appearance, the consequence of the rider's hands moving exactly with the horse's flow and exactly at the rate of his progression. Quiet hands move, no more or no less than the rest of the rider's cabinetry, of which they are an integral part. As a consequence, the hands act as extensions of the seat's motions in all three possible dimensions. In other words, the hands also have horizontal, vertical, and lateral possibilities. By participating in these three directional possibilities, the hands fulfill their functions, identical to those of the seat: they resist passively, yield and drive actively, balance and direct, increase or diminish the rate, and contribute to the readjustment of the level of collection, posture, and bending of the horse.

Therefore, if a rider's cabinetry turns laterally, with the horse's stride, as it should, so as to parallel the horse's shoulder movements with the rider's shoulder movements, the hands will accomplish, by their unity with the torso, what sidereins accomplish during lungeing. The horse alternately arrives on contact and slacks the same from side to side. This feeling accommodates the musculoskeletal behavior of the horse. His shoulders move alternately, and so do his back muscles and hind legs.

The rider who has proper hands must do nothing in particular (except, of course, when using various means to learn to acquire quiet hands), just shepherd the unity of his arms with his torso. As long as the upper arms and elbows are part and parcel of the rider's torso, all will work well. This position also allows the rider who leans back slightly to thrust his pelvis more powerfully forward to sense how the hips and pelvis approach his waiting fists, creating a powerful sustenance of the forehand while driving the haunches under, without pulling on the reins! The "wedging power" of a slanting torso, pressing the pelvis both forward and down, will travel the lower back and pelvis closer to the waiting fists and create one of the necessary contractions on which good half-halts depend.

Let us always be aware that good riding is the result of one isometrically unified rider dancing in harmonious unity with his horse. An "invisible" rider remains inconspicuous by the erect tranquillity of his torso, from which his hanging legs remain adhesively draped onto his horse and from which his lower arms reach forward in the direction of his horse's mouth from the elbow. A rider who rides with upper arms extended ahead of the vertical weight vector immediately destroys the meaning of seat, leg, and hands.

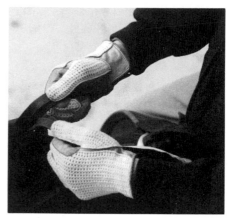

Arthur Kottas-Heldenberg holds the reins. The degree to which hands are closed and the isometric tension of the fists can vary according to the need for subtle resistance or yielding. The real friction for securing a steady and sustained contact on the same spot on the reins is created between the thumbs and forefingers. The rest of the fist is allowed to vary its tone. Wrists must remain relaxed and convey the feelings emitted by the lower arms.

Gloves are indispensable to riding, regardless of the rider's personal preference. Much like what riding boots do for the legs, gloves help generalize the feelings in the hands. Gloves not only spare the rider scuffing, rubbing, burning friction and injuries, they also reduce skin surface awareness and allow the rider to feel the whole horse rather than his own limbs. Equally important, gloves generalize the messages of the hand to the horse, who can discern the messages of gloved hands but not the crudities of gloveless hands. Photo: Charles Fuller.

The seat, consisting of all the adhesive contact areas, should remain passive and adhesive to the saddle. It acts as the communication center. The rider and horse, through the saddle, remain in steady contact. The actual seat contacting the saddle is an area of transmission. It also interprets the torso's activities. The friction area of the seat is inactive, merely providing contact with the saddle. The seat is the point of stability and suspension that allows for the independent mobility of aiding areas elsewhere.

The legs serve the primary purpose of creating impulsion. The rider should not use his legs to maintain his balance in the saddle. The legs should hang and be draped on the horse, not gripping him. The rider should stay in the saddle by virtue of his bodily coordination in such a manner that his perpendicularly positioned torso, pulled down by gravity, maintains him in the saddle.

The legs are used to designate impulsion for longer, extended or higher, collected strides. Legs determine the gait by their various uses. The gaits are also maintained by the use of the rider's legs. Legs work differently in the halt, walk, trot, and canter. This is not a quantitative (amount of pressure) but qualitative (type of pressure) differentiation.

Legs are also the primary aids for bending the horse. They even determine the degree of bending. In summary, the legs control the activities of the all-important hindquarters of the horse.

The body of the rider is also used as a transformer. The impulsion generated in the horse's hindquarters travels forward in his body through his back. These muscular articulations in the horse's back are perceived as motion in the rider's pelvis, which his lumbar back cooperates with in order to keep his seat steady in the saddle. Without these waves of motion in the horse's back, we would sit on a static surface, much like the seat of a car, which gives us no feeling in spite of the motion of the car. The horse makes us feel his motion through his swinging back, through which the impulsion-created energies travel toward his forehand, which absorbs these energies. The horse's front never creates locomotive energies, it merely absorbs and supports those coming from the hindquarters. The back is the bridge that transports these energies from points of origin in the rear to points of termination in the front.

The rider's body sits on this bridge of communication and has the task of transforming these energies. The rider's body absorbs the horse's energies, which come from his haunches, by receiving them in his pelvis and passing them though the lumbar back up to the top of his spine. There, the rider effects change and passes these energies down through his shoulders, upper arms, and elbows to his hands, and through the reins to the horse's mouth.

The body can be used in two different ways in these transforming activities: (1) As weight. The torso can tilt forward or backward from the perpendicular position. It can also rotate slightly right or left in the same perpendicular position. This can also put more weight on one or the other of the seat bones. (2) As power. The rider can flex or relax his abdominal and thigh mucles, thereby indicating degrees of cooperation or resistance to the horse's offered movement.

These activities of the rider's body serve three basic transformational functions: (1) drive, (2) follow and harmonize as an approval, and (3) restrain by passive resistance. A rider's body should always be doing one of these three functions. Furthermore, he should do the appropriate one. Unfortunately, some riders yield to the horse only by following his movement, which they seek to harmonize with at all costs. Such riders are travelers and are ineffective as meaningful transformers of the dynamic energies supplied to them by the horse. Passive resistance begins with legs that are firmly established on the horse's sides in a steady contact. With this contact, the horse is encouraged to continue to work with his hind legs under the weight of the rider while the rider creates an area of steadiness at his calf against which the muscles of his torso can be braced. Then the rider should close the knees and tighten the thighs. The torso should be braced by rendering the abdominal muscles unyielding and by rounding the lower back to send his seat bones forward and heavily down into the saddle. To get the correct feeling, I recommend that you plant your feet firmly on the ground while sitting on a kitchen stool and use your body to elevate the two back legs of the stool off the ground. As you will notice, you can determine how high you wish to elevate the stool legs. Equally, on a horse, you can brace isometrically lightly or strongly. The hands offer guidance and induce relaxation in the flexing topline. Hands hold the terminating points for the horse's energies. As such, they are primarily controlling mechanisms. They absorb the excesses that the driving legs create and the torso cannot handle. As such, they should be the least important, least used, most lightly and sparingly engaged units of the aiding group.

Correctly used hands should never punish, should always be as light and as inactive as possible, and should be coordinated with the movements of human and equine muscles, while the arms remain relaxed.

A young horse may run because he is losing his balance and is falling forward, rolling like an avalanche on his forelegs, gaining more and more momentum as he goes along. The hands should never jerk such a horse's mouth. If a horse is running so, the rider should attempt to slow his rhythm with his torso and circle him frequently on large comfortable circles, on which he can bend and balance at this relatively stiff period of his development.

The quietness of the rider's hands depends on the supple use of all joints, starting with the shoulders down to the fingers. The arm muscles should not pull, the biceps should be relaxed, and the triceps should stabilize the elbows. Again, the hands should be mere extensions of the activities of the rider's seat and should always be coordinated with its horizontal, vertical, and lateral activities. The hands, like the body, will do three kinds of things: drive, restrain, or yield to harmonize.

The most important general concept in aiding is that at all times, all the aiding mechanisms should be in use simultaneously and in perfect coordination with one another. Thus, aiding must be perpetual, coordinated, and used consistently. Even harmonious relaxation is an aid, for it tells the horse something.

THE PARALLEL AND DIAGONAL AIDING SYSTEMS

There are two basic aiding systems based on the coordination of the rider's body. They must be used appropriately and with properly coordinated effortlessness. Riders must always be able to shift from one system to the other, according to what they intend to communicate to their horse. These two systems are called either "bilateral and unilateral" or "parallel and diagonal" aids. I will use the latter pair of terms when describing them.

In the parallel aiding system, the rider applies exactly the same aids on both sides of his spine. He must place his right leg on the horse exactly opposite his left one on the other side. He must use his weight and back muscles the same way on both sides of his spinal column. He must engage his hands identically and, of course, carry them in identical positions and at the same height on both sides.

This aiding system should be in effect when we want the horse to use himself symmetrically in identical ways on both sides of his spinal column. The occasions where that is desirable are fewer than those when diagonal aids are necessary and are limited to the following:

- When the horse is to halt—all the time.
- When reining back—all the time.
- When trotting—only on a straight path.
- When walking—only on a straight path.
- When doing the piaffe.

In all other activities, diagonal aids must be used, because the horse uses each of his sides differently.

The diagonal aiding system should be in effect more frequently than the parallel one. Even during as simple a riding activity as trotting around an arena, riders should make eight changes from parallel to diagonal aids and back. Each of the four straight walls must be ridden with parallel aids, while all four corners should be rounded by a horse that is bent by diagonal aids.

In diagonal aiding, the rider must do different things on each side of the horse. Legs, back, torso, hands, act differently on the right than on the left side. Usually driving is intiated on one side of the horse, creating energy which can be absorbed through the body of the rider, who terminates it on the horse's side opposite from the initiating leg. We say "inside" and "outside" when referring to the horse rather than "right" or "left." The "inside" refers to that side to which the horse is bent or hollowed (laterally). The inside is usually, but not always, that side which is toward the center of the arena; the outside is usually the one toward the rail. During diagonal aiding, the horse is bent, in varying degrees, to his inside. Therefore, if the horse moves in counter canter, he is bent away from the center of the arena and is facing toward the rail. In such a case the "inside" of the horse is actually toward the rail.

Where there is no rail, as in cross-country riding or when stadium jumping through continuous curving lines, the "inside" is always the side toward which the horse is bent. Thus, the horse is always shorter and contracted or "hollow" to the inside and longer and stretched or "full" to the outside.

The rider's legs can be in two basic positions on the horse's sides. The so-called "on the girth position" is slightly behind the girth, the rider's toes are flush with the girth. The so-called "canter position," or "outside leg back position," of the rider's leg is further behind the girth position by about two to six inches. It is called the canter position because it refers to the position required of the rider's outside leg during the canter. It is important to maintain both of these positions with toes well elevated and heels sunk, and continue to ride with stretched calves. During diagonal aiding, one leg is in the "girth" position, the other is in the "canter" position.

THE VARIOUS HAND POSITIONS

The indirect hand serves the purpose of indicating lateral bending to the horse. In this position, the rein is held so that if it were to continue beyond the hand, it would pierce the rider's chest on the opposite side. In other words, if the inside rein is held as an indirect rein, it would connect the inside corner of the horse's mouth to the outside breast of the rider (if the rein were to continue in a straight line beyond the rider's fist). The indirect rein is held near the horse's neck but not crossing over to the other side of his crest. This rein position is usually passive. It should not be pulled backward. In all lateral movements, where aids must always be diagonal, the rider's inside rein is usually used as an indirect one. It is passive and therefore does not act as a rein in opposition to the inside hind leg of the horse, which must carry more weight in lateral movements than the outside one. The indirect rein helps to position the horse's forehand, assist in controlling his shoulders, and contributes to collection.

The direct rein is used to perform half-halts and full halts. It is the hand position designed to communicate effectively the restrictive torso actions of the rider to the horse's mouth. It is the hand that asks and invites the horse's forehand to slow down and wait for the hindquarters to catch up. It is the only hand position that provides the option of passive resistance to the progression of the forehand and must be followed by yielding forward in rhythmic intervals that are coordinated with the horse's shoulder movements. The horse responds to the direct rein by supply yielding his jaw, poll, and neck. The direct rein may go from contact to yielding, and it should avoid restricting and inhibiting the freedom of the strides.

The direct rein connects the horse's mouth toward the rider's hip on the same side. In diagonal aiding, the outside rein is usually direct. In parallel aiding, both reins are used as direct reins. It is important that the activities of the direct rein always be coordinated with the rider's abdominal muscles. The bracing of the abdominal muscles will round the small of the back and cause the pressure of the pelvis toward the waiting fists to increase the contact with the horse's mouth. There should be no tension in the rider's arms.

The leading rein is used most often on young or green horses to offer them exaggerated guidance when needed. The direction of the leading rein is from the horse's mouth toward the rider's thigh on the same side. So it is a rein held slightly away from the horse's neck and directed slightly downward, indicating strongly the track on which the horse is to turn. The indirect rein must be created with a slight "fingernails-up" position of the hand and not fingernails down. It must always be paired with a direct rein on the opposite side. As the horse advances and accepts the rider's legs for bending and turning, this leading rein will no longer be necessary and will be replaced by an indirect rein. The indirect rein helps to place the horse's shoulders, relative to his haunches, in the correct position for any specific exercise.

Now that so much has been said about the aiding system, let me add as a summary that aiding is successful only if the rider offers it through a logical sequence:

1. Rider prepares the horse: warning, usually by rebalancing to the haunches (i.e., an increase in collection). This takes the form of a half-halt.
2. Horse responds to preparation by attentiveness and by assuming more weight on the haunches.
3. Rider aids into the movement.

4. Horse executes the movement correctly: always through a supplely flexed topline and with well-articulated flexion in his joints.
5. Rider confirms the horse's response by yielding: hands give, muscles relax, pelvic structure and legs hang.
6. Horse relaxes and perpetuates the movement: purity of gaits, consistency of rhythm, elevation, suspension of strides and carriage.
7. The rider harmonizes with his relaxed horse in the desired movement, experiencing a partnership, not unlike a dance.

The following table summarizes the correct aiding sequence.

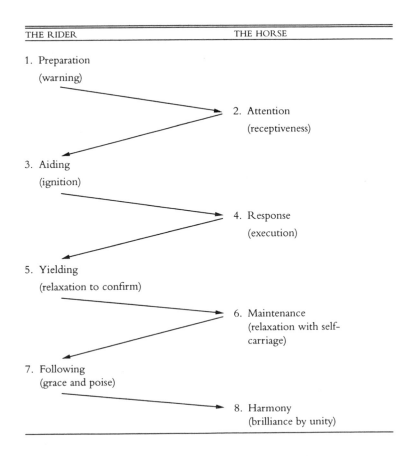

THE RIDER	THE HORSE
1. Preparation (warning)	
	2. Attention (receptiveness)
3. Aiding (ignition)	
	4. Response (execution)
5. Yielding (relaxation to confirm)	
	6. Maintenance (relaxation with self-carriage)
7. Following (grace and poise)	
	8. Harmony (brilliance by unity)

This sequence takes a very short time to perform. Yet, all steps of it must be performed by both rider and horse. If one of them omits one of these responses, the entire sequence must be reinitiated by the rider, who repeats the first step of preparation.

It is tremendously important to yield to our horses. Nothing should ever freeze when aiding; nothing should ever be locked; nothing should ever become static. Riding is dynamic; it is perpetual movement. Good riding shuns confinement. Therefore, it tolerates no rigidity, which is the stopping of motion. Should any part of the rider become stiff, the horse will respond likewise. If any part of either horse or rider is stiff, it spreads to the whole system.

In conclusion, let me state once more that dressage is beneficial for any horse. It is, in fact, therapeutic riding. After all, dressage is simply the natural, harmonious, kindly way of logically gymnasticizing him. Indeed, dressage was developed to help promote the usefulness of any horse. There is no horse in this world that will not benefit from dressage by becoming stronger, more supple, more elastic, more balanced, more harmonious, more attentive to understanding light aids rather than force. All riders can appreciate a horse whose attention span has been increased and who is more trusting of the rider. Any performance can be improved by a more obedient horse who is not only willing but also capable of using himself correctly. That is what dressage aims to achieve.

THE DEVELOPMENT OF THE SEAT THROUGH LUNGEING EXERCISES

Riders have traditionally been evaluated, sometimes praised and admired, entirely on the correctness, and therefore the beauty, of their seat and the imperceptible effectiveness of their influences over the horse.

Horses cannot be improved by giving them physical exercises only. The diversification of work awakens the horse's mind. Movement over open country and acquaintance with varied terrain is indispensable to the development of the horse. Climbing, sliding, moving up and down hills, jumping natural obstacles, stretching over ditches, wading through water, all these and more are the natural tasks for the horse before he is trained in the controlled environment, the manege, the dressage arena. The means toward the desired dressage ends cannot all be found in the small indoor arena.

Analogous to this are the riders who take only "dressage lessons," ride only with long stirrup leathers, sit all the movements, and remain with their horses in small, fenced-in areas. They will seldom become adequate, never really outstanding, dressage riders. A dressage rider is primarily an athlete who must breathe correctly, be strong, yet supple, balanced and coordinated. The rider should have the strength and skills to remain tranquil and absorb the large movements of the horse without looking disharmonious and out of balance. A rider should have muscle tone and strength, but without tightness, stiffness, or tension. The dressage rider has to be, first of all, a horse person who is acquainted with a diversity of equestrian activities, because only by these means can the nature of the horse be discovered. A dressage rider cannot be "made" by riding dressage only. Knowing the feeling of a self-propelled horse that needs no prompting to keep in his gait can best be learned by riding cross-country. The bold and powerful gaits of an alert horse negotiating a natural environment cannot be experienced in a fenced-in arena. To feel rhythm and to judge distance, one ought to ride over cavalletti and jumps. Well-known international dressage riders of eminence rode cross-country and over fences before specializing in dressage and producing the outstanding results for which they are known. Many riders have become international dressage riders after having been well trained in riding across open country and jumps.

Riders should begin their training on the lunge line, while the horse is under the control of the trainer. Even after becoming an outstanding rider, one should be lunged time and time again for the needed athletic adjustments in equitation.

Many things should be done in the saddle during a lungeing lesson. First, the rider should be "sculpted" by words and by actually being placed in the correct position. Legs must be in contact with the horse's sides. Once the rider's legs are draped for stability and adhesiveness of the seat, while the calf is stretched by lifting the toes, they will be able to provide the requisite driving aids. The ankles should be relaxed and mobile, knees turned inward, thighs stretched downward, buttocks and seat bones spread, spinal column straight and stretched upward. Shoulder blades must be flattened into the back muscles and almost touching one another, thereby lifting the rib cage upward so the lungs can breath and the heart cavity is open. The neck should be straight, with the head up, eyes looking straight ahead. Upper arms must hang relaxed, perpendicular to the ground. This is the "basic position," which is assumed on command when the rider is allowed to discontinue an exercise and show the ability to return to a correct, balanced position. This is seen in figure 1, at the walk. The basic position should also be assumed at the trot and canter. There are a few guidelines before beginning work on the lunge line:

1. Do all exercises slowly and in a continuous, fluent motion, not jerkily or abruptly.
2. Start with the lowest parts of the body and move upward. Feet first, then legs, and proceed with torso, shoulders, arms, and hands.
3. Exercise first in walk, then trot, and eventually canter. Almost all exercises can be done in all three gaits.
4. Always start from and return to the "basic position." In lungeing, this means to sit without stirrups, yet with knees in contact with the saddle and the seat hanging down into the saddle adhesively.
5. Intersperse exercises with brief rest periods for the benefit of horse and rider.

In figure 2, the rider has been asked to sit as correctly as he can. He does fairly well, although there are two notable excep-

1.

2.

The photographs appearing here and on pages 59–69 were demonstrated by and photographed by Paul Drake and Susan Derr Drake.

TRAINING STRATEGIES FOR DRESSAGE RIDERS

3.

tions that need adjustment. The lower back is slightly too round (this may be necessary for driving, but not at the halt), which raises the crotch too high and denies stretching and downward pressure on the thighs. The rider's legs are too far forward, showing lack of stretching. The toes are ahead of the knees, which are too high. These faults are a natural consequence of the rounded lower back and lifted crotch. In figure 3, we can see the rider from the front. "Squaring off" as best he can, while the shoulders and arms look square and balanced (neither one is raised nor pushed ahead of the other), we can see that the left knee and heel are stretched longer than the right. The right leg needs more stretching downward to match the left, but before that is done, the rider should be asked to stretch both sides much farther down and to place both legs farther back and down from the hip.

Illustrated in figure 4 is a driving seat with the shortcomings

4.

of a stiff ankle that turns the toes out and pushes too much with the heels, rather than with the calves. The rider has also lowered her head in an attempt to monitor the horse's progress visually. However, the use of the lower back, the tilt of the torso, and the use of pressure through the buttocks and thighs are well illustrated here as commanding driving forces.

EXERCISES ON THE LUNGE

1. An exercise that relaxes and limbers the ankle joints and stretches the calf mucles can be done early in the lunge session by rotating the ankles by describing large circles with the toes. Start inward, upward, outward, downward, inward, etc., rotating both feet simultaneously and ending with toes sharply lifted, heels depressed, and feet parallel with the horse's sides. Always keep the calves in a draped contact with the horse's rib cage.

2. The rider in figure 5 is swinging her legs loosely and freely, in alternate directions, on either side of the horse. This produces awareness of the mechanics of unilateral aids (such as

5.

6.

THE DEVELOPMENT OF THE RIDER'S SEAT AND AIDS   61

7.

in canter departs), opens and widens the seat bones, rotates the hips, and deepens (and widens) the seat. This exercise limbers and relaxes the lower back, making it an antidote for a hollow back. It also helps to correct a collapsed hip position. It helps square off the hips and suggests the feeling of refining the leg contact so that the leg is there for aiding, but without gripping.

3. The very important exercises that develop proper leg position and strong leg aids are shown in figures 6 and 7. The proper positioning of the lower back, pelvic bones, hips, thighs, and knees is paramount to good riding. The exercise that consists of holding the ankles with straight arms, making sure the spine remains straight and the rib cage lifted, will put the knee in the proper deep position. This, in turn, determines the correct placement of all other elements in the seat and legs. Often one must start with one foot at a time before gradual stretching allows both legs to be held simultaneously by the rider, with the torso tall. One should be able to lift the legs up, then keep them there without holding them, thereby freeing the hands for additional exercising. While legs are in that stretched position, the rider should go through many combinations of exercises, such as tilting the torso forward and back or rotating the shoulders. By pivoting the torso around the axis of the spine, the stretching and rotating of the arms can also be added. When stretched enough, slowly lower the legs on the horse's sides until the heel becomes the deepest point, toes lifted well up and placed just behind the knees.

4. As seen in figure 7, the rider finds his balance by contacting the horse only through firmly placed seat bones, by lifting both knees to the height of the hands while pulling firmly on the pommel with the hands to increase adhesion. One must not touch the saddle or the horse with the legs. The straight and vertically stretched torso remains anchored. Riding this way (knees are actually too high in this picture) is important for gaining balance. This exercise develops the sensation that the earth's gravitational pull can keep us on the horse without any need to grip with the legs. This exercise also centers the seat in the middle of the saddle and helps unite the rider's center of gravity with that of the horse in motion. It is an indispensable exercise for the strengthening of the abdominal muscles, without which there is no riding and no half-halting.

5. While the rider in figure 8 has been asked to stretch and

8.

9.

10.

11.

reach as high as he can (evenly, with both arms in short, upward thrusts), he has also been warned to keep his legs stretched down as deeply as he can. This is an exercise for maximum vertical stretching. The spine should be straight, and the arms lifted into a more vertical position than is shown here. The legs should also be stretched more.

6. In figure 9, the rider is rotating the arms in opposite directions, a limbering exercise that can be done either in the manner of swimming the Australian crawl, or in the opposite direction, depending on the posture needs of the rider. The exercise should be done with straight arms (no bend in the elbows) and without altering the deep stretching of the legs. The arm rotation exercise can be combined with others to increase the value of corrections needed; for example, while swinging or rotating the arms, one could tilt the torso forward or back, and even add a sideways pivoting of the torso to increase the limbering effects of the lumbar back.

7. Stretching of the back and side muscles can be accomplished by either reaching across the horse's neck and down (fig. 10) or just reaching down on the horse's shoulder (fig. 11). These exercises are very important (as is the one in fig. 8) for stretching the muscles in the torso. During the stretching, the seat must remain fully centered in the saddle.

8. Figures 12 and 13 show an exercise that contributes to

12.

the ability to drive with the seat. The push from the legs is
coordinated with a push from the shoulders, down through the
lower back into the saddle, so as to urge the horse forward and
apply properly aiding leverage and influence to the back muscles.
First, exaggerate the aid by tilting well behind the vertical while
making sure the legs are kept stretched back and down. The
same position, combined with an exaggerated pivoting back with
the outside shoulder while pushing the inside shoulder forward,
should produce a canter departure through the seat. Following
the canter, we can aid from the trot by "squaring" the shoulders,
by suddenly pushing the outside shoulder forward and bringing
the inside one back. This makes the shoulders part of an imaginary spoke of a wheel that is described by the circle on which
the horse moves, and it brings the horse back to trot. The rider
should learn the effectiveness of the seat through the various
exaggerated torso positions (fig. 13). Leaning back "accelerates,"
while leaning forward to the vertical, but never in front of it,
"breaks" or collects the horse. Awareness of the position of the
rider's shoulders and hips, which should remain parallel with
those of the horse, should be developed through appropriate
exercises. An example of such an exercise could be a rider can-

14.

15.

16.

tering a horse on the right lead and holding the pommel with
his right hand, the cantle with the left, and raising his right knee
up to be level with the cantle.

9. The exercises shown in figures 15, 16, and 17 are done
with the arms moving on a horizontal plane. Flattening of the shoulder blades can best be done with such exercises. Widening and lifting the rib cage upward can also be accomplished. This rider is
following her hand with her eyes as it moves back and forth on

18.

a horizontal plane. The arm should be pushed as far back as possible. Using both arms in stretching and torso rotations (figs. 16 and 17) is most beneficial for relaxing, stretching, and strengthening the all-important lower-back area. This should be done only with the buttocks firmly down in the saddle.

10. As illustrated in figures 18 and 19, rotating the torso causes the seat bones and hips to shift. While shifting our weight to one side can be useful in aiding (canter, etc.), it can also be a sign of a collapsed hip and a crooked seat. In that case, we correct by temporarily rotating more toward the opposite side. If the right hip is collapsed, we should pull the left shoulder backward and push the right one ahead. In these pictures, however, the legs are still too far forward, lacking stretching adhesiveness, and the toes are hanging down with the musculature limp. These are things to be avoided when doing these exercises.

Exercises that are performed on the lunge should be one of two basic kinds: stretching and rotating. Balance is developed by both types of exercises. The instructor should know and assign the appropriate exercises to correct faults as they emerge. For instance, if a rider has a hollow, arched back with the hip bones tilted forward, one should not suggest the exercise of

19.

Earl McFall is doing some of the most essential exercises that help deepen the rider's seat and establish the correct lumbar articulation.

The rider leans back exaggeratedly, behind the vertical, to supply adhesiveness to the seat and tone up the abdominal muscles that hold the seat down. This position teaches the lumbar back how it should feel as it molds to the motion to unite its horizontal sliding with its vertical surrender to the articulations of the horse's back.

Both knees can be lifted, with legs distanced from horse, to anchor the rider on his seat. Then one can alternately raise and lower the knees to "bicycle" into a more supple back and reconfirm the independence of the legs. Or one leg can be pushed backward while the other is extended forward as straight as possible. These exercises also increase the rider's awareness and aptitude to follow the horse's alternating lateral motions.

These exercises should only be done while being lunged. The rider can benefit from them only if he feels safe and is allowed to hold on to the pommel if necessary. The exercises should be done slowly and just long enough not to cause fatigue or loss of balance. Photo: Richard Williams.

folding the arms behind the back and bending backward. That would accentuate an already grave fault. Yet with a slumped-backed rider, this exercise might be very appropriate.

Again, the rider's position should be adjusted for him to feel when the angles are correct. The "sculpting" of the rider at the halt is very important, because a rider understands only what he has a chance to feel. Memorizing correct feeling is indispensable in learning to ride. A rider who is never made to feel what is correct cannot be expected to perform correctly. Teaching riders on the lunge takes a certain specialized knowledge. Such work should not consist of the rider sitting in an approximation of the Grand Prix rider's seat. Often, we see people being lunged and being perpetually adjusted to the "ideal posture." This does not always help achieve the desired goals of lungeing. During a lungeing session, the rider's all-around athletic ability should be developed. Balance, coordination, strength, suppleness, stretching of muscles, and rotating of joints should be encouraged. When a sensible lungeing program is incorporated with jumping, cavalletti work, and cross-country riding, the result will be the development of a rider who is physically capable of aspiring to meet the vast diversification of skills required to become a dressage rider.

THE LOGIC OF THE CORRECT SEAT

Unless the rider sits correctly, the horse will move with pain or discomfort. A deep, adhesive, balanced seat that correctly partners the horse's movement is indispensable for the rider who wants to help rather than destroy his horse. The absence of any discomfort for the horse signals that mutual cooperation between horse and rider can possibly begin. Through a good seat, we can gain the horse's trust in us as a partner and his attention to our wishes. Only a correctly seated rider can apply the aids effectively. By the combination of becoming a harmonious weight and by communicating properly, we may achieve the desired athletic development in our horse.

As in most athletic endeavors, the rider must develop the seemingly contradictory qualities of relaxation and strength. Relaxation allows horse and rider to harmonize, finding pleasure in moving through space in cooperative unity. With appropriate strength in specific muscle groups, the rider can use his aids to communicate with his horse.

Balancing the rider in the saddle is the first and paramount step for him on the way to controlling the horse. As long as the rider fears falling off, or even just losing his balance, relaxation cannot be expected. When losing balance, we instinctively tighten and grip with many sets of muscles, hoping that by strength, we can prevent falling off. Lungeing by an expert provides the rider with the hours in the saddle that give a sense of safety through improved balance. At first, the rider should hold the front of the saddle or a gripper strap and not the reins. The rider will gradually become independent of the need to hold on to anything to secure his balance. Once the rider has stopped losing his balance and slipping in the saddle while riding the basic gaits, he can begin exercises that involve moving various parts of his body independently.

An independently balanced rider emerges after a long process of carefully selected suitable suppling and stretching exercises. Useful stretching and limbering exercises should be done first at the walk, then at the trot, and finally at the canter.

An equestrian earns the name of "rider" by acquiring a balanced and independent seat. Having achieved that, he should be allowed to take control of his horse. Allowing premature control of the horse by the novice rider can cause undesirable habits, and such a rider's seat and aids may never be completely corrected.

CORRECTIVE FAULTS

Here are some suggestions for dealing with the most common faults seen in a rider's seat and aids.

Head Carriage

The rider's head should not be tipped forward or tilted sideways. The neck should be straight and part of an upright spinal column.

The neck muscles should remain relaxed, so that the rider can look slightly sideways without affecting his functions elsewhere. A good exercise is to turn the head from side to side slowly until the chin is placed in a level position above the collarbone.

Torso Position

The shoulder blades should be straightened by folding them back and down to place them flat in to the musculature of the back (not visible butterfly wings) so as to have only a small space between them. This lifts the rib cage (chest out), insuring good breathing and a straight spine. The rider must constantly con-

Earl McFall demonstrates the exercise that straightens the rider's shoulders, stretches his torso tall, and gives a high head carriage. The straight, stretched torso is essential to building the rider's "cabinet," which is the pivotal influence for the increased effectiveness of the seat. This exercise will greatly improve balance as well. Photo: Richard Williams.

centrate on correct body posture even when dismounted—for example, while eating or driving a car. The upper arms must hang in a relaxed manner with straight shoulders, parallel to the spine, which allows the rib cage to be ahead of them. The elbows should feel weighted down as if by lead. (See photo of author on page 239.)

Arm Position

The upper arms should hang (not be extended forward), and the elbows should feel weighted. Do not flare the elbows away from the rib cage. Start by hanging the arms straight down, then bend at the elbows, and put your two fists close together in front of your abdomen. Adjust the reins so that you can hold them in this relaxed position. There should be both relaxation in the arm muscles and tranquillity (steadiness) at the shoulder and elbow joints. Without these qualities, independent hands cannot develop.

To stretch the arms forward from the shoulders, thereby rounding them and making the chest concave and dropping the head forward, is a grave mistake. This faulty position is often acquired by the mistaken notion that the rider must shorten the reins for increased control over the horse. The shortening of the reins to the point of distorting the rider's arm and torso position will actually weaken the seat. When the rider reaches forward for the reins with elbows in front of the shoulders, his seat is debilitated and, with that, the controls abdicated. The shorter the rein, the weaker the seat, the less control. Equally mistaken are notions about shortening the reins to increase collection. As said elsewhere, collection is not a short neck and cannot be achieved without an impeccable seat. Adequate rein length to accommodate the perfect torso position, on the other hand, will increase control and collection. The adhesive seat is the custodian of both.

Wrists and Hands

The wrists should be straight: that is, the back of the rider's hand should be on the same plane (straight continuum) as the back of his forearm. If one assumes the correct position, the large joints of the index fingers should touch when one presses the fists together.

All fingers should be closed. A full fist should be formed, with the fingertips lined up evenly in a row in the middle of the palm. Open fingers can cause the rider to constantly lose the reins and to repeatedly readjust their length. The contact will be upset, altered, and restless. When riders do not learn to ride initially with closed fingers and a closed fist, then at higher levels with the double bridle, they will lose contact with the bridoon and remain in contact only through the curb bit. This often causes overflexing and tensing of the neck in advanced horses. The tips of the thumbs should press down and contact the large joint of the bent index finger. The pressure on the reins should be held between the tip of the thumb and the joint of the index finger, leaving the rest of the fist to moderate its isometric pressures from mild to firm by squeezing. This refinement is an activity for the fist of an accomplished rider on a well-trained horse that can perceive these minuscule signals. As long as movements transmit to the bit without the rider's explicit will and by his design, isometric refinements in the tensing and relaxing of the fists remain meaningless. That sophistication is based on the presumption that the rider's hands are independent and transmit only what the rider explicitly wishes them to transmit to the bit.

The rider's wrists should not be stiff, a fault that is often caused by incorrect angling. They should not be "hinging," either, that is, they should not be allowed to rotate in and out or up and down. The hinging action of the wrist—rocking the fist back and forth frequently—is employed in a misguided effort to soften the horse's jaw. The wrists should simply be straight, quiet, and relaxed. A riding whip may be used to straighten the wrist. Holding the wrist correctly, the underside of the forearm and the underside of the rider's fist should form one flat plane continuously touching the straight whip. Another faulty wrist position causes a pushing of the "thumb down." The line running through the back of the wrist, the lower arm, and the top of the hand should remain straight.

Lower Back and Seat

Do not arch or hollow the lower back. That mistaken position denies the legitimate functions of the lower back, through which the rider needs to follow the horse's motion and monitor the energy coming from the haunches. Riders who press their hips forward ahead of the seat bones, press the crotch down, and slant the lower abdomen over the pommel will never feel the horse's haunches. As a consequence, they can never influence the haunches. They "limb ride" and consequently cannot feel the horse's quarters, cannot sense the functioning of his back muscles (which they pound stiffly by using that position), and will only accelerate by kicking and "brake" with the hands. With a hollow and therefore stiff back, the rider's body cannot be the "transformer" of the energy supplied by the haunches, absorbed through the seat and returned to the horse's mouth in an appropriately altered fashion.

Thigh Position

The rider's thighs should remain flat on the sides of the saddle and should be isometrically toned to stabilize the seat without gripping. They should also be stretched from the hip, with the knees low and back. To enhance the deep knee position and long stretched-calf contact, one of the best exercises is to rise to the trot without stirrups. It will also significantly improve the rider's balance.

Lower Leg Position

The stretching of the calf muscles (ankle extensors) and the ability to contract the muscles around the shinbone (ankle flexors), producing the "heels down, toes up" position, is crucial for stable, quiet, strong, and appropriate driving and bending aids. Without properly stretched calves, there is simply no effective riding! A common fault is that riders wanting "dressage" attempt to ride "that style" by lengthening their stirrup irons virtually beyond reach. The toes must be raised to stretch the calves. Therefore, the stretching of the calves, the flexing of the ankles, all develop

The author, in 1993, schooling a half-pass to the right. Notice the straight, tall posture with the rib cage lifted and the shoulder blades flat. This allows the arms to hang under the shoulder joints, naturally elevate and widen the chest, and anchor the seat by the isometric unity of the torso. This seat allows the rider's adhesively hanging, stretched, and relaxed leg to aid effectively, void of tensions and distortions. Upper legs and knees are included in both the anchoring of the seat and the draping of the legs. Photo: Richard Williams.

in short stirrups. The rider must earn the long stirrups gradually, as he can lower them notch by notch without losing the stretching in his muscles and sinews. His legs should stretch from the hip to the heel and not from the hip to the tip of the toe as in ballet. Stirrups can be lengthened one hole at a time as the stretching of muscles and skills of adhesiveness in contact develop. Riders should start their work on equitation with short stirrups, rising or standing over the knees until the knees sink down and back, steady in their contact position, helping to sink the heels. Eventually, one may practice these skills in the sitting trot and the canter, still riding with short stirrups. This gives a feeling similar to that of going down on your knees in church.

In these three photographs, the author demonstrates what he wishes to emphasize regarding equitation. First, a harmonious balance and the surrendering of the seat to the horse. Second, a rider who "grows taller" from the seat bones up while stretching longer from the seat bones down toward a deep ankle when the horse is asked to lengthen. All work in extensions demands a deepening of the seat, absolute adhesiveness in all contact areas, including the buttocks as well as both legs all the way down to the ankles. The chest must remain expanded, stretched, and wide. The back must remain straight. The rider's torso should be like the torso of a soldier standing at attention!

The image in the mirror shows that the draped legs are in continuous contact throughout their entire length, emphasizing visually that on a bending horse, such as here, the outside leg is positioned behind the inside one, yet without turning the toe out and gripping with the heel. There is no space between the horse's torso and the rider's legs. Only in this way can the horse be bent properly with the legs. Photos: Richard Williams.

The rider's legs represent the most important elements of a harmoniously coordinated aiding system. They are the primary sources of aiding for impulsion and bending. When horses are not on the aids (and consequently not on the bit, either), it is usually because of the ineffective legs of their riders. Ineffectiveness of the driving and bending aids is most commonly due to incorrect positioning and use of the leg.

One common incorrect leg position develops when the thigh and knee are held too tightly, gripping the saddle. Consequently, the rider's lower leg is pushed away from the horse, preventing contact by standing in the stirrup, becoming prisoners of the irons. The ankles are locked stiffly (not rotating with the motion of the horse while aiding) and the toes are turned out. While there is a false "heel down" position, the leg is rendered useless. When working in such a position, the leg aid comes suddenly and from a distance. It is ill timed and reckless and delivers a kicking action, upsetting the rider's seat, not to mention the horse. This kind of leg can neither produce pushing aids (the only powerful yet relaxed aids), nor can it supply rhythm based on supple contact of the calf muscles.

Knee Position

Turned-out knees pinch the seat bones tightly together, contrary to the correct wide distribution of the seat bones on either side of the saddle's spine. The aids produced by legs with turned-out knees may sometimes be rhythmical but banging, giving the impression that the horse is being rhythmically prompted and made dull. Highly visible and rude aids like these will dull the horse and sour him to the aids. There is no chance for modulation in such aids; they "attack" the horse at the same rate all the time. They overaid for the most part, but never moderate appropriately for the occasion.

When the stirrup irons are positioned under the ball of the foot (good for jumpers but not for dressage riders) and the rider is applying undue pressure downward onto the irons, the position will stiffen the legs. The ankle is locked by this, preventing free rotation of the joint, forcing the foot into immobility. The legs will move in an upward scratching on the horse's side. Both heel and knee will be pushed upward by the rider "pedaling down" on the stirrups, like on a bicycle. Meaningless aids develop. The foot should rest on the irons at about the joints of the toes.

With all incorrect leg positions, a great deal of effort will be exerted by the rider to produce a dull horse that cannot interpret the annoyances of rude legs at his sides.

An instructor must step up to the rider to "sculpt him" into a correct position. We can only learn by feeling a position and experiencing the assumption of that position.

Andrew Rymill's leg position is being "sculpted" by the author. Helping a rider to feel how one assumes correct positions is an important part of instructing. Riders learn by feeling, as well as words.

Photo: D. Edmund-Jones/Photosport.

THE PREVENTION OF PULLING
ON THE HORSE'S MOUTH

In schooling horses, pulling on their mouth is unnecessary and causes them anxiety and eventually physical damage. The discomfort and stress to the rider is also enormous, unnecessary, but well deserved. The rider should hold the reins but not his horse. Nature made the horse to balance perfectly on his four legs. The rider's duties do not include lending the horse a "fifth leg," the reins, to lean on. In fact, classical horsemanship cherishes the ideal of a horse in self-carriage. While that concept includes several ideas, depending on the horse's gymnastic development, it always includes the notion of a horse moving free from the rider's encumbrances on the reins. In fact, the reins may do a number of things but not these three: they should not inhibit the horse's liberty to use his limbs freely; they should not attempt to shape the horse's neck and posture; and they should not steer separately.

The reins in the rider's hands are tools and, as with all tools, can be put to good or bad use. Pulling on the reins, even in transitions, is a misuse of the reins. It is possible to think of dressage as desiring the elimination of pulling hands and any painful contact in general. Thus, strong contact through the reins, whether constant or occasional, is counterproductive to the goals of dressage.

Many riders pull because they do not sit in balance, which means they are not in full control of their body and therefore their aids. Often their riding remains ineffective. Words are not sufficient substitutes for feeling through riding. Words can only guide us to situations that will result in proper feelings.

Riding is a sport and, as in any sport, muscle tone, skeletal coordination, and strength in certain areas are all necessary.

During riding instruction, we may hear repeated requests for relaxation. Relaxation of the useful kind can be forthcoming only after the rider has achieved balanced unity with his horse. Indiscriminate or inappropriate relaxation is counterproductive. Certain areas of the body should be relaxed, but others should not be! As riders, we must carefully define each area in order to have an effective seat that can either drive or restrain without our pulling on the reins. No athletic endeavor can be based on total relaxation. People under anesthesia or in a faint are relaxed but are not capable of athletic performance.

In general, the proper and therefore effective seat demands that the rider be silent and present isometric unity from the waist up and be imperceptibly active from the waist down. Some riders who have misunderstood requests for relaxation collapse their torso and grip with their legs. A hyperactive but mushy torso can not remain balanced in the saddle. In this situation, only the strong grip of the lower legs keeps the rider on the horse. In fact, the isometric situation should be reversed!

The rider's torso should be isometrically toned to form his cabinetry. He should be properly stretched, straight in the back, and perpendicular to the level ground. In the torso, the rider should feel isometric muscle tone induced by his own inner toning rather than tensed by the horse's motion. Without isometric firmness in the torso, the "silence" of the torso cannot occur. The horse is moving, and the torso must not only accompany but even partner the horse's movement. The torso should accommodate the horse's movements in all three of its dimensions. The lumbar thrust accommodates the horse's horizontal progression in space. Suppleness in the lumbar back and in the ankles provides for "shock absorption" of the horse's vertical rise and fall with each of his steps as he impacts on the ground. That impact on the ground causes the verticality of the horse's motion. Finally, the rider's cabinetry—that is, his torso, including the upper arms and elbows—should pivot slightly in the exact rhythm of the horse's alternating use of his limbs. The horse progresses with alternating use of his limbs and many muscle groups. Therefore, a good rider's seat becomes quiet in repose precisely because he has learned to accommodate and harmonize with the horse's motion in all of its dimensions: its horizontality, verticality, and laterality. The motions in all three dimensions, of course, emerge as a combination of all three. The way they combine will differ accordingly in each of the horse's gaits.

Let me suggest some things to do when sitting in the saddle. This will necessarily fall short of my personally "sculpting" the rider, but it is all that words can offer:

1. Sit on the saddle without pressing down on the crotch in order to achieve the three-point seat, which has nothing to do with any downward pressure on the crotch. In other words, do not tilt the hips forward, but keep them directly above the seat bones.

2. Do not hollow your back or in any other way arch and stiffen your spine. Sit on your (relaxed, not tensed) buttocks rather than pushing them out behind. Keep the spine straight, which includes the pointing of the tailbone toward and not back and away from the saddle.

3. Tighten your shoulder blades and flatten them into your back so as to have no more than a small space between them; that will stretch the torso up. This is the way to elevate the rib cage and stretch the abdomen. This also, very importantly, stabilizes your shoulders, which in turn allows the upper arms to hang with steady elbows.

4. Flex and firm the abdomen to hold yourself erect. A flat and steady abdomen allows the lower back to follow the movement. The lower back should be relaxed so that the lower spine and lower back muscles can both drive and restrain to perform the half-halt properly. The abdomen provides the deep, adhesive seat so essential to driving and half-halting. Occasionally, lean behind the vertical as an exercise to experience how taut the abdomen ought to be and how it should control the lumbar thrust both horizontally forward and vertically downward. The pelvis and the thighs should hang down on the horse's spine and be draped over his back and barrel in full but lightly adhesive unity.

5. Keep the arms immobilized and cultivate quiet fists. Hands may either be still or yield forward, but both the silence and the motion must occur entirely by the rider's will and design. Involuntary and haphazard hand activities, as well as voluntarily rude activities, are grave riding faults. The hands (lower arms, wrists, and fists) must be mere extensions of the rider's seat only. It is through the stable, well-angled elbows that the horse feels the rider's seat in his muzzle. The buttocks in the saddle convey to the horse most of the rider's weight. Surely, the elbows are very important elements yet not equal to the rider's seat. Yet, the full effect of the seat, that is, its weight plus the activities of the entire torso (the cabinetry of the rider) is fully communicated through the elbows.

Perfectly steady hands are a vital component of correct riding, and that includes straight and steady wrists and fingers closed into a full fist. The lightest contact is not obtained by hinging the wrists or by opening or spreading the fingers. In such hands, there is frequent change, restlessness, inconsistency, haphazard or willful leverage, and loss of contact.

Aiding succeeds through a totally coordinated, harmonized, and perpetual system. There should be a firm feeling of "one riderness" in order to allow for the lightest possible contact. Regardless of how many thousands of miles an underground pipeline supplying water may be or how long an electric transmission wire, if these systems are broken at one tiny point, the system will fail to supply what is needed. Analogously, in riding, if the seat, hands, elbows, or legs fail to perform the proper functions, everything "shorts out" and the aids fail to reach the horse!

Know that all horses can be ridden with the lightest of contact and without inhibition through the reins. It only takes correct equitation and the constant perfecting of riding skills to be effective through lightness, ease, grace, and elegance, totally without force.

THE HALF-HALT

The half-halt is almost synonymous with dressage riding. Classical riding idealizes the perfecting of the horse's balance under his rider, without the force of hands. When properly done, the half-halt is a rebalancing aid without pulling.

The success of a half-halt is dependent on the rider's steadiness and coordination in the torso, for it is based on the anchorage of the seat. The driving aids, so intimately at the heart of a proper half-halt, cannot propel the haunches forward without the restraint of the forehand by a firm anchorage of the seat. The half-halt is an interlude of briefly doubling both the restraining and the driving aids.

A rider must perform half-halts often. Rebalancing the

horse, especially to increase his weight-bearing in his haunches, is at the heart of gymnastic progress. Therefore, half-halts ought to precede all changes required of the horse. These include the very frequent changes from bending to straightening and straightening to bending, such as when riding through corners, followed by the straight lines along the walls of a manege. Also, rebalancing is necessary prior to all transitions, whether they be within the same gait or from one gait to another.

The term "half-halt" carries by suggestion its true meaning and hints at its performing skills. The rider's "upper half," or torso, including upper arms and elbows, acts as a passively restraining force toward the horse's forward progression. Simultaneously, the rider's "lower half" drives the horse's haunches powerfully forward with the lumbar back and legs. Therefore, the sligthly backward-leaning torso, with its braced abdominal muscles, restrains the horse's forehand, while this very position enables the lumbar back and legs to drive more powerfully forward.

The rider's "upper half" is always the primary controller of the horse's "front," which includes the forehand as well as the neck and head. The rider's "lower half" is the primary controller of the horse's hind end, that is, everything behind the saddle: the haunches, the lumbosacral joint, the croup, the lower back, the hind legs—basically, all the propelling mechanisms and the seating mechanisms of the horse.

During the half-halt, the rider's activities also "split into two halves," not unlike the way he "splits" the use of his body into two halves. The first half of the rider's activities concerns the slowing of the horse's forehand in its forward horizontal progression, basically conveying to the horse the desire to halt. As soon as the horse responds appropriately to the invitation to prepare for a halt, the rider conveys to the horse that he "changed his mind" and would rather drive on. It is this creation of a momentary hesitation, followed by an outpouring of reserved energy, that makes the half-halt a dynamic rebalancing gesture.

While a rider might perform thousands of half-halts in a relatively short period of time, no two of them will be quite the same. Only the essence of the half-halt—that it results in an improved balance of the horse—will be constant. The rider's talent, "feel," knowledge, practicing of skills, and experience will determine for how long a half-halt will be performed. The variables are many. The first half, the passively resistant half, can be sustained for one stride or longer. The second half, the one urging a resurgence of energy from the haunches, can also be brief or prolonged. Beyond the timing of these phrases of the half-halt, the severity of the requests for rebalancing will also remain variable. A rider can nearly stop a horse and suddenly pour his energies forward or a rider can just barely straighten and stretch his posture to create a new favorable condition for the haunches to move more forward or upward.

The half-halt is at the heart of the art of riding. It is based on skills and feelings that allow the rider to use himself simultaneously as a transformer of the horse's "staying power" into an "explosion" or renewal of energies. The same torso that speaks of "restraint" to the horse's forehand is the very torso that must be the "propellant" for his haunches.

Finally, the half-halt is only intensifying the rider's influences for the first half of its performance. The second half must consist of yielding and relaxation, to confirm to the horse the rider's satisfaction with his new balance and allow it to be maintained in self-carriage. The first half of activities is by "commission" while the second half is by "omission" of actions. This relaxing second half of every half-halt allows the readjusted energies of the horse to "flow through" him unhindered and to lead to his self-carriage. Appropriate driving must, however, be maintained in both phases of the half-halt.

The half-halt is the result of the synchronized use of all aids in an exaggerated form. Simply stated, it is "doubling everything"! When performing a half-halt, the rider should increase appropriately his leg, torso/back, and rein aids.

The rider will increase his driving leg aids to facilitate improved impulsion, more engagement of the hindquarters. Against this, he will use a retarding back and rein aids. As a result, a shorter but taller-moving horse—moving with more athletic resolve—is more prepared to change something in his position.

Half-halts should be performed prior to all major changes requested in the horse's position. As I mentioned, in good riding,

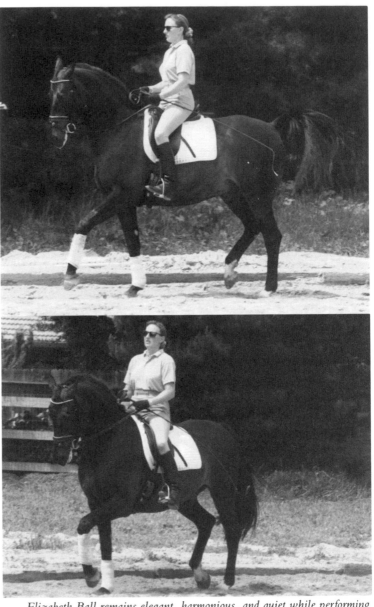

Elizabeth Ball remains elegant, harmonious, and quiet while performing half-halts. These somewhat frontal and side views allow us to observe the draped legs and the adhesive, tall, excellent seat. The performance of the half-halt feels as if one collected oneself, and the horse merely imitates and follows. Increased collection, improved balance, and engagement result from the half-halt. Photos: Richard Williams.

half-halts should be performed with great frequency. To emphasize their importance, we could say that riding is synonymous with the perpetual variation and interaction of half-halting, driving, and harmony through relaxation.

Half-halts are performed in order to make changes easier for the horse and to allow him to change his position without reducing his athletic involvement. Without a half-halt, the horse cannot make transitions (changes in longitudinal position), nor can he bend (change in lateral position), without compromising the major requirements of his athletic performance: relaxation, suppleness, balance, elasticity, and maintenance of rhythm.

Prerequisites to Half-Halting

The rider should be able to ride with an independent and balanced seat. Also, he should have developed effective and coordinated use of his musculature. Because the half-halt's success depends on well-synchronized and appropriately strong or mild aiding, the rider must be faultlessly "on time" with it, as gentle as possible, yet effective and perfectly capable of coordinating it with the movement of the horse.

The horse should be well on the aids, that is, longitudinally flexed, using his back supply to transfer the energies of the impulsion from the hindquarters to the absorbing forehand. He should have an educated mouth that will respond elastically without resistance to both yielding or passively restraining reins. He should, above all, be eager to engage his hindquarters when driven forward, without reluctance or sluggishness. Maturation of both horse and rider must have reached a level at which both are toned and elastic enough to expect of each other smooth, harmonious coordination and partnership.

Half-halts in any movement serve the purpose of suppling. Usually, a horse will have a stiff side and a hollow side. As he moves, he will lean on the rider's hand on his stiff side and not accept the bit on the hollow side. The rider should perform half-halts on the rein that is heavily contacted by his horse. Through his torso and reins, the rider should gently resist the forward progress and then relax contact on the heavy side. The activity should be rhythmically performed to the beat of the hind leg on the stiff side. The most important feature of the half-halt is the fact that it is "half," and therefore terminates each time the horse responds by yielding. For example, when the left leg drives, the left rein contacts, then follow with both left leg and left rein relaxing.

Half-halts in transitions are necessary for a supple arrival from one gait to another. The sign of such suppleness is that the horse needs to change neither his rhythm nor his length when going from one gait to another. When going from a potentially faster gait (canter or trot) to a potentially slower one (walk or halt), repeated half-halts will make for a "soft landing," as the horse moving with considerable impulsion will settle down lightly to a slower tempo without "falling" into the new gait. The first stride of each gait has to be as pure and impulsive as any that would follow it. Only by increased engagement, bending of the joints prior to a new gait, can the horse gather his quarters under the weight to support it correctly. The half-halt allows for repeated yielding, which will ensure an elastic entry into the new gait, uninhibited by a paralyzing, continuously resistant pull.

When the transition occurs from a potentially slower to a potentially faster gait, the half-halt serves as a preparatory warning device. It also facilitates improved engagement of the hindquarters. Thus, the prepared horse will be making a few more engaged steps which make him more capable of lifting up into a trot or canter, rather than merely pushing foward and falling through the forehand into these gaits.

Half-halts in lateral work should be employed to prepare each bending. Actually, every corner should be preceded by executing a half-halt. Without this, a horse usually does not bend, but instead falls through each corner stiffly. On lateral half-halts, diagonal aids are used. Thus, a half-halt before a corner should be performed with the inside leg driving and the outside rein maintaining contact.

Depending on the horse's natural suppleness and elasticity, on his gymnastic development and on his responsiveness to the aids, half-halts may be repeated more or less often. An advanced horse that is moving well in a full bridle will respond to half-halts before they transmit from the seat to the hands, which is to say, the horse will respond to the leg and seat aids primarily.

Half-Halts Lead to Self-Carriage

When an improperly trained horse leans on the bit and over-contacts, he will be forced to bid the musculature of his body against the rider's stress-causing hands. No human athlete could develop his body if it were engaged to force a locked door open by constantly leaning against it in a paralyzing brace.

Riders must insist on a contact so light that their hands merely transmit the isometric conditions and the position of their torso through the reins to the horse's muzzle. The horse should be able to read the rider's mind through the bit rather than being either held or steered by it. Self-carriage is a very serious requirement in classical equitation. If a rider cannot control the horse's haunches, tempo, and balance with his seat alone and without the pulling actions of his hands, he cannot gymnastically improve his horse. At all stages of training, the horse should remain in perfect balance without the rider's powerful connection to the bridle. Neither the rider nor the horse should hang on to the bit. It takes two to pull: if the rider blames the horse for pulling, he must remember that his horse is blaming him for the same. No one can pull on a string with force if the other end is not tied to something. An untied string cannot be tightened because it will follow the puller.

Training a horse without confinement and restraint through the reins will allow him to balance in self-carriage. This is the foundation for the future sophistication of the self-carriage concept. When a horse matures and develops gymnastically in self-carriage, he will volunteer to maintain the gaits without the rider's prompting. Therefore, the most sophisticated manifestation of self-carriage is when a horse can be asked to perform any gait, any figure, and any level of engagement that he voluntarily maintains until aided to change out of it by his rider. A sophisicated horse will maintain the gait, proceed on the figure, and maintain his posture just as his rider asked, as if by himself. He will not need step-by-step prompting and continuous pressuring by his rider. He will continue to perform "by himself" voluntarily because he is free from fear and inhibition and knows that he can trust his rider to not disturb his balance or impede his motion. A horse trained in such a manner, one in self-carriage, will always be free to engage his haunches and, as a consequence, remain light in the forehand. Such a horse will be free to engage for maximum performance his haunches, carry his neck in the most graceful posture, and work as if his proud performance were his own idea. A horse in self-carriage may be asked for passage and will maintain it until his rider asks him for a change, to perhaps a halt, or canter, or trot.

The horse in self-carriage is one working on his four legs, without borrowing the rider's hands as a "fifth leg." He is allowed freedom of carriage limited only by the accomplishments of his haunches. He always maintains his balance, with his rider's mild assistance, through half-halts. He promotes and prolongs his gaits, figures, and level of engagement willingly without the rider having to labor.

Self-carriage verifies the purity of the horse's schooling. If a rider cannot yield one or both of his reins without his horse rushing, breaking gait, or diminishing engagement, the horse is not trained correctly and is leaning on a "fifth leg." Self-carriage can be developed only by riders who are anchored in the horse's movement on their seat rather than connected to their horse through the hands, anchored in his mouth. Horsemanship has always been evaluated by the rider's ability to present his horse in self-carriage, hanging down from his seat and torso without any stress on the reins.

THE SEAT—SOME OBSERVATIONS

The following illustration can aid visually our understanding that the harmonious seat results from balance, relaxation, and appropriate flexion. Certain parts of the body should be relaxed while others must be flexed!

Note in the illustration that, in my opinion, harmony through the seat is not only a by-product of balance, relaxation, and flexion, but also is synonymous with controlling the horse's actions.

A balanced seat is the "vertical seat," which appears to be "leaning behind the vertical" because the nape of the neck and the shoulder blades should remain behind the seat bones. The

term "vertical" implies a vertical spinal position. The neck of the rider as well as his tailbone are both part of the spine. In order to produce a weight vector perpendicular to the ground, the line from the shoulder joints to the tailbone, rather than the line descending from the shoulder joints to the crotch, should be vertical. The weight of the torso acting perpendicularly downward should be able to propel the pelvic structure horizontally forward in front of the spine. The rider progressing horizontally harmoniously results from his utilization of his weight's vertical gravitational pressure transformed through the lumbar back into a horizontally forward thrusting pelvis.

An incorrectly sitting rider with an arched back hollows and tenses the lumbar area and pushes the buttocks out behind the movement, which will cause his own abdomen to undulate and rock forward and back, acting as a shock absorber. In such a case, the rider's weight and driving force will fall toward the crotch and cannot enter the saddle to influence the horse. The sense of direction in the seat will come from feeling that the weight of the shoulders back and down arrives in the saddle at the back of the seat, pressing the seat bones forward and downward toward the withers in the direction of the horse's movement.

THE COLLAPSED HIP

The collapsed hip, a very common manifestation of a number of serious faults in the seat, has its origins in the anatomical problem of being asymmetrical. We are built differently on each of our sides; we even have different organs lodged on different sides. We are certainly right- or left-handed, depending on functions of our central nervous system. As a result of one side predominating, our musculoskeletal progress also develops unevenly.

Yet, the goal of most athletic endeavors is to achieve trained (learned) ambidexterity. We certainly propose ambidexterity as one of our major gymnastic goals for our horses: "Straighten your horse and ride him forward!"

To diagnose a collapsed hip, one observes the rider from the front and from the back. Let us suppose that the rider's right hip is collapsed. Then this is what one would see:

1. The right stirrup looks (or is) shorter, the right ankle is stiff with the toe turned out and down more than on the left side.
2. The right knee is higher and more forward than the left one.
3. The right seat bone is pushed toward the center of the saddle while the rider "hangs away" from the horse's spine to the left of it.
4. The whole torso is shifted to the left of the horse's spine, while leaning at an angle to the right.

To compensate for the majority of the torso's weight being to the left of the horse's spine, the rider attempts to regain his balance by lowering his right shoulder and leaning his torso to the right. This will make the rider appear concave to the right and stretched taller on his left side. In such a position, the rider sits crookedly. Since riding is based on harmony, such a seat would impair progress.

Collapsed hips are a direct consequence of specific stiffness in the rider. Stiffness may be limited at first to an isolated area but will inevitably spread to other parts of the rider's body. The collapsed-hip syndrome is usually caused by ankle stiffness initially. If a rider cannot absorb the motion of the stirrups by properly resting his toes on them, following them with supplely rotating ankles, the ankles will stiffen. Supple ankles are a result of correctly positioned legs that hang parallel with the horse's sides. By posting unevenly, by sitting into the hollow side of the horse, or by maladjusted and/or uneven length of stirrups, riders with stiff ankles turn the foot out more or press down with one foot more forcefully on the stirrup. This slight change in that small ankle area can push one entire side of the rider off to one side, out of balance, and produce a collapsed hip!

By sitting on a chair at home, putting both feet on the floor, then pushing the right toe down, pulling the heel up, one can feel the right seat bone move to the center of the chair and the hip collapse. In the chair, one can reproduce the whole syndrome.

To correct the problem, one must eliminate its cause. Therefore, learn to mobilize and supple the ankles by following the motion of the stirrups. Lift the toes up and sink the heels down. The collapsed seat bone side should be pushed forward. Take all leg contact away from the saddle and ride in a walk (later in a trot) with both legs lifted away from saddle contact. (See lungeing exercises for a more complete description.) Feel how the seat bones can be pushed forward into place and how the lower back must work in order to keep them there!

In all turns, arcs, and circles, where the horse is expected to bend, one ought to ride with the inside bone pushed forward and down. We feel heavier on the inside seat bone because when bending the horse, the rider's outside knee and thigh must be pushed back and down, steadying the lower leg on the outside slightly behind the inner one in order to bend the horse. The heels must stay down to secure stretched calves.

By riding with the outside leg properly back, one automatically feels heavier on the inside seat bone without leaning on it. Then push the inside seat bone forward, downward, inward, and not sideways toward the center of the saddle.

THE RIDER'S INDISPENSABLE SKILLS

Because it is based on communication between two living organisms, riding must include not only the rider's "talking" but even more importantly his "listening." A rider's awareness of his horse's mental and physical state, indeed, should determine what and how much he asks of his mount. Therefore, the truly talented riders are recognized as having "feel," which depends on the talent for being a living antenna that picks up all communications the horse sends. The magic of perception and awareness, supplemented by intelligence, compassion, and empathy, can induce the rider to proper actions. For a knowledgeable observer, this soon becomes apparent. When schooling his horse, the good rider should "make sense" to an onlooker. An informed observer should be able to understand what the rider is doing and even predict what he will do. Most good things happen in silence. A noisy coach who dictates every move produces riders who are incapable of sensing their horses. They grow to rely on verbalizations from a coach rather than feelings from their horse. A dependency may be fostered between coach and rider whereby the coach becomes a crutch to lean on or an antagonist to resent. In the process, the horse and his communications are sacrificed and even ignored, the pleasure of riding not discovered. Indeed, the intoxication of riding is not in the process of aiding, but rather in the thrill of monitoring the horse's responses as pleasant verifications of successful communication.

A rider should always be fully aware of the horse's well-being and his horse's communications. He must also react to them with knowledge and insight. Knowledge comes by practicing riding, coaching, reading, watching, and discussing. More important, however, is the insight and wisdom gained by empathy toward the horse. Empathy, putting it simply, is the ability to put oneself into the position of another, to focus on the needs and interest of another rather than on one's own. The most sophisticated behavior, the most civilized and mature inner life of any person, is based on his ability to be "outward" rather than "inward." The rider ought to train himself to think the ways his horse does.

We can start by imagining that our horse is in a state similar or analogous to that which we experience when dreaming! We are aware of situations while dreaming, but do not know how we got into them. Nor do we have the power to change the circumstances or to extricate ourselves from those situations. We have pleasant, even thrilling dreams but also nightmares. They come about without our having much control over them, and when they proceed, we have little to do with the outcome. Yet we react to them, impulsively, even instinctively. We seldom react to dreams rationally or logically. We can neither analyze them nor form a synthesis. We cannot manipulate them. But we remember them well. We react to these dream memories emotionally. We fear nightmares, we palpitate, we sweat. Horses do, too, when the rider gives them nightmares! Horses are neither smart nor stupid in human terms. They are neither because when they surrender to the rider's controls and to his will, they enter a dreamlike state. Are humans smart or stupid when dreaming? Neither. We just know pleasure and pain; we know we are victimized by it. We know that physical discomfort brings on nightmares. Ride a horse into a pleasant dream. Make him remember the thrill of it. Ride only so long as it is pleasant and induces in the horse a dream. In a nightmare, a few minutes are much too long!

Rationality is based on logic. Logic is based on synthesis and anlaysis. Horses do not have these capabilities. So do not treat them like people. This is why conditioning has a very important role in riding and teaching a horse: that which is undesirable must be promptly eliminated and that which is desirable must be promptly rewarded. Good schooling should guide the horse to do what is desirable and to habituate correct responses. When things go well, riders become mesmerized with awe and pleasure. That prevents some of them from petting their horse. Always reward when things feel good and do it without breaking the magic!

Any absence of pleasure is already a mild form of punishment for the horse. Both reward and punishment play an important part in his training. They are essential features of the aiding system. While rewards should be bestowed on the horse after he has complied with a request, punishment should follow disobedience.

Basically, there may be four reasons why a horse does not perform what the rider has in mind: the rider's aid was not understood; the horse was not physically or mentally ready to comply with the rider's wishes; a sufficiently advanced horse, receiving correct aids, willfully disobeys them; or the horse evades the rider's influence by playfulness.

In the first two instances, the horse is incapable of performing what is requested because the rider aided incorrectly or he overdemanded. In both cases, the rider is at fault and no punishment is due the horse. In the latter two instances, however, the horse deserves some form of punishment. (See pages 254–255 for a discussion of this.)

Three

The Athletic Horse

Becoming an athletic horse is not done by food alone. The formal education of any animal, including the human, is heavily influenced and even determined to some degree by heredity. The animal is born with a genetic package of assets and limitations. Formal education should address a horse that is limited by his inborn abilities, aptitudes, talents, and potential. He will also have experiences prior to the beginning of his formal education. Consequently, the horse's background warrants some attention.

The genetic makeup of a horse is very important in determining how much education the horse will be able to receive. It determines how well the horse will perform. The best upbringing, the best education, the best training will not eliminate hereditary shortcomings, whether they are of a physical or mental nature. This is the reason why selecting the right young horse for our educational purposes is paramount to riding and competition success.

The upbringing of the young horse from his birth to the time his formal education commences is of great importance. The best hereditary traits can easily be thwarted, inhibited, or ruined by incorrect upbringing. A young horse can easily be

By nature, the horse is made for running. He is most beautiful when free and in flight. The canter is the most efficient of the horse's gaits. Here Attila, as a young stallion, shows his joy in flight and suspension. The horse should have space in which to move freely. This is essential when he is growing and not yet ridden. Even the ridden horse needs freedom for daily exercise, but never by being taken to a corral or turn-out ring and chased around by whip-cracking attendants. Raise and maintain your horses not by food alone, let them also live by moving. Photos: Susan Derr Drake.

physically stunted and mentally ruined long before he is mature enough to receive formal education or training. Damage in early life can cause shortcomings that are difficult to overcome and correct.

Like all living organisms, the horse exists in several contexts as a result of his interaction with his environment. The horse's "present" condition as we work with him in training does not exist in a vacuum. It represents two relevant dimensions: (1) The "present" of the horse is a result of his past; his memories, in particular. By the same token, his present is becoming the past of his future; whatever we do to him now, he will remember. (2) The horse will always spontaneously interact with his current environment, which, while training, includes us.

Therefore, to experience his world sympathetically is the first and foremost principle in the upbringing of a horse. We must consciously adopt an attitude of empathy toward the horse. We should try to experience the world (including ourselves) through his senses and as if through his thinking. This attitude presumes not only a willingness to empathize and an eagerness "to play at being a horse," but also a solid academic knowledge of the horse's nature.

To know our goals for the horse and chart our course to fulfill them constitute the second most important element of a successful training plan. Goals should be formulated in a hierarchical pattern. The cumulative, overall, paramount goal should always to be to develop our horse's innate potential to its utmost. If we select our young candidate horse properly, then his potential will guarantee that, as he develops it, he will also fulfill our competitive ambitions, as if by coincidence. Lesser, interim training goals will have to be designed for years, months, weeks, daily lessons, and even minute to minute. Since training is hierarchical, lesser goals must always be supportive of greater ones. We cannot hope to succeed in a year's program unless we do those things from minute to minute that will enhance and contribute to the yearly goal. In a brief outline of training suggestions, I will suggest major goals for about a one-year period.

From birth to six months of age, a foal is nurtured and nourished by his mother; therefore, his life is with his mother. They may be part of a herd of broodmares and foals or they might be in an area just as a pair. In either case, they should be in a large area where they can move about at leisure and at their chosen gait. Food should be plentiful and include natural pasture. When herding to pasture is necessary, it should be done at a leisurely walk, allowing opportunities to feed all the while.

From six months to two years of age, the weaned foal ideally should join a herd of similarly aged youngsters. The horse is a herd animal with well-developed social instincts. For his un-folding, the society of other horses is essential. Competition horses shying from others, kicking at others in a warmup ring, reveal great social inhibitions and resultant impairment. Horses raised correctly in a herd usually will not exhibit such undesirable and abnormal behavior. While sheltered overnight in a more confined and well-protected area, the young horses should re-main free (untied) and together in their shelter. During the day-time, and weather permitting, they should be herded out to pasture for the day's duration and back at evening time. As they grow older, both the length of the herding distance and the quality of its challenges can be increased gradually. The morning and evening herding times are those of purposeful exercise. Young horses should travel an ever-increasing distance on their feet and be moved over terrain that will contribute to good hoof and joint development.

These twice-a-day exercise periods should present physical and mental challenges in the form of small climbs, slides, ditches, ravines, brooks, ponds, logs, etc., as the local terrain naturally offers. Should the area be void of surface challenges by nature, herding paddocks should be constructed that will contain ob-stacles built to accommodate the desirable exercises.

From two to three years of age, formal schooling of the horse begins. The young horse should be separated from his fellows periodically and eventually, for most of the time. He is tamed and made accustomed to human companionship. He should receive a halter to wear, be groomed, housed in a separate box or paddock, and his hooves trimmed and shod. He becomes familiar and, if handled properly, friendly with people.

At first, he should be handled in the halter, then eventually lunged. At first, he will be lunged from the center of the circle. His balance will develop, and his familiarity with and love of people result in his obedience to his handler. Once the young horse obeys verbal commands given from the center of the circle on which he is lunged, he can be trained to accept two lunge tapes. The second tape is added around the outside of his body, running below his tail and above the hocks and leading to the handler, who holds it in the center of the ring. Lungeing on two tapes, or long reining, adds to the control of the horse, especially encouraging him to bend onto the arc of the circle. It also prepares the horse for the next step in his training. Care should be taken to use lunge lines (tapes) that are sufficiently long for this purpose (i.e., 10 meters, or 33 feet). Great care must be taken to avoid accidents whenever handling a horse. However, when lungeing a horse, potential for mishaps and accidents greatly increases. Riders must never be in "shooting range" of their horse's hind legs, never stay within kicking range of a horse. As a matter of principle, riders and handlers should not spend time behind the girth line of a horse and do all passing from one side to the other in front of the horse.

The horse is warmed up daily on the lunge tapes from the center of the circle on which he works. Later, he should also be driven from behind by long reining. The two tapes are held and handled as if driving a horse hitched to a buggy. The trainer must follow the horse on foot at an ample distance to prevent being kicked. He should aim to teach the horse to walk straight in front of him without excitement. Anytime the horse deviates from the straight line of his progress, the trainer must step directly behind him, making himself invisible, and insist on the horse's continued trust in him. All this work must be done without threatening the horse. When the young horse lunges well, both on a single tape controlled from the middle of a circle and from double tapes being driven from behind, he is ready for the next step of his education.

The horse should then be driven in a buggy or cart. There are several good books on how to teach a horse to pull and what proper equipment should be used while doing so. The importance of driving a horse from a buggy, or rather his pulling something, is enormous. As you have gathered by now, during each step of the horse's training, attention is paid to both his physical and mental development. By driving a horse, he will be straightened. He will develop his muscles further, while developing strength and stamina. He will acquire rhythm, especially through periods of trotting. He will develop the trotting muscles. He will be able to perform transitions that are gymnastically important for muscle and joint development. The horse will become supple, especially through transitions. He will learn to accept the bit and the handling of aids that communicate to him through complex equipment. Mentally, the horse's attention span will increase. He will be expected to keep his focus on small but meaningful communication signals. He must submit to his driver through trust. From the buggy, his handler can communicate to him, place demands on him, and intensify meaningful gymnastic exercises.

Driving is a great pleasure to the horseman and teaches him good hands and the use of the whip as an aid rather than an instrument of punishment. Being driven should be a joy to the horse. Pulling a light buggy or cart should be no strain; yet, the pleasure of traveling on straight stretches at a good clip, liberated from a tedious lungeing circle or the boredom of walking on two long tapes, should encourage his impulsion and zest.

From three to four years of age, the well-founded horse should move under saddle with his rider on his back for the majority of the training time. The horse can still be lunged to warm him up in order to supple and relax him before each session of riding. He can occasionally be driven from a buggy. At the age of three most of his training time is spent under saddle, and he becomes a riding horse. The foundation of his career as a sport horse functioning under a rider is now being laid. The horse should move in a generous frame, free of hindrances and interferences from the rider. The rider should concentrate on harmonizing with his horse. This is not a simple task, for the young, saddled horse will lose his balance often. He will be uneven and insufficient in his gaits. He will rush. He will "fall through" turns. He may be stiff in his joints, reluctant to use his muscles, tire easily, and resist. These are all the expected symptoms of the shortcomings that are due to lack of physical fitness. To help the horse, the rider must sympathetically follow the shifting center of gravity of the young horse with his own center of gravity, in order to harmonize. The rider should plan to ride his horse over open country as much as possible. Freedom, both from the rider's restrictions and from confinement in a small arena, is essential. Under the foreign weight of his rider, the horse will be gymnasticized and find his balance best by moving over irregular terrain, by climbing, sliding, and taking small leaps.

About two or three times a week, the horse should be gymnasticized in an arena. These sessions should include cavalletti work. (Good books on cavalletti work are available for you to consult.) The arena work should be more demanding mentally, but less demanding physically than the cross-country work.

This year in the horse's training is critical for his future career. It is during this time the horse learns all the basic aids. His rider must teach him the meaning of these aids. Therefore, being overdemanding is a mistake. The literature that is concerned with how to train young and green horses is vast and should be consulted.

From four to six years of age, the horse should be "generalized." His education should be that of a combined-training horse's training. He should be dressaged, moved over open country, and jumped in an arena. Horses should not jump higher than four feet before they reach four years of age, for their joints can be overtaxed and permanently damaged. The time has come for working the horse more intensely.

Competition may be pursued during these two years. The horse should learn all about the competition environment, including the mental state of his rider. All competition environments alter the behavior of both rider and horse.

At age six and beyond, the horse has reached full maturity. He should be appropriately specialized. In order to pursue greater demands in performance, time spent with the horse must be focused on particular tasks. The horse will either be more suitable for dressage or jumping or for continuation of combined training. One of these areas of specialization should be selected and pursued with the appropriate training.

The great competition athlete is a horse that is raised through motion and exercise. In a species that survived by flight, the "survival of the fittest" will favor those individuals who grew up moving.

THE COMPATIBILITY OF JUMPING AND DRESSAGE

For a long time, jumping has had a wide appeal for riders. Dressage continues to gain in popularity as more and more riders are introduced to it. The question of whether dressage and jumping are compatible will invariably surface. Jumping enthusiasts are being exposed to the competitive appeal of dressage, and it is therefore necessary to respond to this question.

Paraphrasing one of Oscar Wilde's witticisms, questions are often more important than the answers. Questions reveal needs, and therefore deserve our full attention. Perhaps some of the following are reasons for questioning the compatibility of dressage and jumping.

Some riders do not know what dressage is. They may have read some highly technical books on the subject that did not mention anything about its applicability to riding in general. They also may have witnessed some "dressage demonstrations" that had no more in common with dressage than the ill-applied use of the term. Such demonstrations may have displayed a confined, inhibited, hindered, and unhappy horse that was forced to do something unnatural, thus producing a feeling of uneasiness if not disgust in any tactful rider.

Then there are equestrians who would like to pursue both jumping and dressage but wonder if by doing both with the same horse they may not diminish their chances to reach the top. Our culture and our education suggest that success and attaining perfection can only be the result of specialization. Not knowing really what dressage is all about, these riders may think that it is so vastly different from jumping in goals, ideals, methods, and principles that it will endanger their horses' chances for success.

Related to the above reasons is the extreme rarity of horses that compete successfully in both dressage and jumping events. This, in a way, may suggest that there is a vast discrepancy between dressage and jumping. But this is not really the case, since when riders are prepared, we may see horses successfully compete in both disciplines.

Dressage and jumping are not only compatible, they are, in fact, complementary. Let me substantiate this seemingly bold statement. During my European equestrian education, I was not aware of anyone of sufficient expertise who did not agree that dressage and jumping are indeed compatible. As far as I am aware, the great equestrian authorities agree with this tenet.

Equestrian experts agree that there is only one basically correct way of riding. Originally, good riding was not developed for competitive purposes. Today, however, in most industrialized societies, the horse has ceased to be a beast of burden and a means of transportation. Consequently, its development is shaped according to sporting needs. The horse's needs are the same as those in the past. As was the utilitarian horse of the past, the sport horse of our times must be athletically and correctly developed in order to improve considerably over his natural state, which represents only his potential.

The one correct way of riding is often called the "classical" riding form. The rather pompous term "classical" is justified by the fact that the origins of this way of riding are found in the writings of Xenophon. Something that has endured that long, including the equestrian tradition, deserves to be called "classical."

Even more relevant to our topic than the antiquity of the classical riding form is the fabulous wealth of accumulated knowledge, all of which is based on the wealth of past equestrian experience. It promotes the ideals, goals, and methods that have proven most effective through centuries of trial and error. In the past two thousand years, everything has been tried, feverishly debated, keenly contested, and daringly experimented with. Millions of known and unknown equestrians strained their minds and bodies to find out what should be done, how it should be done, and why it should be done in order to achieve the most desirable results with their horses.

Basically, this is what we have inherited: Ideally a person should become an equestrian because he loves and respects horses and feels a need to dedicate himself to their well-being. Therefore, the goal is to develop horses on their terms, at their natural gaits, through their natural tendencies and by natural means, in order to unfold their natural talents to the utmost degree. The role of the equestrian is that of an educator. He should always be guided by empathy toward his horse.

The goals of classical horsemanship are guided by the ideal of developing a horse that will live long, in good health, and will stay consistently useful and happy while serving his rider. This fundamental goal can best be achieved by a concurrent and gradual development of the horse's physical and mental potential.

For our contemporary sporting purposes, a horse should be physically developed to move evenly, in correct balance, with enthusiasm, and straight in all his natural gaits. He should be able to lengthen (extend) and shorten (collect) his strides without losing balance and maintain an even rhythm. Therefore, he should neither run nor slow down but rather shift his center of gravity to maintain an even rhythm in bold impulsion. The horse should be able to carry his rider with a minimum of exertion and without any stress. He should conserve his energy by his improved athletic ability, which includes the development of correct muscles and the strengthening of his joints. As a consequence of his training, he should have a relaxed elastic movement resulting in a comfortable and harmonious ride. In short, he should become an athlete of great strength, yet so coordinated and supple that outstanding performances will appear effortless and poised.

Mentally, a sport horse should be aware and obedient. Trust in the rider results in relaxation, which in turn develops into obedience. Kind, perpetual, reasonable, consistent, and sufficiently strong communication will increase the horse's attention span and awareness. The physical and mental development of the horse should proceed hand in hand, reinforcing one another, and should show a tendency to gradual improvement.

The methods of classical horsemanship were developed to serve the ideals discussed and to achieve the fundamental goals described. They are based on a harmonious understanding between the horse and the rider. Such understanding can be achieved only by constant communication between them. Meaning is introduced into these communications by the rider, who perceives and perpetually evaluates his horse's responses. He also responds to the horse's communications by meaningful, consistent, gentle but sufficient aids. Because the rider reserves the initiative to create desirable changes, he is in command.

THE THREE DISCIPLINES OF CLASSICAL HORSEMANSHIP

Today, classical horsemanship promotes three disciplines of competition: (1) combined training, (2) stadium jumping, and (3) dressage. World Championship titles as well as Olympic medals can be earned in these competitive disciplines. Most horses seen in any of these three competition disciplines have been trained in accordance with the principles of classical horsemanship.

The outstanding horses that compete internationally share certain characteristics both physically and mentally regardless of the discipline in which they compete. In other words, an outstanding horse could almost invariably compete successfully in either combined training, stadium jumping, or dressage. Any horse with good conformation and proper upbringing may very well be suitable for competing in any of the three international events; it is his specialized training rather than potential and talent that will determine the area of his competitive participation.

Riders who wish to specialize may be guided in the selection of their horses by the following standards, provided the general suitability of the horse has been established:

- A horse of exceptional beauty and elegance, with superior gaits, offering outstanding natural balance, suspension and fluency in motion, will be particularly suitable for dressage.
- A horse that shows outstanding jumping ability and an exceptional sense of rhythm, timing, observation, and courage will be a good candidate for stadium jumping.
- A horse that shows stadium jumping ability and also has robust health, excellent legs, stamina, courage, strength, and great gallop will make an excellent prospect for combined training.

Notice that the bascule of the jumping horse is analogous to the longitudinal flexion of the dressage horse that is on the bit. The profile view shows the stretch and flexion of the top neck muscle, with the sun highlighting it, while the shadowy lower neck is a gullet. The flexed muscle connecting to the shoulder blades is visibly stretched, just as it should be during dressage work. The frontal view enables us to evaluate straightness and balance by checking the symmetry of the horse's body and his use of the limbs. The power to suspend and float in flight comes from the haunches, as do all the horse's propellant energies.

Photos: Susan Derr Drake.

JUMPER, DRESSAGE, OR THREE-DAY HORSE

The foundations should be the same for all of them. Horses that are selected for athletic careers ideally should receive identical basic training for a period of two or three years after saddling. If specialization occurs too early in a horse's development, the horse will likely never deliver a truly outstanding performance.

The purpose of this discussion is not to describe in detail the proper athletic foundation of a horse. A horse that has been saddled as a three-year-old should be trained until he reaches the age of six years with one goal only: his general development. During these three years, the horse should be moved over open country, exercised over cavalletti, and jumped over single and combined fences from trot and canter, and gymnasticized in the dressage manege. All of these activities, with the exception of the actual flight over the fence, fall into the category of dressage gymnastics. As long as the rider is in total control of his mount, he has the chance to improve him. It is only during the time when the horse is airborne in flight over the fence that the rider exchanges his control for fluent accompaniment, offering the horse complete freedom from interference. Consequently, the correct foundation of a horse's training is laid through dressage.

From age four to six, depending on the development of the horse, his training should include participation in competitions. The most appropriate form of competition for this period of training is Combined Training events, since it contains all three phases. Specialized experts will evaluate the horse's gymnastic development in the dressage arena; others will judge his movement in the open country. Finally, he will have to prove himself in the stadium over the fences.

Since Combined Training events are offered less frequently than dressage and jumping competitions, the horse may be shown during this period of its development more frequently in both dressage and stadium jumping competitions.

The main objective of this period is testing and evaluating the horse's progress. The horse should move with great impulsion. While showing zestful forward urge, he must remain at all times under the rider's control. He should perform with energy, yet without showing stress and strain. He should be supple both longitudinally and laterally, able to shift his center of gravity in order to extend or collect his strides (longitudinal suppleness), as well as make controlled transitions from gait to gait. He should be able to bend in his entire body in both directions on arcs (lateral bending), to travel on curved patterns without losing balance or impulsion.

The horse should be mentally alert and obedient. He should be aware of his environment, of his rider's aids, and of his own body. He should submit himself to the rider's guidance. He should allow the rider's influences to permeate and control the position and activity of his body.

Undeniably, these physical and mental attributes are necessary for a well-founded jumper, and are only achieved by proper dressaging.

THE HORSE'S SPECIALIZATION

At the age of six, horses may become specialized by continuing to compete in only one of the three phases. At this time their athletic development will allow specialization. There is seldom time and energy left for either the rider or the horse to continue competing in all three phases. However, riders and horses who have the time and energy to spare should continue to specialize in the competition that tests diversity, the Combined Training events.

Only outstanding horses are worth specializing, for others will not produce outstanding results regardless of the effort. At the time an outstanding horse is being specialized he ought to be able to do the following:

- Successfully compete in the Third or Fourth Level AHSA Dressage Test.
- Compete and place on four-foot-high jumping courses.
- Complete successfully the Intermediate Level Combined Event Test.

If the horse is not capable of performing as suggested, then he has serious athletic limitations, an incorrect foundation, or an incompetent rider.

Now let us examine the continued compatibility of dressage and jumping after specialization has taken place.

THE THREE-DAY HORSE

Horses and riders who continue to compete in Combined Training Events internationally, in World Championships, and in the Olympic Games have always demonstrated that knowledgeable dressage promotes outstanding jumping performances. Within three days, they prove time and time again that a well-trained horse can perform a supple dressage program elastically; then, the next day, go over a strenuous and speedy cross-country course with solid jumps; and, on the third day, show stamina, courage, and impulsion by jumping a stadium course with considerable finesse.

Successful riders who specialize in jumping sophisticated stadium courses are aware that the fences are not the determining factors for success! What leads to success in stadium jumping is how the horse is brought to each fence, how he departs from fences, and how he responds to his rider on the ground between fences. The results of stadium jumping competitions are decided primarily on the flat ground and only secondarily by the flight over fences. Riding a jumper to success is done on the flat. The flight and the subsequent clearing of the fence are determined by the rhythm of the horse, the correct length of his strides, the degree of his impulsion for push-off, his undisturbed attention and concentration, his use of the correct musculature, the correct bending of his joints, and his response to the rider's commands, allowing the rider to ride him to the correct takeoff points, with the correct impulsion, in the correct stride (collection-extension), and with a suitable degree of longitudinal flexion. These requirements for proper flight in jumping are all worked out by gymnasticizing. Indiscriminate and perpetual jumping of fences will never prepare a horse for great achievements in stadium jumping.

These drawings permit some degree of comparison between the actions of a jumping horse at the highest level of performance and those of a dressage horse at the highest level of his gymnastic accomplishments. The drawing at top left shows the moment when a horse is so thoroughly anchored on the haunches and elevated in the forehand that the haunches act like a crane lifting the forehand—indeed, the horse's entire body—off the ground. Strength, skill, balance, and coordination defying gravity.

The drawing opposite top calls attention to the increased power of the haunches, which is due to the utmost collection preceding this phase of the jump. That collection enables the horse to propel his entire body into flight.

The drawing opposite below can be studied to discern further similarities between these horses. The bascule of the jumper landing on the forehand after flight and the analogous flexion of the dressage horse are retained by the neck. The head of the jumper is slightly raised to reduce the weight impact on the forehand, to prevent collapse or cartwheeling, and to enable the haunches to tuck under for the support of the very first stride.   Drawings: Chaille Groom.

JUMPING, AN EXTENSION OF DRESSAGE

Jumping is one of the "figures" in dressage. There is not much difference in preparing a horse to take a fence correctly or to perform a piaffe correctly, for doing either requires similar physical and mental development. They both require a total and harmonious control by the rider. Jumping is essentially a dressage movement. A stadium course is basically a dressage test. Of the two tests, dressage and jumping, the latter is the more difficult. Jumping a course calls for faster responses and coordination, more radical shifts of position in order to maintain harmonious unity. Then why is it that so many horses jump courses successfully without having been properly dressaged? First of all, because of pure luck. Secondly, because for a while, even mistakes can lead to superficial success. Also, because people can afford to ruin talented horses and dispose of them while the horses' careers are still in their infancy. And, finally, because the poorly gymnasticized, yet successful, jumper performs far below his natural talents.

THE CLASSICAL "AIRS ABOVE THE GROUND"

The ultimate in dressage is demonstrated by the riders and horses of the Spanish Riding School in Vienna. At that institution, the "airs above the ground" are still taught to horses and shown to spectators. At the same school and also in the Grand Prix Dressage Test, the other sophisticated dressage movements are displayed by horses. These movements are demonstrations of the ultimate physical and mental achievements of an athletic horse. They are gymnastic exercises that, however difficult, are possible when a horse is developed correctly, in accordance with the general principles outlined in this book. Like dressage horses, jumpers show extension and collection. They perform pirouettes at the canter. They sit down on their hindquarters in extreme collection at the moment of takeoff, as dressage horses do when performing a levade. Jumpers will take leave of the ground and suspend themselves in air much as dressage horses do when performing the capriole or ballotade.

Thus, even at the level of the greatest specialization, the horse that jumps a high obstacle must use his body in a way similar to that of the horse performing *haute école* movements in the Spanish Riding School. They are both talented athletes, developed correctly to display their highest inborn capabilities. Indeed, this is the task of the true equestrian, the full development of the natural potential of the horse. Whether he displays the results of his artistry over fences or in the dressage arena is a matter of taste and temperament.

Four

Longitudinal Flexion

Horses instinctively pay attention to all stimuli in their environment. That behavior is part of their natural "survival kit." They have keen senses, especially smelling and hearing, that aided them through millennia noticing approaching danger. Once danger was monitored by these suspicious senses, the powerful, speedy runner took flight in defense. Horses that pay little attention to their riders and a lot of attention to everything else in their environment behave as their ancestors did in nature. Let such behavior serve as a warning that the horse is getting ready to take flight.

GAINING THE HORSE'S ATTENTION

A horse that is inattentive to the rider is behaving somewhat untamed. "Dressage" is an untranslatable word, precisely because it denotes more than training. The term also describes taming!

When a rider begins gymnasticizing a horse, he is coming into contact with an untamed animal that heeds the commands of natural instinct. The most important initial task is the taming of the horse. Even after the horse is tamed for the purposes of human use, we continue to encourage further submission to human will. Ultimately this results in undivided attention and unquestioning obedience. From the untamed natural horse, to the totally obedient horse, the road is a long one, and to travel this road requires wisdom from the rider.

The most fundamental result of taming is the replacement of inborn instinct-dictated reactions in the animal with rider-inspired reactions. Such results depend on two prerequisites. One is the earning of the horse's trust. The other is the horse's understanding of which reaction is desired by each request of the rider. These are in sharp contrast to the horse's unthinking, unfeeling, instinctively coded reactions to environmental stimuli.

The trusting horse will submit willingly to his rider's wishes. He will obey his rider's commands joyfully. Trust, resulting in submission and obedience, must be earned by the rider, for it can never be demanded or forced. A rider can earn the trust of his horse by being kind, understanding, patient, reasonable, and, above all, consistent in his actions. People only earn the horse's confidence by the same methods that earn them the trust of other humans.

The horse's understanding can be developed through educational principles that are also found in human education. Intelligence cannot be given through education. It is an inborn ability. Yet, it can be awakened, encouraged, sharpened, and put to desirable use. Intelligence has a lot to do with discipline. It can be utilized to replace random, unpredictable actions by consistent, predictable, and focused activities. Such desirable mental developments depend on an increased attention span, the ability and willingness to concentrate.

It is this concentration that is the epitome and ultimate manifestation of all taming. Concentration is the very capstone of all that has gone before into the building of foundation and structure. Submission, obedience, trust, awakened intelligence, curiosity all result in a horse concentrating on the wishes and commands of his rider. Once this mental development has been achieved, once concentration upon the rider replaces random reaction to environmental stimuli, then the horse is tame. The tame horse will not fidget, prance around, or be preoccupied with stimuli other than those initiated by his rider.

STRETCHING TO FLEXION

The lowering of the horse's head and the stretching of his neck are very important tasks during the early stages of training. Therefore, concern with this aspect of the training is wise and commendable. Even later, throughout the horse's career, he should be capable and eager to stretch first forward and then gradually downward as he is encouraged to do so by his rider. Whenever the rider commences a "free" movement—that is, free walk, free trot, or free canter—the horse should stretch his neck forward, then gradually lower it. While in competitions only free walk is asked for, during training sessions, the free trot and canter should be practiced briefly as an effective rewarding device.

We must remember that when aiming at stretching the horse's neck, we also desire the stretching and elevating of his back; without the former, the latter cannot occur. I will suggest some ways for stretching a horse's topline.

Fundamental to all stretching strategies is the ability to slow the horse down. Horses that carry their necks and heads up, drop their backs down, and move with stiff joints are usually moving too quickly. When slowed down and aided in rhythm to maintain active engagement in the hindquarters, most horses will lower their necks, relax, and elevate their backs.

The slowing down of the horse should be done by the rider's weight and abdominal muscles, never forgetting the importance of the shoulders in adding weight to the seat. The rider's hands and the reins held by them should be mere cushioning extensions of the torso.

The hands can do a variety of things in coordination with the body in order to relax the horse's back and neck and lower his head. The hands can stroke the horse's neck while holding the reins with a closed hand. This stroking activity stretches the reins initially by alternately lengthening the distance between the horse's mouth and the rider's seat. However, soon the horse will react to this invitation by stretching his topline with a lowering of his head position. From then on, especially if the rider can continue to slow down the horse, he will contact the reins by gently filling the rider's palms while stretching his neck forward and down.

At first, the rider invites stretching by passively holding the reins with a light contact, releasing them gradually to a longer contact. Then, as the horse relaxes with these mild, even, and sensibly forward acting reins, he will stretch toward the bit. When that happens, it will be up to the rider to decide how often he wants to repeat the stretching. As the horse understands the reins through this exercise, he will round his topline to seek elastic contact with the bit. Once longitudinal flexion is steady and habitual, stretching should be cultivated during transitions.

Another way to encourage the horse to accept the rein contact and lower his head can be performed as follows: The rider places both hands on his thighs by pressing his fists down on them. That will bring both reins down and slightly apart, away from the horse's neck. The reins will be low and steady as if they were sidereins, yet kept sensitively alert to maintaining mild contact. They may also be spread wider toward the rider's knees. Care should be taken to do this with bent elbows. Many horses who cannot relax and balance will find this gentle "frame" acceptable and will yield to it at the poll and jaw. As soon as that happens, the rider should yield on the inside rein, maintaining contact only with the outside one.

The yielding of the inside rein simply means that it should be gently stretched forward, allowing the horse to stretch forward and down to seek contact with it. The yielding should be a forward stretching, not a dropping of the rein into a visibly hanging position.

As the horse is relaxing into these lowered "sidereins," the rider should reward him by lengthening both reins by about an inch. It is as if sidereins had been readjusted to suit a longer neck. This lengthening of contact should proceed step by step as long as the horse remains on contact. The moment the soft-contact chewing stops, the horse's nose stretches out and his neck stiffens; it should be taken as a sign that the reins have become too long and that they no longer communicate.

Ideally, a horse can be relaxed to the bit and stretched

Fred Weber and Wertherson exhibit a rarely seen, entirely correct longitudinal flexion. The photograph captures the "grounded" diagonal pair of legs
approaching the moment when they, too, will leave the ground for the coveted
moment of suspension.

Everything is remarkable about this presentation of Wertherson: the topline
correct; the musculature stretched, "liquid," and allowing the movement to
blanket the horse in his entirety; the limbs gaining the ground unhindered. The
freedom, elevation, and elegance of his locomotion are the result of the correct
longitudinal flexion. The horse is not just moving, he is carrying his rider.
The motion is "uphill" from the hocks to the poll. The neck is not confined
and therefore is an eminent example of flexion through stretching rather than
as an evasion of pain. The horse moves through his unconfined neck toward
his bit. The front hoof predictably will land under the horse's nose, which will
travel precisely over the hoof as it impacts on the ground.

Freedom and balance create this grandiose posture that enhances the horse's
ground-gaining ability and amplification of motion. Note that impulsion, the
increased activity of the joints, is obvious, and therefore the extension can be
executed slowly. Haste is the enemy of impulsion. Slow and articulate, cadenced
and generous, the horse produces motion as art.   Photo: Cappy Jackson.

through his topline by asking him to stride deeper toward his center of gravity. While doing so, however, he should wait for that stride with his forehand. The rider must drive the horse, yet make him understand that he is inviting the forehand to wait for the hindquarters to catch up.

With proper coordination, the horse will surely understand that if he shortens his body, he can carry the rider in comfort. He will flex the joints of his hindquarters, arch his neck, and bridge the locomotion of his hindquarters with the supporting forehand through an elevated, rounded back that swings. The horse will tuck his pelvis forward by rounding his lumbar back and flexing at the lumbosacral joint. The rider will contact the rein where it connects to his seat in a normal position and will begin to drive. Should the horse respond to the driving by speeding up, the rider will half-halt and insist on a slower tempo. When the horse has shortened his frame through flexion, the rider will yield minutely with the inside rein first and continue to drive. Gradually, the reins will be lengthened again, yet only enough to forestall speeding up. The horse will gradually understand driving to be meaningful for shortening his body rather than for prompting him to speed up. He will lower and lengthen his neck, elevate his back, and stay in contact by seeking the rider's hands.

LONGITUDINAL FLEXION

"The horse on the bit" is a misleading expression, yet it is one we are accustomed to using and, by consent, we pretend to understand, in spite of its mischievous suggestion that it has to do with the rider's hands and the horse's bit exclusively.

Being on the bit is the most important concept in classical horsemanship. Only a horse that contacts and accepts the bit and moves toward the bit is athletically correct. Using a human analogy, let me suggest that there is a great difference between people who are moving about in a grocery store buying mustard, for example, and those working out in a gymnasium. Both are moving and are engaged in some mental activities, but only the one working out in a gymnasium is improving himself physically and mentally. He will show muscle development and skeletal coordination that one cannot acquire by shopping for mustard. Likewise with horses; just by moving a horse around, the rider traveling, the horse covering ground without using himself properly, no improvement can take place. One can only make athletic and gymnastic improvements if the horse is longitudinally flexed. Therefore, the horse must be flexing toward the bit before any gymnasticizing can take place.

Being on the bit, or longitudinal flexion, as it should be called, has to do with the total horse. When a horse is on the bit, his skeletal position as well as his use of his muscles changes. To be on the bit connotes relaxation, suppleness of muscles, elasticity in the joints, elegance, and obedience. That is both the foundation and the substance of all dressage work. The most important feature of a horse on the bit is that he is longitudinally flexed, thereby becoming a shorter horse, capable of moving deeper under his own weight with the hindquarters, lifting the weight up rather than pushing it forward. The longidutinally flexed horse is well poised to carry his rider, and therefore will be able to surrender his haunches to the rider's will and become obedient rather than subservient to force.

THE HORSE ON THE BIT

The "horse on the bit" is an unfortunate expression because it is potentially misleading. Long accepted as part of the classical "terminus technicus," however, its use will continue. There may have been times when all "terminus technicus" led to consensus because those who used them understood their colloquial meaning. Now that the equestrian educational backgrounds are increasingly diverse and the number of riders considerably greater, equestrian understanding of terminology may also differ depending on the source from whom it was acquired.

If one were to test the phrase "horse on the bit" on a person not involved in riding, they might interpret its meaning in unfortunate ways. Therefore, it is worth offering some thoughts on this important phrase and the subject it deals with.

A definition of the concept includes a horse that is longitudinally stretched, thereby allowing the energy of his hind-quarters to travel unencumbered through his entirety without blocking it by tensing of muscles. A longitudinally stretched horse is, coincidentally, flexed. However, flexion is not sufficient to produce the correct equine movement unless it is part and parcel of stretching the spine by way of stretching the nuchal cord, a ligament that spans the horse's length from his poll to the dock of his tailbone.

Contributory to as well as resultant of this ligamentally induced spinal stretching is the horse's ability to flex some muscles whose flexion is indispensable to correct locomotion and carriage when a rider is added to the horse's weight package. These muscles interrelate in a complex system of "sympathetic responses" such that if one of these muscles is flexed, a group of others will join it and also flex. The horse's top neck muscle is one of these. If a rider succeeds in flexing it, not just the poll, which is merely a joint with no ability to expand or contract as muscles do, the rest of its "sympathetic muscle group" will also flex. These include the abdominal muscles, which carry the rider's weight and allow continued freedom of articulation of the back muscles (swinging), and the muscles in the croup and buttocks, which push the stifle joint forward and upward.

Therefore one can activate the flexion and elasticity of this important "sympathetic muscle group" either by starting with the relaxation of the horse's neck, sending his neck and head forward and downward, or by sustaining his posture but increasing the activity in the muscles of the haunches, which propel the stifle and ultimately convey the energies of the hocks.

Therefore riders can create the flexing of the horse's top muscles, which induce longitudinal flexion and relaxation through stretching, by starting either at the horse's front (most suitable for tense and fast horses) or at his haunches (most suitable for lazy, sluggish, weak, and therefore slow horses). In any case, riders need to stretch the horse, not merely flex him. For flexing is possible by a short, tense, inhibited horse too. Stretching eradicates tension and forestalls inhibitions of movement and posture.

Flexing the poll is not a goal. By itself, flexing the poll is useless. However, when the proper muscles are flexed through their stretching, the poll will also necessarily flex as a by-product. Flexion at the poll does not induce longitudinal stretching, and flexion at the poll is valid only as an inevitable by-product of longitudinal stretching.

Correct longitudinal stretching rounds the topline and enables the horse to move in his entirety, not just with the legs. The same stretching gives the horse the ability to absorb the shock that is caused by the impaction on the ground.

None of the above is possible if the horse were to be literally "nailed to the bit." By nature, genetic instinct, the horse is a claustrophobic creature that will "break out of bondage" at any cost. Instinctively, he will respond to pressure with counter pressure. The rider pulling on his mouth will be countered by a horse pulling on the bit. To pull against confining and restricting hands, the horse will bid his structure in its entirety. Muscles tense, ligaments stressed, and joints stiffening, the horse will use all his strength and power to fight confinement. The mouth not being meant for painful intrusion but rather for the pleasurable activities of eating and drinking, the rider's inducing of pain will produce enormous tension in the horse. This will not be limited to the physical efforts to "break out of bondage" but will include mental anxieties that are manifested in shying, bolting, kicking, grinding teeth, pulling lips up, clattering teeth, sucking the tongue back, hanging the tongue out of the mouth, and all other unsightly and auditory signals of anxiety.

Horses "nailed to the bit" will naturally respond by stiffening first their muscles, then their joints. All this will result in a deterioration, not an enhancement, of the basic gaits. There will be unsuspended, choppy, shuffling strides, the very antitheses of amplified, suspended, elastic movements of softness and easy grandeur.

Therefore, let us think for a moment what is *really meant* by the "horse on the bit."

The contact is something the horse does, not the rider! The rider merely teaches, encourages, and tutors the horse to contact. He does this by yielding with hands forward, providing for an expansion of the frame and the lengthening of the neck. After the horse contacts the bit, the hands should become passive, stable yet soft to confirm and reward the horse's action.

The horse should seek a contact with the bit precisely because the rider liberates, rather than confines, him through his contact. By yielding on the reins, the rider approves and verifies to the horse his correct contact.

The purpose of allowing the horse (not the rider!) to seek and contact the bit is to form a termination point that defines the limit of his stretching and the termination point of his energies. This enables the rider to communicate through his seat to the horse's forehand his wishes regarding the horse's producing a desired posture, carriage, speed, and cadence by his energies properly harnessed from the haunches. Through the bit, the horse should be aware of his rider's mind, better understand his intentions, and even sense through the contact with the bit the activities of the rider's seat.

In order for the seat to communicate to the bit, the rider must sit in the correct posture. This must include a still and vertical upper arm and elbow position, which helps to sustain a passive, isometric resistance. This is indispensable for the motionless stability of the rider's torso and arms, which will enable the horse to "step through" the rider's torso and monitor his seat. The rider's seat is comprised of many more elements than his seat bones and buttocks. The composite parts of the seat, when combined in action or passive resistance (inaction), will amount to far greater effectiveness than segmented, partial use of these elements would permit.

The seat is much more than the sum of its parts (Gestalt) because it includes the manner in which these parts interrelate from moment to moment.

Contact is certainly not:

- A feeling of force connecting a human fist with an equine jaw.
- A sense of holding a wall against which to push the horse.
- A point of inhibition of the liberty of movement in the haunches and forehand.
- A point of confinement that can force the horse to invert his neck and by that infuse tension to all other sympathetic muscles.
- A point of pressure or a sense of anchoring a horse, around

which he can desperately pivot by "fishtailing" with his
haunches.
- A fifth leg that he can lean on as a crutch.

RIDING TOWARD THE BIT

Without wasting time, we can always initiate riding the horse
forward toward the bit; that is, to create and moderate the degree
of longitudinal flexion. Indeed, if one can consistently produce
longitudinal flexion on any horse with any problem, then one
is really a good rider! That is what riding is all about: the ongoing, perpetual process of sending the horse forward toward
the bit. This suggests the great secret: The horse never arrives
on the bit. He should never take hold of it, pull or hang on it,
or use it as a crutch. The secret is the continual sending of the
horse toward the bit. Only through the resulting longitudinal
flexion can one achieve the proper position and muscular relaxation and skeletal balance in which the horse's gymnastic development can properly take place.

When one drives the horse forward toward the bit, the bit
should elude ever so slightly the horse's "arrival" on it, his taking
hold. This allows the horse to step forward without fear of
hindrance by pulling and the accompanying pain. The horse's
forward (but not running) thinking depends very much on his
courage in working toward the bit. The bit must suggest and
represent to him a resilient opening, a yielding and elusive co-
munication, rather than a literal contact. A tense, restraining,
pulling rein results in an open jaw, tense neck and back muscles,
and ugly, apprehensive, stiff, choppy strides.

This brings to mind that classical schooling creates a horse
in self-carriage. It is we, dressage devotees, who are supposed
to be the upholders of the classical tradition of "all with the seat
and leg and nothing with the hands." We are the promoters of
beauty through freedom and impulsion. We are the ones who
do not ride with strength but with understanding through natural
and consistent communication. We seek to ride a horse who
lacks pain and is happy. All of these goals depend on a yielding,
elastic rein contact! By yielding, the reins should participate in

Steffen Peters rides Udon in self-carriage, which is obvious from the level of engagement of both the airborne legs and those grounded in support, and verified by the unencumbered posture of the neck and the flexed top neck muscle. Perhaps most telling are the impeccably synchronized actions of the diagonal pairs of legs. Those impacting on the ground are indeed parallel. Notice the limbs that are airborne: the trajectory of the front hoof is twice as high as that of the hind. That is the way it ought to be. Self-carriage is at the heart of correct training and depends on the rider's ability to sit straight, perpendicular, and tall. Mr. Peters does. Photo: Cheryl Erpelding.

the consistent promotion of forward engagement of the haunches.

When the reins restrict, they should be part of passive resistance. They should feel as if you are drawing a violin string through a cube of butter, while your pelvis is thrust forward toward them, fists steadied to allow the seat to advance toward them.

As soon as softness and sensitivity have been established, we must consider strengthening the horse to ride him toward the bit, and to do so we must think primarily of slowing his tempo. Many horses have been ill-trained to respond to the leg aids in only one, incorrect way: run ahead. Instead, early in his training, the horse should understand and trust the leg to mean something other than "Hurry up." Slow your horse down with half-halts. We can only teach a slowly moving horse the concept of moving away from leg pressure sideways with all or part of his body. That is precisely the reason for teaching turns on the forehand and haunches from the halt! Later, when we teach shoulder-in, leg-yielding, or any of the two-track movements, slow the horse down. Horses who hurry cannot experience engagement, the increased articulation of their joints. They cannot relax for fear of losing balance, and must sometimes resist in self-defense.

When a horse moves slowly, we can move his front end (shoulders) or hind end (haunches) to one side, by design. When our horse is crooked without permission, we straighten him by the very same methods used to bend him. If, for example, he is moving with his haunches always to the right, apply the aids to produce a haunches-in left on a straight horse. If a horse is crooked to the right, he may momentarily straighten but might soon resume a crooked position. Repeat the exercise, because with each straightening, you induce changes that will ultimately reduce his crookedness. Liken it to uncoiling a spring: you loosen it gradually until you have a straight piece of wire in your hand. The horse cannot straighten all at once; he needs repetition and time. If he had the properly developed musculature and equal ability to stretch and contract on both sides, he would not need straightening. Crookedness is a manifestation of uneven development, first in the muscles and later, if not corrected, in the joints. So one must be very patient in straightening the horse and waiting for proper development that only comes with time and repetition.

In order to flex, the horse requires a degree of collection, however minimal initially, and once achieved, allows for increased collection.

A horse on the bit is a horse longitudinally flexed, a horse submitting to the rider's aids. This athletically efficient posture promotes the horse in athletic progression.

When a horse is longitudinally flexed, he becomes a shorter

animal, being able to stride deeper under his center of gravity, a more compact mass that he has a chance to lift, rather than push. In this position, the horse yields at the poll, arches his neck, however mildly initially, relaxes his belly muscles, elevates his back, and bends the joints of his hindquarters more acutely when in motion. When the horse is flexed, he becomes attentive to the rider and he finds the position more comfortable for carrying his rider. He becomes calm and pleased. He will find it easier to carry the shortened bulk with his more relaxed muscles and will be eager to further obey the rider's aids. He will respond to "whispering" rather than "shouting" aids of the rider's legs, weight, and hands. He will feel supple and easy to command. He will be attentive, coordinated, relaxed, and flexed. For this reason, when the horse comes to the bit, there is a feeling of "What a different horse!" As if by magic, all the difficult things become simple. It is as if a deaf and dumb animal has become perceptive, conversational, and intelligent.

The horse must always be invited to accept the bit from the haunches toward the forehand; that is, by primarily driving rather than by restraining aids. It is interesting to note that being on the bit always denotes a certain level, however minor, of collection. The moment a green horse has stepped deeper under his weight, lifted himself somewhat off the ground into relatively greater suspension, elevated his back, lowered his neck, and flexed at the poll, he has, to a certain degree, collected! From then on, the degree of collection can be gradually increased with proper gymnastic training. As the muscles of the horse become more supple and his joints more elastic, he will carry more and more of his weight on the hindquarters, lightening his forehand. His body will shorten, he will suspend higher in his movements, and become slower yet more elastic in his motion. All this starts with the first moment of infinitesimal collection called "accepting the bit": the longitudinal flexion.

There are several ways in which a horse can be ridden to the bit, and only a rider with diversified experiences will easily find the most suitable way for the particular horse he is working with. Three fundamental means are used to stretch the problem horse toward the bit.

THE CROOKED HORSE

A horse that is moving above the bit because he is crooked needs only to be straightened and he will step up to the bit instantly. A rider who can align the horse's spine by controlling the relative position of the horse's forehand to his haunches will access the hind legs. Once the spinal alignment is secured, the rider should drive to load the horse's hind legs evenly. This activity includes the slowing of the horse until his strides on both sides are equal to the length the horse performs with his shorter-striding hind legs. Even length and height of strides with both hind legs are dependent on the rider's abilities to align the horse's spine, as well as his ability to sense how to even up the strides of the hind legs. This important activity was turned into the age-old advice, "Straighten your horse and ride him forward." Indeed, in misinterpretation, this is being "translated" into running horses off their legs at top speed. The admonition, however, was meant to address the cognoscenti who knew its meaning to be "Spinal alignment, followed by equal use of the hind legs" yields the "straight horse, moving correctly forward by loading the hind legs evenly."

THE RUNAWAY HORSE

A horse that is running because he finds his rider not a weight but a frightening burden will need to be slowed down through repeated half-halts in order to flex toward the bit. All horses can be slowed down through half-halts, the rider indicating a desire to walk. Just before the horse walks, the rider must yield on the reins, without losing contact, however, and allow the horse to slowly trot on. If repeated, this will convey to the horse that he may trot, but slower. Eventually, he will relax, find his balance, feel a more harmonious rider accompanying him, and will gently accept contact on the bit. On a rushing horse, it is essential to slow the tempo to the point where the horse allows himself to be drivable! As long as the rider travels on a running horse like a passenger and dares not contact his horse's sides with his legs, the horse will not flex to seek the bit.

THE LAZY OR WEAK HORSE

The lazy, weak, tired, or young horse will often go behind the bit, rejecting contact by overflexing his neck, tucking his nose in, head hanging with his profile behind the perpendicular line to the ground. He will appear relaxed but will continue to push rather than lift his weight and, therefore, will dwell on his forehand. The rider should powerfully drive this kind of horse to encourage contact with the bit. When the bit is passively presented to the horse, forceful forward driving (even with touches of whip) will entice him to seek contact with the bit by stretching his neck. At once, the rider must lighten and make the contact more pleasurable. The rider invites a contact by presenting the bit to the horse. Then he drives until the horse becomes so active with his hind legs that he needs to extend his neck. Then, the rider's hands lighten but do not relinquish the contact, which is now maintained on the horse's initiative.

The three basic ways of stretching the horse toward the bit discussed here most commonly refer to horses that were not started correctly. These horses are the most commonly known objects of instruction. However, the green horse needs none of these methods if started correctly from the beginning! Let us briefly outline how one proceeds with such a green horse.

The weight of a horse standing under the rider is distributed as follows: two-thirds on his forehand and only one-third on his hind legs. In motion, originated in the hindquarters and received by the forehand, the same proportionate weight distribution will prevail on a green horse. Therefore, if a green horse is only driven or allowed to run without controlling him by a light rein contact and even half-halts, he will shift as much as three-fifths of his weight onto the forehand! By all means, this should be prevented, the goal being, of course, that as the horse develops, proportionately more and more of his weight should be carried by the hindquarters. The increased weight bearing of the hindquarters is collection.

To begin with, walk the horse at a slow, even pace with long, generous strides along the walls of the arena. Wait until he lowers his neck, reaching toward the ground with his nose, elevating the back. At that moment offer light contact on the reins temporarily and in a while release it and continue a free walk.

Repeat the contact on the reins for longer and longer periods of time, planning to release (yield) the contact only when the horse's neck is deepest in its downward search with his back highly stretched. As the horse learns that he is rewarded by lightness when he elevates his back and as he builds his confidence in the rider's hand, which never confines him or discomforts him with unusually long periods of contact, he will begin to seek the feel on the bit as soon as the rider invites him by contacting the reins.

Still at the calm walk, the horse will gradually relax his neck muscles, yield at the poll and jaw as soon as the rider presents the bit to him with his light contact on the reins.

Now begin to work on a circle, usually starting on the left side, with a diameter of about 10 meters (half the width of an arena). Bend the horse around the inside leg at the girth, placing it not too far back to avoid pushing the hindquarters out, and keep the inside rein holding a light contact. Allow the outside rein to strengthen its contact mildly. This strengthening will occur if the outside rein is held exactly as it was on the straight line. Because the horse, by bending on a small circle, will become longer on his outer side, the contact on that rein will be strengthened there by the horse. Note that this effort will supple the horse's muscles on the outer side rather than, as commonly supposed, on the inner, hollowed side! As a result, the horse will now step deeper under the weight with the inside hind leg, slightly elevate his neck, relax at the poll and jaw, and mildly raise his back on long and generous contact and move in mild collection.

After the horse has been working on the bit at the walk and on circles in both directions, continue with a combination of exercises:

Contact at the walk, as described. Then trot and immediately ride the 10-meter diameter circle at the trot. Make sure your inside leg provides aids for impulsion and regularity of rhythm while the outside leg guards against drifting, held steadily further back. As you return to the wall, make a transition to the walk. Repeat the exercise, but only once the horse walks on contact and not before!

Again walk on contact, trot, and immediately ride a half-circle (10-meter diameter), returning to the wall on a straight, inclined line (changing hands), and walk upon reaching the wall. Soon the horse will remain steadily on contact with the bit both during the walk and the trot and during transitions from one to the other.

The young horse's initiation to the steady acceptance of the contact terminates much later with the riding of a figure eight pattern. This is ridden so that each circle of the figure is 33 feet (10 meters) in diameter, thus placing the figure eight across the width of the dressage arena, changing direction at the center line. Walk on contact, bend the horse onto your first circle, then trot. Walk upon reaching the center line. Bend the horse on the other circle, wait until he surely bends to the arc of that circle, and only then trot. As soon as you reach the center line, walk again. Repeat. It is important to understand that the rider must wait at the walk until the horse bends on the arc of each circle before trotting the circle. When this last exercise is done with steady and light contact between rider's hand and horse's mouth, the horse is on the bit and the foundations for serious dressage work have been laid!

The effort to ride the horse toward the bit should start within days after the young horse has been mounted by his rider. When pursued correctly, with utmost patience, lightness of contact, and a great deal of rewarding, the horse should accept a contact within two to four weeks! If a green horse is not correctly started and is not encouraged to carry his rider in the athletic position (longitudinally flexed on the bit, on the aids, in balance, etc.), the likelihood of his becoming an "evergreen" will be sadly increased.

Longitudinal flexion of the horse refers to the horse's flexion throughout his entire length. This is something we humans never experience because of our posture while in bipedal locomotion. However, when doing a sit-up, we do an analogous abdominal contraction that stretches, rounds, and elongates the back muscles. This includes the analogous rounding of our neck, rounding our back, and, through lumbar tucking, tucking our pelvis forward. A horse in longitudinal flexion is effectively doing a human's "sit-up" and can travel in that posture. Because the horse creates all of his locomotion in his hindquarters, he cannot correctly propel himself forward without proper and total engagement of his body. In order to engage totally, he must expand or contract with his muscles throughout his body. This muscular articulation facilitates longitudinal flexion. This flexion begins at the fetlock and runs through the joints of the hindquarters that enable all locomotion, and communicates the movement through the back muscles to the front. There, the impulsion is fed into the navigational, balancing areas of neck and head, and terminates at the horse's mouth.

Longitudinal flexion results in relaxed but well-rotating joints and active, supple musculature. In turn, they contribute to the creation of great impulsion yet controlled energy.

Longitudinal flexion further results in an improved ability of the horse to (1) carry his rider in correct balance, i.e., move with correct weight distribution on all four legs both on straight lines and on arcs; (2) shift the center of gravity of the composite weight toward his hindquarters, which are the only source of locomotion, thereby making movements more effortless and liberating the forelegs for higher and more suspended motion; and (3) increase his powers of collection and extension. This means that the horse's ability to lengthen and shorten his strides will increase in all natural gaits without having to alter the rhythm of his hoofbeats. In other words, the horse will cover greater or shorter distances per unit of time without either rushing or slowing down. Both rushing and sluggishness tire the horse and make the rider's travel uncomfortable.

Balanced movement is the foundation of all correct riding achievements. Only a longitudinally flexed horse can move in balance. This is difficult to achieve, considering that most horses "fall" to the forehand when free on a pasture. They lack sufficient musculature, strength, and know-how in balancing their own bodies correctly. When the foreign weight of the rider is introduced, the horse will unavoidably "fall" further out of balance in order to keep himself upright on his four legs.

By "falling," we do not mean that the horse literally falls down to the ground! Rather, we mean that the horse is incapable of maintaining a balanced distribution of weight on his four legs. All horses have to be gymnasticized before they can maintain a correct distribution of weight at all gaits while performing figures. However, there are horses with such superior conformation that they have "natural balance" and move evenly, lightly, and supplely when free of the rider's weight.

The horse's hindquarters are the source of his impulsion; therefore, the rider must seek to control them. The only way to do this is to flex the horse longitudinally. The best exercises for improving longitudinal flexion are transitions. It is important to know that transitions can take place from gait to gait (i.e., trot to walk, etc.) and also within the gaits by extending or collecting the horse's strides. The most collected gymnastic exercises are the collected walk, the piaffe, and the pirouette at the canter.

To be sure that readers can better understand the importance of correct longitudinal flexion in appropriate visual images, I have selected the photographs overleaf for their correctness in what they show and for their great beauty. The rider, Melissa Simms, is the head rider and trainer at the Egon von Neindorff Reitinstitute in Karlsruhe, Germany. She is riding Serafino, a Trakehner stallion, the son of the famous sire Tenor.

RIDING RANKS AMONG THE ARTS

Being a living tradition, the art of riding survives only as long as those cultivating it have a passion for purity. Living traditions cannot be assimilated solely through books and films; they live through their practitioners. If we were only to read about dressage but not practice its principles, the art could disappear. Unfortunately, the gymnastic principles of dressage are often compromised by either ignorance or complacency.

Recognizing and rewarding that which is correct and punishing that which is false is the primary function of judges. They are not just responsible to the contestants in the show they judge, but also should serve the art they evaluate. The rider who is successful represents the closest approximation to the ideal that the judge is there to uphold.

Not only what is being said, but also who says it matters. Those contestants who hold dressage dear will appreciate a judge

A

B

Melissa Simms, head rider and trainer of the Reitinstitute Egon von Neindorff, Karlsruhe, Germany, on the Trakehner stallion Serafino.

C

D

138

A. *Flexion must be the result of stretching the horse's topline from the dock of his tail to his poll. The elasticized muscles should stretch the ligaments and the spine of the horse. All longitudinal flexion must be the result of stretching, including the longitudinal flexion that occurs during collection. Stretching through the topline has horizontal and vertical dimensions. At the beginning of training, as well as throughout the horse's gymnastic career, stretching must begin by lowering the horse's head by sending it forward and down.*

Of course, the horse must always be urged to stride under his center of gravity. To send the horse's head forward and down does not put the horse on his forehand, provided the rider keeps the horse's haunches energetically engaged. One can see in this picture that the horse steps with his hind leg into the footprint left by his forehand on the same side. His stifle moves ahead of the point of his hip.

The horse's back is expanded, raised, and relaxed. This makes it high, supple, and articulating with the movements. The neck is sinking from the withers and the withers are the highest point of the horse. The neck is lengthened to stretch down, forming the mildest arch. The middle of the neck is lowered and the arch of the neck is reaching the maximum horizontal and minimum vertical posture possible. The head of the horse hangs from the well-protruding flexion of the top neck muscle, under which the dark line of a gullet can be observed. Most important, the horse's face hangs perpendicular to the ground, with his nostril well ahead of his eyeball. The forehand is free and steps well ahead of the elbow with a freely swinging shoulder. The horse is not behind the vertical nor on the forehand.

The result is full stretch, complete rounding of the topline, relaxed hanging head and tail. Perfectly synchronized diagonal pairs of legs move with clarity of footfall. The rider's balance is exactly over the horse's center of gravity. Exemplary leg position insures the straightness and impulsion of the haunches.

B. *The horse remains stretched but begins to upright himself to accommodate a working trot. The haunches are more engaged, which makes the strides not just longer but higher.*

The horse's back remains high, round, and supple, his neck remains unencumbered to show its natural length and strength. The poll is raised by a neck just as long as that shown in picture A but is carried less horizontally, more upright. Increased vertical lifting of the limbs adds to the suspension of the gait. This in turn creates the increased verticality of the horse's neck carriage relative to that seen in picture A.

Here again one can observe the impeccable clarity of the parallel position of the diagonal pair of legs: right hind and left front. Because he has been allowed to maintain a stretched topline and the natural length of his neck, the horse can maintain his balance and develop the haunches. The clarity of his gait is obvious and, of course, that is the goal of training.

C. Having acquired balancing skills, muscular strength, and strength in the joints, the horse can now be asked to collect the trot. The most important thing to notice is the lack of any restraint, confinement, or manipulation of the horse's neck in shape or size. As this picture shows, the horse must be allowed to carry his head wherever he needs to as a result of his body posture and the nature of his strides.

The strides are obviously amplified by collection and not destroyed by being minimized. The horse holds his poll as the highest point of his body, with his face slightly ahead of the vertical, because the joints of the haunches have increased their flexibility and can carry the rider higher. The hind and front legs lift with greater suspension from the ground, resulting in increased cadencing of the trot. Still fully stretched, free to stride forward, relaxed and poised but in improved balance, the horse can now shift his center of gravity toward his haunches. As the haunches sink on softer joints at the time of impaction on the ground, he will correspondingly raise his poll and show higher knee action. The elevation of the forehand should not be, and is not done here, by the rider's hands. Instead, correct and gradual work and the proper use of seat and legs create the collected trot. Collection results from the simultaneous increase of engagement of the haunches and the shifting of the center of gravity back toward them.

D. The greatest collection that can be achieved at the trot is the piaffe. This picture shows the most important features of this movement. The horse assumes the weight on his haunches. All his joints are elastic, strong, and therefore well flexed. Notice the sinking on the fetlock, hock, stifle, and hip of the left hind leg, which supports the weight on the ground. Observe the soft, elastic, well-bent joints of the lifting leg on the right.

Most important to notice is the lowering of the point of the croup, which results from the rotation of a flexing lumbosacral joint which in turn pushes the pelvic structure forward and under. The lumbar back muscles behind the saddle are strongly stretched, and push the pelvis forward and down to compress the haunches. The forehand shows freedom and elevation, as it should, at the withers. The tall arch of the neck, carried as nearly vertical as conformationally possible, lifting the poll also as high as possible and positioning the horse's face slightly ahead of the vertical, are all the result of the increased flexion of the hind leg joints which simultaneously causes the proper sinking of the haunches. The horse remains calm in mind and relaxed in body. His head still hangs from the top neck muscles and his frame, carriage, and position are all volunteered and not forced.

Now, once again, visually recollect the following principles. The rider sits with a straight back, shoulders back and down. Her upper arms and elbows are part of her seat. The hands are low, relaxed and the contact soft. The reins never inhibit, restrain, shape the horse's neck or encumber the horse's movements. The rider's legs are back under her seat bones, with her toes behind her knees. The heels are lower than the toes. The calves are stretched, draped, adhesive, precise, well honed. The horse, therefore, performs from the seat and legs and is permitted to contact softly.

The horse is always calm and relaxed. His body is stretched through his topline. His haunches are active to amplify his strides both horizontally (ground gaining) and vertically for collection. The rider is in total control of the haunches and therefore can influence the horse's posture. The rider can stretch the horse lower and longer or can upright him at will. Elasticity and suppleness result from the rider's ability to change both the horse's body's length and the length of his strides. The combination of the rider deciding on a desired body posture with a corresponding stride proves the horse's obedience.

The arching of the horse's neck is determined by the horse's "navigational" needs and not contrived or forced by the rider. The closed, relaxed, quiet mouth seeking quiet, light contact with the bit testifies that the horse is obeying the leg and seat aids properly.

During all stages of the horse's training, according to need, he should periodically be stretched with his head sinking forward and down. The stretching and sinking of the neck must be controlled from its base at the withers. Those riders who rock the horse's head from side to side with short, confining reins will merely pull the horse's mouth toward his chest, with his face behind the vertical, the poll pointing toward the ground and the neck rising upward from the withers to a bulge, to break at the fifth vertebra. The arching of such a neck is not a continuously even curve. The incorrect, painful coiling of the horse's neck into a "bow, tightened by a bow string too short" will disengage the haunches, damage the gaits, and deny the rider their control.

Photos: Dr. Ulrich Schmitzer.

who scores the rider according to principles. Such a competitor will appreciate the comments that will help him abandon the wrong directions in his riding. The serious rider is dedicated to the art of dressage and will accept Machiavelli's dictum "Guard the end"; i.e., pay attention to the result. Ultimately, the rider who contributes significantly to classical horsemanship is the one who wins internationally. Who would not trade a hundred blue ribbons won at county fairs for an Olympic gold medal?

The Training and First Level tests follow one another with gradual and small changes of gymnastic sophistication. In these levels, a rider needs a horse with three good gaits and in horizontal balance and good rhythm, to show that he has accepted the aids and works with relaxation and pleasure under the rider. Often riders who show Training and First Levels already do all the Second Level exercises in their daily work. Those who compete will agree that their daily work includes quantitatively and qualitatively more sophisticated work than the tests call for. In fact, during the early stages of training, the tests are, indeed, simpler than the daily work should be.

This is not the case at Second and Third Levels. The gymnastic evolutionary distance between the First and Second Levels is far greater than that dividing the Training and First Levels. In fact, Third Level represents a different gymnastic concept altogether than what was required previously.

At Third Level, both collection and extension are required in all three gaits. In that sense, on this level aspirations of Grand Prix requirements begin. Sophisticated lateral bending exercises are also called for. The two-track movements include demands to displace both the shoulders and the haunches of the horse. Requirements call on the horse to perform all three gaits in medium tempo and demonstrate them over short distances, yet distinctly enough to differentiate from both the collected and the extended modes! Thus, the constant controlled changes of the horse's strides from lengthening to elevation (collecting) are required to be shown with fluid efficiency.

At Third Level, the horse should show the ability to stretch and contract his musculature, thereby enabling him to lengthen and heighten his strides. He must make taller steps with more distinct rhythm and therefore show cadence, being airborne without fear of losing balance. He must be able to shift his center of gravity toward the haunches and begin to lighten the forehand and present a taller carriage. The Third Level, if done well, is a rather beautiful test that has inherent spectator appeal similar to that experienced while watching the Grand Prix.

In Second and Third Level tests, only that which is energized from the haunches and moves freely forward toward the bit through a loose and articulating back succeeds. Collection cannot be induced by pulling on the reins. It cannot be cajoled by lifting the horse's head up, shortening his neck, or any other manipulation with the reins. A horse cannot move freely and correctly when held in front while being driven from behind. Riders should remember that positive one and minus one equals zero: pulling on the horse and kicking him simultaneously create nothing but a tense, confused, alarmed horse with an open jaw, rigid back, and fast, pushing, mincing, short steps—the antithesis of the elastic horse we wish to create!

When horses raise and lighten the forehand they do so by rocking upward at the withers—not merely by having the poll held high with an artificially shortened neck. They can work upward with the withers only when the haunches have engaged and lowered. Horses can engage the haunches and elevate their forehand only when they use their back and neck muscles correctly: stretched, flexed, relaxed, and loose. The ultimate lightening of the forehand is seen at the levade, the withers rock back and up. The horse never lightens his forehand when being pulled up at the head. Everything comes from the flexibility of the joints of the haunches, which allows the horse to tuck the pelvis and to lower his croup. Like a crane lifting objects high, the collected horse is anchored on his haunches and is liberated to lift up his forehand.

The horse should "playfully" assume collection in self-carriage and collect from the rider's lower back influence and rise in front of him toward supple reins. The collected horse feels shortened in length and tall and as if losing rein contact by being so incredibly light precisely when collecting. Collection is forward suppleness, not retardation and restriction.

Fewer riders pass to Fourth and higher levels of competition. And that is why, once again on Fourth Level and above, we can see more correct performances. The Third Level seems to be the crisis level, the one where scores of riders fail—the eye of the needle through which no thick threads may pass. So let us remember that at Third Level, dressage arrives, by testing both collection and extension.

THE MEANING AND PURPOSE OF COLLECTION

Collection occurs when the horse shifts his center of gravity toward his haunches. In a sense, "collection" is a relative term. It refers to any change in the horse's tempo, depending on the shift in his center of gravity. Whenever a horse becomes shorter in length and taller in his posture, his legs lifting higher, therefore with shorter strides than before, he is "collected." Collection is relative to the degree to which the horse assumes weight on his haunches. To some degree each rider collects the horse, even the youngest and the greenest. Even on the very first occasion a horse is ridden, he will need to be slowed down, even halted. Even at a "primitive" stage of collection, by merely slowing the horse, the essence of true collection presents itself because the horse shifts the center of gravity toward his haunches. Collection is not the shortening of the horse's neck by pulling. A shortened neck may even prevent collection.

In another sense, collection refers to a specific way of executing the basic gaits: walk, trot, and canter. The meaning of collection is more specific because the standards that define collection in the gaits are absolute and recognizable. In fact, collection in all three gaits is so specific that it is recognizable by the horse, by the rider, and by knowledgeable observers.

THE CHARACTERISTICS OF COLLECTION

In collection, the legs lift higher above the ground and therefore, coincidentally, move in shorter strides. However, a horse that only shortens his strides without lifting his legs higher is not collected. This will slow progression but should not change the rhythm. The hip, stifle, hock, and fetlock joints rotate supplely

Steffen Peters schools Udon in piaffe. It is not the rider but rather his horse that is active. The tranquillity of the rider, with his seat becoming part of his horse's relaxed back, is exemplary. Observe that the rider's seat includes all contact areas from buttocks downward, as it should. This allows tactful aids to engage the horse rather than those that divert or confuse him. Clarity, precision, tranquillity are stamped on the rider. The piaffe, the highest collection attainable at the trot, is simultaneously the highest attainable collection prior to the horse moving on to "the airs above the ground." Increasing the collection in piaffe will naturally result in the horse sitting down into a levade. The levade is always preceded by piaffe work. Here one can see the importance of the lowering of the croup as the horse yields the lumbosacral joint and adds its all-important flexion to that of the joints in his limbs. The horse is anchored in the haunches by this rounding lumbar back, pelvis thrust forward and under, and the sinking on supple but strong joints toward the ground on the right hind leg which here supports him. The eye can easily trace the line of engagement through flexion from the right hind hoof all the way to the poll: uphill.

In this movement of ultimate collection, one visually perceives the horse's hind legs gathering under in their approach toward the muzzle, where the kinetic energies terminate in the horse's contact with the bridle and result in the elastic bowing of the entire equine structure. Photo: Terri Miller.

and with increased articulation. The majority of the lifting action is by the hocks. That is why exercises for strengthening and animating the hocks help to develop collection.

The leg supporting the horse's weight on the ground sinks as the joints in it yield softly to the weight on them. Like a compressed and coiled spring, the strengthened joints of the horse allow for sinking in order to cushion the impact of the strides. Supple joints of a collected horse, like a coiled spring, produce more suspension than do stiff legs. A truly supple and collected horse feels soft-striding yet springy, enabling a rider to aid and accompany his movements effortlessly. Supple horses inevitably appear elegant with an effortlessly composed rider in the saddle. Watching supple performances, one sees the horse carry his rider as naturally and effortlessly as he carries his own skin.

A collected horse uses strong and supple joints with great accuracy and economy. An effortlessness should accompany the

In this remarkable pictorial sequence of a canter pirouette to the left, Arthur Kottas-Heldenberg, Chief Rider of the Spanish Riding School in Vienna, Austria, demonstrates mastery of collection. As always, with his inimitable elegance, this rider participates inconspicuously in the horse's motion. He never just sits on top of a horse but always sits in the motion of the horse. This "insider's view" gives the best riders that wonderful insight into not just what to do, but also how much of it to do. The lowest point of the stretched legs is the heel. The hands are very low and gentle, making it obvious that collection is not a shortening of the neck by restraining hands, nor is it based on a lifting leverage of hoisted hands.

This slow, calm, even, balanced, concentrated, and well-flexed horse carries his tranquil rider. The impeccable throughness of the topline, the softly flexing joints, and the balance shifted toward the haunches allow the beautiful pirouette to emerge. First of all the horse must be collected. Then, the turning into a pirouette is just a matter of choice of pattern.

Notice the increased flexion of the joints, including those in the lumbar back. The posture of the neck and the carriage of the head are exactly commensurate with and a result of the engaged hindquarters. The rider does not shape his horse but controls his energy, which in turn gives the horse his shape. Photos: Charles Fuller.

1.

2.

3.

4.

5.

6.

7.

8.

TRAINING STRATEGIES FOR DRESSAGE RIDERS

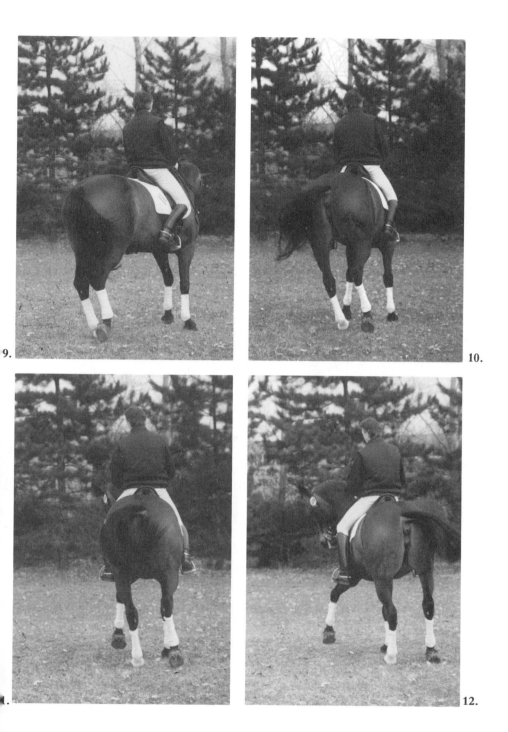

LONGITUDINAL FLEXION

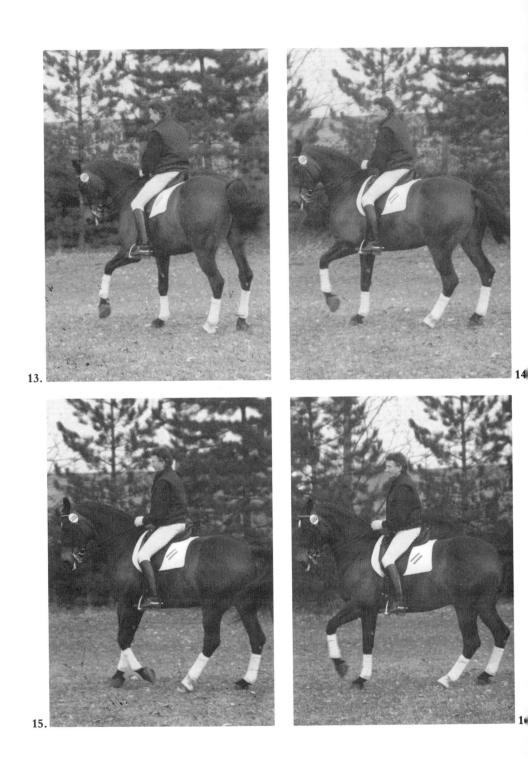

13.

14.

15.

16.

TRAINING STRATEGIES FOR DRESSAGE RIDERS

17.

most difficult tasks, and there is a feeling of effortlessness rather than working at the exercises.

The lumbar back muscles of a collected horse tuck his pelvis forward and under. The croup is lowered. The lumbosacral joint flexes to push the pelvis forward. This allows the propelling muscles to increase the articulation of the joints. The lumbar back muscles must be strong and the rest of the back relaxed, loose, swinging, and stretched. Back muscles that stretch and swing also strengthen and carry the rider effortlessly. This promotes the compacting of the body, with an increased erection of the neck, and also allows the center of gravity to move toward the haunches, or, conversely, the haunches move forward and under the center of gravity. This process is dynamic and perpetuates collection.

As the center of gravity shifts backward, the forehand is liberated from its task of supporting the majority of the composite weight of horse and rider. Lightness of the forehand increases the elegance of carriage.

The horse becomes shorter in length yet taller-moving. He remains stretched through his back and over his topline into a keener flexion. His shorter mass is, of course, easier to support for the haunches and easier to lift upward into suspension. The horse moves upward and forward.

The shoulders move more freely because the horse no longer dwells on them. In ultimate collection, in a levade, there is no weight on the forehand. As a result of collection, the withers bounce upward with each stride, which is most evident during passage. Coincidentally, because the horse's neck and head happen to be in front of the elevated forehand, the neck arches high and the head is carried in the highest position.

The horse's profile will appear vertical (perpendicular to the ground) as he continues to flex toward the bit. He should continue to carry his head high with the neck muscles emerging from the withers and he should use the top neck muscles from which he can hang his head down. If the head is supported by the lower neck muscles emerging from the chest area, the carriage is incorrect and the horse's head appears to be supported by being "shelved up" rather than "hanging down."

Of course, the elements of collection described above should occur simultaneously. They are mutually supportive, reinforcing one another, perpetuating and improving the degree of collection as a result of their interplay.

As these qualities of interacting collection occur, we must remember that collection develops gradually and slowly, based on the stretching and strengthening of muscles, the rotation and suppleness of joints. These combine into the accuracy of motion that represents economy of energy. The gradual gymnastic work that cultivates relative collection will eventually succeed in creating absolute collection. That is why we should focus on the ideas that serve as the means to the end goal of collection.

As much as driving the horse forward is paramount, every day's work should include episodes of collection. When collecting the horse, do it through half-halting and always approve obedience by an elastic giving forward on the rein. Never lose rhythm. Maintain a perfect, constant rhythm while working in one gait. Most riders rush their horses in the mistaken belief that they are getting impulsion. Slow the horse down to give him a chance "to sit down on his haunches." Relative to whatever forward driving goes on in the general effort to activate the

Guenter Seidel riding an exemplary trot. Observe the softness of rein contact. The tall seat stretching up to a tall head carriage and down to a sunken heel. Low hands supply a yielding contact. The horse in elegant, supple self-carriage. Tall at the poll due to such well-engaged haunches. The diagonal pairs of legs move in absolute synchronization. The airborne legs show the trajectory of the forehand's hoof moving twice as high as that of the hind leg's. The unity seen here is born of empathy with the horse's needs and harmony with his motion. Photo: Cheryl Erpelding.

haunches, the rider must also periodically shorten the horse's strides. Often gymnastic riding goals are pursued in the wrong order, or prematurely. Extension comes from collection. Good collection, on the other hand, cannot develop without extensions. Thus, just as we collect as a means to gain extension, we may also do a variety of exercises, without necessarily collecting a gait, and thereby improve collection.

Let us suppose that the goals include developing collected gaits, but the horse is not yet ready to produce truly collected strides.

The greatest enemy of collection is the misguided belief that the horse's front end (neck and head) should be raised up by the rider's hands (reins) in order to lighten the forehand. The shortening of the horse's neck produces pain, and consequently resistance and false carriage. When superficially perceived, a collected horse may strike some people as being distinguishable by its elegantly arched neck and high head carriage. They do not realize that this is not the cause but rather the by-product of collection. Collection takes place in the haunches because it depends on the horse's ability and willingness to increase the articulation in the joints of his quarters to assume more weight. The misunderstanding that by shortening the horse's neck one can collect is analogous to putting the cart in front of the horse. In other words, such belief is based on a confusion of the symptomatic result with the fundamentals that caused it. The only defining criterion of collection is an increase of weight-bearing in the haunches.

Here is a simple analogy. You want to sweep some crumbs into a dustpan. As you sweep the crumbs with the broom toward the dustpan, you must move the dustpan back slowly in order to gather the crumbs. The ratio of the speed of the receding dustpan to the speed of the vigorous broom approaching is the key to the success of picking up all the crumbs efficiently. Both of your arms are working to get the crumbs collected into the dustpan. Both move the crumbs forward. One arm with the dustpan is "tempting" the crumbs to arrive by receding from them, while the other arm with the broom is "urging" the crumbs to go forward into the pan. This activity suggests collecting something that it is pushed forward toward a receptacle—something that is not stationary but yielding. The collection occurs without anything ever stopping the motion of the crumbs forward.

Similarly, we collect the horse's energies that are generated in his quarters. We cannot shape the horse, only his energies. We cannot collect him by shortening his neck or lifting his head up; that would be reshaping the horse by force. We cannot carve or cast his body. We cannot shape him in his stall. We can only ride the horse's energies, never his bulk. The energies are supplied by the haunches and shaped by the half-halts of the rider. The rider is the transformer of energies received from the haunches through the back. Energies absorbed and understood are returned to the horse in a modified form.

To find and feel the correct ratio between driving the quarters and restraining the progression of the forehand without tensing the rein contact is the art of collecting. The half-halt is not named so in vain, for half of the aid should ask for a halt, and when the horse is responding by gathering himself toward the halt, the other half of the half-halt sends him forward as if the rider changed his mind. The horse understands the suggestion to collect when the aids are increased. He should be asked to "come back" on his haunches, and when he almost halts, he should be "restarted" by the continuation of rhythmic aids. As all half-halts are resolved by yielding, do remember that after the transition to collection is performed, the horse must be encouraged to continue in self-carriage.

The most severe problem with collection occurs when the rider believes it to be gained from the horse's neck and head carriage. We are trained to manipulate by hands and verify the results by sight. We always "fix things" with our hands and grope to balance and steady and grasp to feel in contact with whatever we are doing. We watch intently and visually "feel" things happen. The natural tendencies, coupled with schooled skills reinforcing them, hinder us in riding in general and in collection in particular. Riders find the horse's neck and head readily accessible to manipulation. The hands through the reins maintain a physical connection with the head of the horse. The reins represent many powers through leverage and pressure that can potentially cause pain to the horse. Through the reins, the horse's head can be lifted, turned, and manipulated. Thus, the horse's head becomes a "doer's paradise," because as soon as the hands "do," the horse's head visibly reacts. Manipulation is rewarded visibly.

The haunches, on the other hand, cannot be directly touched and manipulated. We have not yet invented (and hopefully never will) a mechanical device that would lift the horse's hind hooves and enable man, through straps or something, to jerk them forward or upward. We have our seat and leg influences acting on the horse on his back and sides. Those areas are distant from his haunches, which are, of course, behind and below the areas we directly contact with the seat and legs. There is no actual, physical contact between the rider and the horse's haunches. Yet, we must clearly communicate information to the horse that will precisely affect the activities of his haunches.

To achieve a sensitive communication process with the horse takes a long period of consistent and insistent aiding. The horse's acceptance of the aids must be diversified and his submission to the aids well confirmed in order to collect effectively. The driving aids of the legs and seat are vague to the horse because they are indirect and conceptual aids! Having no direct physical force acting on the areas they address, these aids will only be obeyed by the horse after he makes the conceptual leap of understanding their intentions. Thus, we must first convince the horse that when we do something to his sides with our legs, we really wish to affect the action of his hind legs, his source of locomotion. To transfer sensations felt at his sides and through the saddle to affect the action of his haunches is a trained, conditioned response for the horse. The real neuromuscular responses to the rider's leg and seat cause tactual stimuli, which are transferred, later quite predictably, as their meaning is refined, to the horse's haunches.

When the rider's leg actions are ignored by the horse's haunches, the conceptual leap has not occurred and the meaning should be reinforced by the light use of the whip. Used this way, the whip is the "spark" that jumps a thought from the rider's mind to the horse's mind. The stimulus of the whip should be light and symbolic, always void of pain, to invigorate the haunches because the horse's instinct already suggests flight. The horse then begins to understand that the legs' demands must energize the haunches. The whip should always be used in conjunction with the leg.

The instinct to take flight, however, might create a new challenge. The horse might misinterpret the driving aids, particularly when supplemented by the whip, as a wish by the rider for more speed, and turn to running. Speed is the enemy of impulsion and engagement. By speeding, the horse can escape impulsion with strides that become short, fast, choppy, and tense. Impulsion depends on slow but ample rotation of the joints, which thereby allows energy-efficient, long, ground-gaining strides. Impulsion is a result of increased articulation (flexion and rotation) of the joints, which is manifested in slower rhythm, yet amplified strides.

The horse is on the aids when he submits to driving aids without rushing from them. Upon receiving leg aids, a well-trained horse will first energize his flexion and accommodate the rider with a posture commensurate to the engagement in the haunches. He should never run from the legs. Only a horse with tolerance for leg contact will lengthen or collect his strides in a consistent rhythm. Bending rather than drifting sideways away from the leg contact is also based on trained leg contact tolerance. The half-halt is an indispensable aid for increasing the horse's leg contact tolerance.

CORRECT BENDING IMPROVES COLLECTION AND COLLECTION LEADS TO ENGAGEMENT

The half-halt is a near synonym for dressage riding. Without it, the horse could not maintain his balance when asked to shift his center of gravity. Gymnastic riding is successful only when the horse can shift his center of gravity horizontally, vertically, and laterally, without losing his balance.

When driving a horse forward, we must discourage him from running faster by the necessarily frequent and skillfully applied half-halts. The horse's understanding of the leg aids should become more sophisticated as time passes and training progresses. Instead of resulting in speed—in effect, the faster rhythm of footfalls—the horse should learn to differentiate the various effects of the rider's legs and produce appropriate re-actions, running being one of several inappropriate ones. Correct reactions include lateral bending or increased engagement of the haunches.

The rider must use both legs all the time. When bending a horse, both function in highly important roles. Never can a rider bend a horse "with the inside leg." To bend a horse, the rider should use steady, continuous outside leg pressure behind the girth in order to press the horse's quarters inward. That "curl-ing" of the part of the horse behind the rider is done with the outside leg slightly behind the position of the inside one, but still with the calf stretched and heel pushed down. This position of the outside leg toward the rear is accomplished by pushing the knee back and down, the power coming from the well-

Arthur Kottas-Heldenberg showing exemplary aids for bending a horse, around the inside leg but with the outside leg. The "exhaling" inside rein is invisible yet detectable by the curve-shaped contact on the outside rein. The rider's shoulders parallel those of the horse's and his hips parallel the horse's hips. The rider's spine is perpendicular to the horse's spine both from this frontal view and from a surmised side view. A rider should not tilt his spine back or forward. Nor should he bend it to one side by lowering one of his shoulders. Here is the perfect example of a seat all riders should emulate.

Photo: Charles Fuller.

stretched calf. The inside leg of the rider has a double function. The inside leg is placed in the normal vertically hanging position, to define the area "around which the horse is to bend." In addition, the inside leg provides the aids to create the impulsion necessary for bending.

When moving through corners (arcs) and curves, the horse should be bending and therefore using his hind legs in slightly different ways from each other. The inside leg flexes more at the hocks while the outside flexes more at the stifle. A laterally bent horse steps with his hind legs toward the hoofprint of the forehand on the corresponding side. Often, we see stiff horses crossing with the inside hind leg under their body toward the hoofprint of the outside fore, as if in a leg-yield; the outside hind leg, of course, is spinning off the curved pattern outward. A properly bent horse, however, will track correctly with his hind feet, because he uses them slightly differently. While bending, the horse contracts and shortens his inside muscles and lengthens and stretches his outside muscles. He shifts the center of gravity to the inside of his spine. Both of these attributes depend on increased inside hock activity.

Imagine an analogy in human terms: stand on your right leg and lift your left knee high as you extend both arms sideways. You will realize that with your left knee high (analogous to the horse's left hock), your body will develop a bending posture to the left. Notice also that your balance is maintained in spite of your standing on your right leg alone because your left knee is up and your torso is contracting on the left and stretching on the right. Bending the horse in good balance, one's inside leg drives his inside hock to increased bending.

Only the specialized positions and activities of the rider's legs will produce proper and consistent lateral bending in the horse. Lateral bending is paramount to arriving at collection. One cannot develop collection by riding in collected gaits. Collection is developed by means other than by solely practicing collection itself. All knowledgeable riding is made up of various means leading to the desired ends. Therefore, one achieves a Grand Prix test not by riding a Grand Prix test every day, starting with the green three-year-old and "drilling" it into him. This analogy, far-fetched enough to be grotesquely comical, makes its point strongly. We do not achieve passage by riding passage; we do not achieve collection by riding a "collected" trot on an undeveloped horse. One of the many means—indeed, one of the most important means—to collection is riding with proper bending. When bending, as mentioned above, the horse must use the inside hock differently than he uses the outside hock. Bending is unilateral (one-sided) collection, and it is a most important building block in producing genuine bilateral collection—equal on both sides.

The shoulder-in, one of the finest suppling and therefore collecting exercises, is primarily concerned with intensifying the horse's bending through the mobilization of his inside hock. That is why the pulling of the inside rein during a shoulder-in is its very negation. The entire movement is designed primarily to address the inside hock, therefore it must not be inhibited in its potential action by a restrictive inside rein. Through the shoulder-in, the rider can "sweep the horse's inside hind under" by doing the exercise in mirror images, that is, repeating the same on both reins, until strength, courage in lateral balance, eventually produce a perfectly soft and harmonious result when both hind legs sweep under, as if they both simultaneously do the shoulder-in, but now on a straight track. Behold collected trot!

The ideal dressage horse, which moves forward with minimum effort producing maximum efficiency of impulsion on a straight line, is developed through the means that include frequent bending. Through bending, the horse is elasticized, making it possible for him to move straight and efficiently. Similarly, the medieval sword-makers of Baghdad or Toledo tempered their steel until they could produce swords with blades bent to a full circle. The blade, which bent to the circle either way, was the blade so well tempered that when straightened, one still knew it was supple rather than stiff. When straightened, the supple and flexible sword wielded the maximum efficiency!

Only the horse that can collect—its haunches inward and under—can extend efficiently. When such a horse extends, whether to a medium trot or to a fully extended trot, he gives the rider a feeling that he is sinking down behind while climbing up a staircase two steps at a time with his front end. The animation and freedom of the forehand make the horse dance upward "tilling the air." The animation and the effortlessness of this kind of motion have such a hypnotic effect on the horse that he seems to act as if he could maintain this activity eternally! The horse finally becomes self-propelled, self-risen in the front, in full flight upward and onward with so much kinetic impetus that the rider becomes a mere supporter of the action by accommodating it as a harmonious partner. The feeling is that the horse rides itself through the rider, who merely lends his weight as a medium of balance and stability through which the horse can send his energies unencumbered.

An arched neck does not by itself denote a horse on the aids. Being on the aids helps to become part of the momentum of evolution toward collection (out of which comes extension) and engagement. A curved neck, an arched neck, an overbent neck, a "broken at the third vertebra neck," or a neck in any number of wrong shapes is not ridable! The neck incorrectly held by the horse or falsely developed by a rider will prevent the rider from controlling the horse's haunches. Equally, ill-shaped necks will prevent the horse from connecting his haunches to the forehand. The neck is symptomatic of what the haunches are doing. False position, wrong development in the neck, will testify to the same in the haunches.

Through bending and, in particular, correctly performed two-track movements, the horse assimilates the correct meaning of the rider's "collection leg aids." For instance, when the horse understands that during a shoulder-in the rider's outside leg pressure prevents it from speeding up or "uncoiling" to evade by straightness, while the rider's inside leg supplies a rhythmic aid for impulsion to increase the hock action, then the horse connects the leg aids toward the bit. Being on the aids is essential to gymnastic development. Being on the aids depends on the horse understanding the leg aids correctly, rather than refusing them by rushing away from them or by stiffening against their contact.

ENGAGEMENT ON THE AIDS

Bringing the horse to the aids is done primarily by driving leg aids and only secondarily with the concurring seat and derivative hand aids, as they all work together in a system. The horse cannot be engaged through the hands, not because I think it is wrong, but because it is physiologically impossible. This is not a matter of style, emphasis, method, or taste. It is a fact of objective physiological data.

When the horse is properly on the aids, the neck coincidentally arches and the poll flexes as part of the total longitudinal flexion. On top of the spinal column of the horse, following its entire length, runs the cervical ligament. At all times, this ligament should be fully stretched. When it is fully stretched, not only does its elasticity and resultant swinging activity increase, but it also will elevate the horse's back. To elevate the back, a rider ought to lower the cervical ligament at both of its ends; that is, have the horse "tuck his haunches under" and stretch his neck forward and down simultaneously.

That is why just "showing the ground" to the horse, effectively lowering his head, is not enough. One must also simultaneously drive his haunches farther under him. The cervical ligament, and the back, will fully stretch and elevate only when both ends of the ligament are approaching the ground!

When the haunches engage more, then the biceps femoris muscles perform a major function and visibly press the stifle farther forward and upward while lifting hocks higher in their rotation, a lesser function. These muscles, running on the back side of the horse's rump, are observable at the walk, trot, or canter as they "tuck the haunches under," that is, they pull the back end of the ligament tight. The front of the ligament is attached to the horse's skull and can be stretched by riding the horse's head forward and down while engaging the haunches and tucking the pelvis. Without this activity, the horse is physiologically incapable of carrying the rider properly and developing gymnastically.

Once the back has been elevated, then the horse can balance himself. Thus, the correctly stretched horse, driven correctly by the rider, will "hang his head" from the muscles at the top of his neck just below the crest, the splenius primarily and the semispinalis capitis secondarily. The horse does not need to support his head carriage by "shelving it up" with the brachiocephalic muscle of the chest. On the longitudinally flexed horse, regrettably referred to as being "on the bit," all other muscles also automatically relax and move with a great deal of flexion or stretching to create ample, loose, effortless locomotion. These relaxed muscles can be observed "playing" in ripples under the fine summer coat of a correctly moving horse.

The greatest hindrance to driving the horse properly comes from riders stiffening their legs. Gripping the horse with tight legs, pinching heels pressing on his ribs, or banging legs are incorrect leg positions and deny aiding. Riding with the seam of the boots in contact with the horse's side is a bad habit held over from the "beginner stage" when the rider needed to grip in order to balance himself to stay on. Often quietly elegant legs are confused with tight, gripping legs. The horse cannot monitor tight legs as aids and will sour to the pressure, which he will interpret as a meaningless second girth.

Weight on the horse's sides will be tolerated much as he tolerates the weight in the saddle, but gripping legs cannot modulate and therefore never "converse." In human terms, tight gloves do not communicate what gently squeezing hands can. Tight legs also create pain and discomfort much like tight shoes. In fact, with the passing of time, the pain induced by both tight shoes for humans and tightly gripping legs for horses sharply increases and gradually approaches the intolerable level.

In preceding chapters, I have written about the incorrect use of the rider's legs, including the rhythmic upward "scratching" of the horse's sides by rocking the toes down on the stirrup irons and scratching or digging the horse with the heels upward. The correct pushing aids depend on correctly placed, stretched, and draped legs that are hanging in relaxed yet continuous contact with the horse. Such a leg position can only be maintained if the ankles are relaxed, flexed, and can rotate to absorb the horse's motion.

Rhythmically repetitious, yet not visibly obvious, forward-driving aids are the only legitimate driving aids. Of course, they must coordinate with the properly anchored seat. While learning correct driving aids or while teaching them to the horse, the frequent and light use of the whip is necessary. The horse must react to these rhythmically light and harmonious aids and if he "forgets" to react, a rider must remind him with a touch of the whip. The whip serves as a conduit from the rider's mind and will to his horse's mind and helps to create submission of the haunches. It is much better to insist on the horse's attention to the aids early than to nag at him for years!

Effective aids are not exhausting to the rider and not souring to the horse. The horse is capable of flicking a fly off his skin and therefore can tune to the lightest aids if that is what you teach him. The horse can and should always pay attention to the rider while working, and should also be given frequent rest periods. The horse's ears should not point forward but should be relaxed and slightly slackened back—a position indicative of attention to his rider. The horse's eyes should not stare forward or roll sideways as if observing objects but rather look as if in a daze with an inward vision. As soon as the horse goes off the aids, tune him back with a stronger application of seat and leg aids.

We can ride neither forward nor sideways by physically displacing horses with force. That is, we cannot push them around. Regardless of how much power a rider may use, he cannot force the horse to do anything. No amount of strength can compel the horse to do anything. The simple reason is that the rider is not on the ground. Being seated on the horse, the rider becomes analogous to the horse's own body parts. Therefore, a rider is as helpless in influencing the horse's direction or impulsion by muscle power as his own earlobe is in determining where he should go and at what speed. Thus, muscle power and force will not ride the horse. Schooled aids will, and they might as well be light and harmonious. Since the horse has the neurological aptitude to react to very slight stimuli, he has the mental aptitude to perceive mild stimuli and differentiate between them for a sustained period of time. He has an excellent memory. Use of force and power will only stiffen the rider and horse. Sensitive aids will result in exquisite communications. If a horse pulls, remember that it takes two to pull! If the rider unpulls by yielding one rein at a time, the horse cannot and will not pull. Horses will learn anything. They will learn to gymnasticize on light communications just as easily as they will learn to do the same by harsh and heavy communications.

To increase the horse's attention to the leg aids, two-track exercises are the most valuable. Two-track movements have terrific gymnastic value. Nothing else "brings the horse into the aids" more firmly than obedience to the complex two-track aids.

To build the horse from the hindquarters forward is not lightheaded idealism. It is a physiologically predetermined, compulsory training commitment. The effort begins as soon as one succeeds in gaining the horse's attention to the forward driving aids. As soon as the horse accepts the legs without rushing, on the lightest aids he should produce the result of slower but greater rotation of the joints in the haunches. Nothing good can be developed from the horse's mouth backward. The way is forward and upward in a slow rhythm in order to finally create a tall carriage.

Another method for collection is through "longitudinal engagement activity." First of all, a rider must feel the gait of the horse and harmonize with it. This is easiest in the trot, but the same applies to the walk or canter. This activity provides a short diagnostic period during which the rider is a listener monitoring what the horse offers. Awareness of relaxation, submission to the aids, balance, rhythm, and impulsion allow a rider to produce desirable change.

The goal of aiding is always the "disturbance" of the status quo. A rider cannot disturb something he does not monitor and understand. He should ask for a change only according to need. Often, improved impulsion or regularity of rhythm may be the most important needs. A rider must begin to ask for longer or higher steps than those the horse volunteers. That is, a rider should lengthen or shorten the horse's base by extending and collecting the strides.

Work on improving the gaits by lengthening and shortening the base, and alternate between the two modes. Extend the strides to the utmost that the horse can offer in pure rhythm and then collect as much as you can, without slowing the rhythm. It is important that the horse move forward fully stretched and instantly when asked. He should increase the amount of weight assumed by his haunches to "come back" when half-halted into collection. Gradual transitions in these exercises of going from extension to collection can weaken, while crisp ones with demarcation can increase their gymnastic value. Use hands, only in passive resistance, well connected to the rider's pelvic structure and with the perpendicular torso pressing down to balance the horse back into collection. With every repetition, the aids should become much more refined because the horse's understanding must be verified and rewarded. The horse will learn to respond quickly and to add longer periods of suspension to the gaits.

Steffen Peters demonstrates one of the most difficult movements to execute correctly: medium trot through a corner! The horse carries him obviously uphill from right hock to poll. He is bent in a beautiful continuum throughout his spine and with obvious bending through a relaxed torso. He exhibits enormous, ground-gaining strides with freedom and elevation, and absolutely synchronized limbs. Light hands neither shape the bend nor steer through the corner. The horse is properly bending from legs and seat.

To ride deeply into a corner at a medium trot and to succeed in producing a picture such as this is a documentation of correct riding theory made visible by effective equitation in practice. Photo: Cheryl Erpelding.

Further schooling of collection and resultant extension can be done on a circle 20 meters in diameter. This circle is one of the most important patterns on the way to Grand Prix. Incidentally, if one had to, one could train a horse in an arena that is a 20-meter circle. I am not recommending that type of confinement; however, in the nineteenth century, the Empress Elizabeth of Austria rode in a 20-meter diameter circular blue tent and achieved sophisticated results.

When riding a medium trot, the horse's hind legs must pass over the hoofprints left by his forelegs. In that sense, the medium trot is an extended trot with modifications. In the medium trot, in contrast to the extended, the horse is not allowed to stretch his topline to full length and therefore some of the shoulder action of the horse is kept in reserve. The horse is not allowed to fully extend in the shoulders. Thus, the medium trot is ample in length but not fully extended to the horse's utmost stretching ability. In the medium trot, the taller neck position and the higher but shorter use of shoulder action "compose" the horse into a very energetic and elegant movement. His haunches are well engaged but produce higher steps and a distinct lightening of the forehand, bouncing the withers up and lifting the knees higher. The medium trot is the bread-and-butter exercise on the way to Grand Prix. Without the medium gaits, the proper muscular development that produces the proper skeletal rotation just does not develop. The Grand Prix is born of development in the medium gaits. They build a strong, athletic body. The 20-meter circle is a wonderful gymnastic tool that, being a continuous line, allows the perpetual flow of motion. Riding the medium trot on the circle can give the trot special significance in furthering the improvement of balance.

For the development of medium gaits, a sense of "perpetual motion" is highly important. Riders feel that working often in medium gaits is detrimental, hard work. Remember that just a century ago in Paris, London, and Vienna and in the world's other metropolises, horses were driven in medium trot across cities, pulling their passengers in carriages to dinners, dentists, theaters, and shopping—maintaining the tempo for miles, clock even, and on pavement.

The medium trot has the distinct signature of great engagement and impulsion in the quarters, combined with a slow and elevated motion of the forehand that "waits" for the arrival of the haunches. That relative restraint in the forehand, in relation to the reach of the haunches, defines that wonderful forward yet upward bouncing motion that gives the feeling of a horse rising in front of the rider's thighs and sinking behind his seat bones.

The passage is born out of the medium trot. Both the strength and the skills needed by the horse for passage develop from medium trot work. Once the horse is ready for it, a bold half-halt during a medium trot can make the horse collect into passage. Medium gaits discourage speed or shifting the weight onto the forehand.

I hope that riders will engage their horse by using the three fundamental methods I have recommended here: put the horse on the aids, teach him the meaning of light legs, and use bending and two-track exercises. To increase his impulsion and confirm his balance, use transitions from longer to shorter strides. To stabilize the rhythm and build overall athletic and muscular development with skeletal proficiency, ride the medium trot on a circle.

RIDING STRATEGIES FOR THE ENGAGEMENT OF THE HORSE

Engagement is a concept that has several closely related meanings. In the general sense, engagement occurs when the rider succeeds in shifting the center of gravity backward toward the haunches of his horse, and that is, of course, collection. It also occurs every time the rider succeeds in making the horse improve upon whatever he is being asked to do at the time. As the process continues, the rider is perpetually seeking to shift the center of gravity backward and perpetually demanding a finer output from the horse. Thus, the final and specific definition of engagement appears: the maximum output by the horse in performing any gymnastic exercise asked of him. That presupposes that he is supple and elastic and capable of shifting his center of gravity toward the haunches as well as maximizing his athletic output all the time.

Shifting the horse's center of gravity toward his haunches should remain a perpetual effort in the rider's daily work. The horse's center of gravity is "naturally" on the forehand, as the bulk of his chest, rib cage and forearms, neck and head, are far heavier than the bulk of his quarters. Thus, a horse at the free walk will have three-fifths of his composite weight over his forehand. With considerable imagination, which is rather useful in all learning, we can propose that the horse is like a carpenter's level and has a bubble in him floating forward or backward to show us when he is "level," or horizontal. Imagine your horse this way as you ride and "feel" for his center of gravity or, rather, cultivate the center of gravity of his motion. For you cannot shape your horse, only his energies! If you propel him energetically enough that he supports more than half of his weight with his haunches, taking more than half off the forehand, you are engaging your horse.

Obviously, in working for this kind of engagement, the most useful daily exercises are the transitions, both from gait to gait and within the gaits.

During transitions, there are two curious things to note. First, transitioning from extension to collection, or from a potentially faster to a potenitally slower gait, such as from trot to walk, actually shifts the center of gravity backward. Yet, if a rider manages an upward transition with the center of gravity staying relatively close to the haunches, he gains greater gymnastic value because engagement of the horse is more improved by upward transitions. Second, the center of gravity will, by necessity, have to be shifted backward more efficiently if the horse is bent in a lateral movement. Thus, doing extension-collection-extension exercises on a 20-meter circle will have a higher gymnastic benefit than doing the same along straight lines.

Demanding of the horse that he do better than before is the indispensable job of the rider for each minute spent in the saddle. This implies that while in the saddle, the rider has concentration and focus, which allow him to sense, feel, and know every moment what his horse's performance level is. Feel what the hindquarters are doing and monitor the energy level all the time. Be accurate in monitoring and, most importantly, be punctual in reacting to any moment of slacking on the horse's part. This should be the attitude of the rider who demands performance from the horse beyond what he has volunteered. However, over-demanding leads to fatigue and mistrust.

Engagement is born of an uncompromised focusing of the horse's energies. Presumably, the rider has acquired the correct seat and aids, without which there is neither stability nor close-enough leg contact and seat to control the situation. Whatever the horse is doing at the moment, the rider should ask him to do it better. In short, the rider's continuous task is maximization of the horse's output. If the horse walks, there is surely a better walk that could be produced. If bending a horse on a circle, there is surely a chance for a better, more continous bending and for better impulsion than currently offered. If the rider extends the trot, he could surely try for a longer stride. In the half-pass, the straddling of the legs could surely be deeper with a greater bend.

Interestingly enough, horses are not only willing and capable of producing better quality than before, but they can learn that there is consistency in this demand and will habituate putting put out more as the training progresses. Then, when you have an off day, when the "flu is going around," you can still compete on a horse that is accustomed to putting out a great deal of performance because he has consistently been asked to do so. The rider does the horse a favor by demanding a lot because a horse that moves with maximum efficiency will do it with minimum effort and wear and tear.

Maximum performance of all the gymnastically important exercises with minimum effort is the ideal task of the fully developed dressage horse, as shown on the Grand Prix level. Years spent shifting his center of gravity toward his haunches and years spent maximizing his efforts from moment to moment create perfection of balanced coordination, elasticity, and suppleness on which this performance is based. Brilliance of performance arises from consistent schooling for engagement.

Therefore, on the highest levels of gymnastics we look for a horse that can perform each task called for to the ultimate extent of his natural abilities. For instance, if an extended trot is asked, the horse will extend his trot to the longest he can reach with his particular conformation and while remaining in perfect rhythm and balance. The same horse, when asked to perform

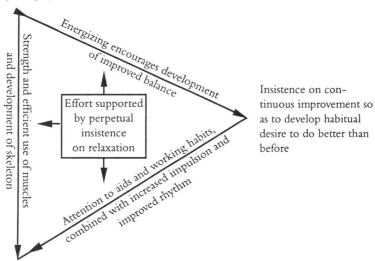

Demand for the shifting of the center of gravity backward through transition work (longitudinal principle) and bending (lateral principle)

Strength and efficient use of muscles and development of skeleton

Energizing encourages development of improved balance

Effort supported by perpetual insistence on relaxation

Insistence on continuous improvement so as to develop habitual desire to do better than before

Attention to aids and working habits, combined with increased impulsion and improved rhythm

Willingness and ability to maximize performance at all times

the piaffe, is not expected to show his engagement by extending his strides to their utmost conformational limits. Quite the contrary, his engagement is proven by the complete absence of advancing over the ground while remaining active in a trot-like motion. Piaffe is more akin to passage than to trot. Transitions from one to the other must be faultless in rhythmic regularity. Similarly, while a well-engaged half-pass is evaluated on the depth of straddling with the legs, a continous bending in the spine, and cadenced, airborne, sideways floating strides, we do not desire similar movement on the straight wall. In summary, that which is the sign of great engagement in one movement is not necessarily the ingredient of engagement in another. Engagement is evaluated by the performance of the essence of each gymnastic movement. So, if the essence is length of stride, then *length* is how we would predominantly measure engagement. And if the essence of the exercise is the lowering of the haunches such as is the case in piaffe, then lowering the haunches is very important in determining the degree of engagement in the performance. Engagement is the ultimate goal of dressage riding. Those riders who consider it their daily riding duty to induce their horse to do better and to step under more than ever before will go to the top.

The diagram shown on page 171 is a visual expression of the hierarchy of engagement work.

Five

Lateral Bending

The horse's neck is naturally more supple than his bulky trunk, which includes a relatively unyielding rib cage and heavy musculature. A horse can remain rigid throughout his trunk and still bend his neck to reach a fly or scratch his body way back. However, correct lateral bending occurs only when the horse is evenly bent throughout his body, along his spinal cord.

At the beginning of dressage training, the major task is to teach a horse to carry his rider in balance on a straight line. The horse should move evenly and straight without pushing his shoulders or haunches in or out, his hind legs following the forelegs so that the horse's spinal cord remains the center axis from which the hoofprints are equidistant. The rider should never become a passive traveler, and even on a running horse, he should keep his legs intimately in touch with the horse's sides, teaching the horse the concept that he may move only under conditions of aiding.

Most of the time, a horse moves on a bent line. Only seldom is there a straight path to move on. In our small riding arenas, there are two long walls and two short walls where a horse should move straight. Otherwise, most riding is done on various

Arthur Kottas-Heldenberg, Chief Rider of the Spanish Riding School in Vienna, Austria, is maintaining his horse at even bending of the spine and even loading with the hind legs. Here one of the greatest riders of our time is succeeding with all the principal tasks necessary for the "straightening of the horse": the horse is longitudinally flexed from hocks through to the bit. He is simultaneously evenly laterally bent to the right. Observe that the rider's feet hang parallel to the horse's sides to ensure fine calf aids and the outside leg is inevitably back, where it should be, for controlling the bending.

Photo: Charles Fuller.

arcs and circles or in the combination of them, whether it is jumping or other gymnastic disciplines that the rider may pursue. Lateral bending can be practiced qualitatively in two different ways.

The simpler lateral exercises are those done on circular lines, while the horse's hind legs continue to follow in the direction of the corresponding forelegs. These are called "single track" lateral exercises. The path of the horse proceeds on an arc. Such is the case with all the corners of a riding arena, since they are parts of an incomplete circle. To that, we can add the riding of a full circle, which can be of any size, usually larger for a stiffer, novice horse and smaller according to the horse's ability to bend as he improves his suppleness. Then we can ride serpentine lines, which are more difficult than simple circles, because the horse is asked to bend from side to side in succession. Finally, we can ride figure eights, which are rather difficult to do well, as the horse must sustain bending for a long while on each side, yet is given only one straight step to change the bend from one side to the other side.

The progression should be from simple to complex in riding on arcs, from a simple circle, to serpentine, to the figure eight. We also proceed from generous arcs to tighter, smaller ones as the horse's ability to bend onto them in a continuum improves. Note that the horse should be tutored in lateral bending at the walk first, then in trot, and, finally, in canter.

The more difficult or complex lateral bending exercises are done on multitracks. These require that the horse's hind legs do not follow directly into the footprints of the forelegs on the corresponding side. Rather, the horse will leave either three or four distinct traces of hoofprints behind on the ground. In general order of difficulty, these exercises are as follows:

The shoulder-in and shoulder-out exercises can only be done at the walk and trot. In shoulder-in, we ask the horse to bend around our inside leg, stepping with his inside hind leg toward the footprint of the outside foreleg. As a result, he leaves three tracks behind and bends the joints of the inside hind leg generously by striding deeply under his center of gravity. The horse progresses in the direction of his outside shoulder, however; he bends opposite the direction of his progression: to the inside.

This is the only multitrack movement where bending opposite the direction of motion is required.

The shoulder-out is the reverse of the shoulder-in. It is not necessary to do it, for by changing hands a rider can supple equally both sides of the horse with shoulder-in alone.

The haunches-in and haunches-out exercises are a little more sophisticated in their demands on the horse's musculature than the shoulder-in and the shoulder-out.

In the haunches-in, the horse is once more bent evenly around the rider's inside leg. He moves toward the side on which he is bent with his hindquarters displaced inward away from the rail. The forehand proceeds along the rail. The outside hind leg of the horse strides toward the footprint of his inside foreleg.

The haunches-in can be done in all three natural gaits: walk, trot, and canter. However, I discourage practicing it in the canter. Horses have the natural tendency to canter crookedly, usually with their haunches in, anyway. This is highly undesirable, because it allows the horse to avoid bending his joints correctly and causes him to move in stressful lack of balance. Indeed, the rider must teach and encourage his horse to canter very straight. Thus, the haunches-in at the canter, while horses are eager to offer it, should be avoided.

The haunches-out, just like the shoulder-out, is an exercise that is not necessary to practice, as it can be replaced by changing hands and performing a haunches-in, again in the opposite direction.

The half-pass is a more sophisticated lateral bending exercise than the previously described ones. It serves to strengthen the horse's use of his hips, stifles, and shoulders, as opposed to the shoulder-in, which aims to strengthen the hocks for-collection and suspension. The haunches-in strengthens the stifles and the lumbar back most.

In half-pass, the horse moves on a diagonal across the arena, with his bent body somewhat parallel with the wall toward which he progresses, yet with his inside shoulder slightly leading. The horse is once again bent around the inside leg of the rider, proceeding in the direction of his bending. Most important are the maintenance of the forward urge and the evenness and clarity of motion. Half-passes can be done at the walk, trot, and

Arthur Kottas-Heldenberg is showing a correct haunches-in exercise. His finely draped inside leg is there for the horse to bend around and to maintain his impulsion. In this movement, the horse's hooves ought to leave four separate tracks on the ground, which is only possible if the bend is as great and continuous as seen in this picture. Notice that the neck must continue forward on the path of progress without being pulled inward from it. This important element during the haunches-in keeps the horse's inside shoulder leading, denying the evasion of leaning to the outside shoulder to escape engagement. As with anything accomplished with great mastery, this complex exercise is presented by the rider seemingly in repose. Mastery begins when effort ceases to be obvious.

Photo: Charles Fuller.

canter and should be done in all three gaits. The horse moving in half-pass will leave four tracks behind on the ground. It strengthens all the joints, especially the hips, and therefore, will improve the horse's ability to extend his strides.

Pirouettes are also lateral bending exercises. They can be performed only in the walk and in the canter. While pirouetting at the walk is a relatively simple gymnastic exercise, doing the same in canter is one of the most difficult. Young horses can soon pirouette at the walk, but only the most advanced horses will be able to do the same at the canter, usually some years later.

At the pirouette, the horse is asked to turn around his inside hind leg. Both hind legs are to remain active, but on the spot where the movement was started. One can ride quarter, half, three-quarter, or full pirouettes, depending on the horse's level of advancement. During these turns, the horse is gently bent around the rider's inside leg toward the direction of the turn.

The following is a summary of some of the properties of lateral bending:

- During all lateral bending exercises, horses are evenly bent along the entire length of their spinal column toward one side. The "inside" is the hollow or contracted side of the horse. The other side, called the outside, is stretched longer and feels "full."
- While lateral bending exercises can never be done with a straight horse, their purpose, however, is to help straighten a horse. Lateral bending exercises have a very high suppling value, which ensures the eventual development of the desired straight-moving horse.
- There can never be any successful lateral bending without the horse first being longitudinally flexed. In other words, lateral bending can occur only when the horse is accepting the leg aids for increased flexion in his joints without hurrying. This elevates his back, rounds his topline, arches his neck, and allows his head to hang while seeking the bit.
- While longitudinal flexion is a prerequisite to lateral bending, each reinforces the horse's ability to do the other. Hence, successful lateral bending will consolidate the horse's ability to remain in longitudinal flexion, which in turn will make this prerequisite position more often available to do additional lateral bending exercises.
- Always repeat each lateral bending exercise in both directions.

Arthur Kottas-Heldenberg demonstrates the suppling values of two-track exercises. The photographs at the trot show the increased assumption of weight by the horse's inside hind leg during half-pass. The photograph of the walk (upper right) shows how the exercise supples the horse's shoulders by straddling with the forehand. All two-track exercises will strengthen, therefore supple, the joints of the horse. Continuous body bending is important. To show how it succeeds, these pictures were taken from various angles, from outside, straight on, or inside the horse's progression.

Photos: Charles Fuller.

Never exercise the horse's hollow or stiff side more than the other. Always "mirror" lateral exercises and do it in close succession. For example, circling to the right should be followed by circling to the left.

- Always combine longitudinal and lateral gymnastics. All transitions are powerful longitudinal flexing and balancing exercises. Riding transitions after each lateral exercise makes for a successful combination. As an example, ride a half-circle right in the trot and reaching the opposite rail, depart into canter on the left lead. Or pirouette left at the walk, and then depart at the canter on the left lead when the pirouette is completed. The possible combinations are infinite.

Gymnastic riding can be meaningful only when a planned strategy is pursued by the rider. No exercise should be done on the spur of the moment and without due preparation. During riding, a quick succession of changes may indicate well-planned gymnasticizing. There is no specific value in endlessly riding in the same gait, on the same line, in the same exercise for a long time. The frequency of transitions is in direct proportion to the value of gymnastic development in the horse.

THE TWO-TRACK MOVEMENTS

Two-track movements are so called because while doing them the horse's forehand will travel on a different track than will his haunches. Depending on which two-track exercise the horse is performing, he may leave three or four tracks with his hoof prints.

Two-track movements may be placed into two different categories:

The shoulder-in and the shoulder-out by themselves form one category. These are the only two-track movements in which we bend the horse opposite from the direction of his progression. For example, when performing a shoulder-in to the right, the horse must continue to move in the direction of our left hand and knee, even though he is required to be bent to the right. The shoulder-out is identical to the shoulder-in—the horse is

Arthur Kottas-Heldenberg riding a shoulder-in (photo on the left) *and a half-pass* (photo on the right) *to demonstrate exemplary bending to the right. The photographs taken from these angles "inside the movement," and not from straight ahead, in order to make the perfect bending of the horse more obvious. Continuous spinal bending produces continuous body bending. The "body building" of the horse depends on the precision and consistency of his bending. The rider's superb seat makes it obvious that all bending is with the outside leg back and around the inside leg, which remains the custodian of impulsion and rhythm. This bending position of the legs necessarily and correctly places the rider more onto his inside seat bone. Especially in bending, the rider's shoulders and hips must always parallel the shoulders and hips respectively of his horse.* Photos: Charles Fuller.

counter bent, that is, bent toward the wall along which he moves. The designation of whether a shoulder-in or a shoulder-out is being performed depends entirely on which way we bend the horse relative to the wall of the manege. The "inside" is always the side on which the horse is hollow or contracted regardless of whether he is shoulder-in or shoulder-out. "Inside" does not refer to the arena, it refers to the horse's bending. The shoulders are displaced inward and move on a line inward from that of the haunches. If the wall is on the side he is bent away from, we have a shoulder-in. If it is on the side he is bent toward, we have a shoulder-out.

The haunches-in, haunches-out, the half-pass, and the pirouettes form the other category. All of these movements belong in the same category because in all of them, the horse is asked to proceed in the direction toward which he is bent. The aids, therefore, are very similar in these movements. They differ only in intensity and application because different degrees of bending, suspension, and collection are expected. The mildest bending is required in the pirouettes to allow for more turning activity; maximum collection, balance, and skeletal displacement. The half-pass demands more bending and great suspension. Bending at the haunches-in is the greatest, with maximum muscular stretch and minimum skeletal displacement required.

In all lateral movements, the seat should remain an inactive anchorage without any pushing or rocking gestures. That is, a rider should neither shove forward nor gyrate sideways with the lower back. Stay perpendicular, without leaning forward or backward. Do not tilt the torso inward or outward. Do not try to push the horse away with the torso. Do not stiffen or raise one shoulder and do not look down or at the horse's head. In two-track movements, the most important aids are the legs. Their effectiveness depends on a well-anchored seat. The leg aids are felt by the horse only in their relative strength, and that depends on the steadiness of a deep, adhesive seat. The reason for this is that we are on the horse and not anchored on the ground!

Any straight but flexible object can be bent only when it is affected at a minimum of three points. Place your riding whip on a table and try it. The whip is a particularly good instrument of analogy to the horse because it has a heavier, less flexible butt end and a highly flexible thin end, which is analogous to the horse's neck. Try to bend the riding whip as if it were a horse's spine. Put your thumb on one side of the whip at its middle and bend the whip around it by pressing on the opposite side of the whip, near its two ends.

This experiment will demonstrate that the horse must be *bent around* (but not with) the inside leg. The inside leg supplies

The canter half-pass to the right schooled by Arthur Kottas-Heldenberg. These photos illustrate correct longitudinal flexion combined with good lateral bending and show the proper posture of the neck. One clearly sees (especially in the photo farthest left) the arching flexion of the top neck muscle with the neck's bending position supported by parallel muscles flexed, coming up from the side of the neck. The poll supple, the head hanging, the horse's relaxation, are all visible because the horse's muscles are correctly used in the support of his posture. Notice that the rider's hanging upper arm forms a pronounced angle at the elbow with the lower arm, which belongs to his horse. The outside rein contact is indeed just a contact, and not pulling, and therefore the hands of a giving rider are being sought by his horse. The proper use of outside rein is crucial for the correct definition of the horse's lateral bending.

Photos: Charles Fuller.

the impulsion and determines the rhythm and the point around which the horse must bend. The inside leg is analogous to your thumb on the whip. The horse is *bent by the rider's outside leg*, which is placed back and in a continuous pressure contact. The outside rein is offered to welcome the horse's light contact, which he finds due to the stretching of his outside neck muscles. This stretching outside contact is the main feature of bending, not the pulling of the inside rein.

To continue with the whip analogy, try the following with your fingers still working the riding whip:

- Push the whip only with your thumb, that is, the inside leg. It will remain straight yet drift sideways—a leg-yield or drift, but not a shoulder-in.
- Add the pulling of the light end of the whip, that is, the inside rein to the pushing of the thumb, that is, the inside leg. You get neck bending with a straight torso and outward swinging haunches.

Both of the above experiments demonstrate two common evasions to bending! With only two of the bending aids, the horse may go sideways, may drift from the legs, but he will not bend in his entire length and will not exercise his inside hind leg, flex his joints, or stretch and contract the appropriate muscles. However, if you bend the horse with the outside leg, around the inside leg, stretching the horse into the control of the outside rein, you will achieve bending.

In all two-track movements of both categories, the rider's outside leg remains responsible for the bending. In the shoulder-in, the haunches must be kept on their original track in spite of the shoulders being taken off the original track. The shoulders are moved on to an inner track away from the wall. The outside rein should be as steady, neither tight nor slack. The inside rein is rendered resilient to encourage forward progression, particularly the deeper striding forward and across by the inside hind leg. The rider's inside leg is rhythmically active, in a perpendicular position.

In the pirouette, half-pass, and haunches-in, the bending aids remain the same. While executing them, the horse must

Steffen Peters riding the half-pass left at the trot. This is a remarkable picture for showing utmost engagement by maximizing the straddling of the horse's legs and obvious suppling of the shoulders. The deep straddling of the hind legs shows how the horse's hip must sink forward and under and how his lumbar back must exert supple muscular support to achieve this challenging progression. The exact parallel positions of the diagonal pairs of legs are exemplary. The bending of the horse, his energy, his amplification of the stride while gaining ground sideways, and his elasticity in producing the grand straddling are wonderful achievements. Photo: Cheryl Erpelding.

travel in the direction toward which he is bent. Therefore, the outside leg assumes a double role: it bends the horse as well as encourages the sideways displacement of the horse. The inside leg remains identical in its position as during the shoulder-in. The feeling is that the rider "receives" the horse with the inside leg and keeps the rhythm with it. The inside rein continues to encourage resiliency and is suppling, by yielding in small rhythmic allowances that open the gates to progression. A restrictive inside rein will cause a stiff-necked posture with a tense, low back and even tilting of the head.

When teaching two-track movements, slow down the tempo to communicate that you want your horse engaged on his haunches. When the horse has eventually understood these movements and built the strength and skills needed to perform them, he will do them with proper impulsion and collection. Do not allow your horse to run away from the leg aids. Ride with leg and rein contact on both sides to influence bending. Otherwise, the horse may speed at the unexpected use of these aids. You must slow the tempo of the horse and place your legs into their bending positions before asking for two-track movements. Without preparatory half-halts, the exercises will not succeed.

We often ask for two-track movements after preparing the horse through corners. This presumes that the rider can use the corners to intensify bending and collect with a half-halt before the performance of the two-track.

In summary, remember that all two-track movements can best be divided into two major categories. One includes shoulder-in and shoulder-out—the only two-track movements in which the horse does not bend in the direction of his progression. In the second category are all other two-track movements, grouped together because in all of them, the horse bends toward the direction of his progression. Thus, the haunches-in, the haunches-out, the half-pass, and the pirouette are included in this latter category.

We should also remember here that the shoulder-in and haunches-in have twin counterparts: the shoulder-out and haunches-out respectively. Beyond this similarity, they further resemble one another in that they emphasize the displacement of either the front (shoulder-in and -out) or the quarters (haunches-in and -out) relative to the line of progression. Thus, they encourage the development of body control with the goal of straightening the horse and moving him evenly forward.

The Similarities in All Two-Track Movements

The most important similarity in all two-track movements, from the point of view of the horse's gymnastic development, is that the horse must bend in all of them continuously and evenly along his spine. When he does not bend continuously, but instead bends more at the very flexible neck, the horse will evade bending in the rest of his body. In fact, the horse's offer of an exaggerated neck position is an evasion to bending.

In all two-track exercises, the horse's balance greatly improves as he learns to cope with the new experience of displacing his center of gravity. We greatly improve the horse's muscular flexibility, manifested in longitudinal flexion, as he stretches his musculature on one side of his body and contracts it on the other. As these movements combine the sideways-moving balance displacement with bending, their combined effect strengthens the entire organism as "body building" does and also elasticizes the horse's joints. Without two-track movements the lumbar back of the horse does not gain the strength and agility to lower the croup and compact his haunches by sinking on increasingly flexible joints. All of these athletic improvements result in a horse moving more powerfully, with increased suspension manifested in cadence and, of course, grace in movement.

From the rider's point of view, there are additional values in the two-track exercises. These exercises have a special value in increasing and refining the horse's submission to the aids. They increase his attention to the details of the aids and separate the meaning on both of his sides. Because of the required use of unilateral aids in two-track movements, the refinement of understanding between horse and rider through these exercises may be likened to a conceptually abstract conversation by someone learning a foreign language.

During two-track movements, the rider's outside leg should always be positioned farther back than the inside leg. This outside leg on the horse's long and stretched side must be pressed back and down at the knee, while keeping the calf stretched and the heel down. If the heel rises up and the lower leg approaches a horizontal position, the positioning of the leg becomes ineffective. However, if the outside leg is positioned back correctly, it will fulfill its major function of keeping the horse's spine bent by controlling his haunches. Coincidentally, the outside leg positioning is the answer to a question often asked: Which seat bone is more heavily weighted during two-track movements?

The answer is obvious when the rider aids correctly! Anytime the outside leg is positioned back for bending the horse, it inevitably places the rider's inside seat bone more adhesively down and forward. In fact, the outside seat bone may feel as if it has risen up somewhat, into the buttock muscle, and left the saddle in favor of doubling the weight toward the inside seat. Thus, while schooling on two-tracks, the rider always sits on the inside seat bone, which is always the one on the horse's hollow or short side.

The Rider's Hands During Two-Track Movements

During two-track exercises, the horse must cross one hind leg in front of the other. On the side on which the horse's hind leg crosses over, the rider's hand must yield the rein in a gesture indicating opening the gates to forward progression. Crossing with a hind leg is not all we hope for. We aim to achieve a well-engaged crossing: one with a high, yet deep stride.

During a shoulder-in, the rider's inside hand must yield as the inside hind leg crosses to allow for increased engagement! In all other two-track movements, it is the rider's outside hand that yields to permit the engagement. The hand opposite the yielding hand remains as an indirect rein, a rein of reference; it is stable, but light in contact.

Suppling must be based on yielding. When a rider misinterprets suppling as a pull-back on the jaw and then a pushing of the hand forward, he is mistaken. Suppling must yield the already light contact without any pulling preceding or following it. To yield, simply deny contact with the rein on one side and do it without visibly slackening the leather.

When yielding is done artfully, it is done in rhythm with the horse's stride. The suppling rein should yield exactly at the time when the horse's hind leg on the same side lifts off the ground. The steadiness of the rider's seat and aids, the sophistication of their quietness, cannot be overemphasized. Establishing the "feel" for yielding and supporting on the opposite rein depends on the rider's ability to anchor correctly and to use the aids as a comprehensive, interrelated system.

The Use of the Leg Aids to Supply Rhythm and Impulsion

On the horse's long side (outside), the leg is steady and positioned in the "behind the girth" position. On the short side (inside and hollow), the leg is in the usual, perpendicular "girth" position. Most of the aiding for impulsion is supplied with the rider's leg on the horse's hollow, contracted inward side. Therefore, during the shoulder-in, the rider's inside leg must aid for both the crossing of the horse's inside hind leg and the impulsion. However, in the other two-track movements, the impulsion leg, being on the inside, is not also responsible for the crossing of the legs.

As a matter of general principle, when aiding a horse in any two-track movement, you can help improve his balance best by staying in balance yourself. Leaning to either side denies the horse the chance to understand the leg aids and leads to frustration and a loss of balance due to fear. The rider's spine should remain perpendicular to the horse's spine. Therefore, riding straight toward a mirror is very helpful. Even during coaching, some riders doubt that they are tilting to one side.

Remember, a rider cannot shape the horse, only his energies! When riding on two-tracks, you are giving the horse's energies a sophisticated new "shape" that can only be sculpted correctly when the horse supplies sufficient energy to be shaped. Never contrive the horse's shape with the reins. By allowing his impulsion to flow through his entire body, the horse will perform his best and will inevitably be gymnastically proper.

All two-track movements, with the exception of full-passes, are asked for in the AHSA tests.

The Four Goals of Two-Track Movements

The shoulder-in, haunches-in, half-pass, and pirouette share a common gymnastic purpose: the engagement of the hindquarters of the horse. The desired result is, first, an increased ability to collect as the horse develops an acceptance of more weight on his hindquarters.

The second is the marked strengthening and subsequent suppling of all joints, including those of the forehand. Without taxing, flexing, rotating, and bending these joints, the horse can not amplify his basic gaits and gain the strength required for increased suspension.

The third is to improve the horse's lateral balance. The skills of riders and horses develop together in their abilities to deliberately adjust the relationship of the forehand to the haunches. Two-track work completes the sophistication for absolute straightening of the horse. The correct bending of the horse remains essential. This is at the heart of controlling the spinal alignment and ultimately the straightening of the horse.

The fourth purpose of schooling on two-tracks is to increase the horse's mental obedience through attention to detail and added sophistication to his harmonious coordination.

The Suitability of Gaits for Two-Track Work

The half-pass can be performed in all three gaits. When developing it, the order of training should proceed in this way: from the potentially slowest to the potentially fastest gait. The skills are easiest to teach to the horse at the walk. At the canter, however, he will find the execution of the movement the easiest.

The pirouette can be performed only at the walk and the canter. Some riders "pirouette at the trot" with their advanced horses by performing a piaffe, during which the horse rotates around his hind legs. This movement is not called for in any test, and it is done for the purpose of lightening the horse's forehand, creating more engagement, and improving balance and obedience at the piaffe.

The pirouette at the walk should be taught long before it is introduced at the canter. The pirouette at the canter is proof of the highest collection in that gait and therefore is the most sophisticated of all canter exercises. The pirouette at the walk is much simpler and should be practiced at the early stages of training to introduce the horse to the idea of increased engagement and obedience to unilateral aids.

Similar to the half-pass, the haunches-in can be performed in all three gaits and should be introduced in the order of walk, trot, and canter. I do not recommend its practice in canter, since most horses have a tendency to canter with their haunches-in as an evasion to engagement. Insisting on a haunches-in in canter would therefore add to, rather than diminish, this natural tendency to move crooked in canter. However, the exception could be the haunches-in ridden on a circle or even on a diminishing circle. When done knowledgeably, this could be a preparatory movement for the canter pirouette. This helps to establish bending, the tucking and lateral flexibility of the lumbar back, and the suppression of the croup.

The positioning of the horse is very similar in the half-pass, pirouette and haunches-in movements: the horse should be continuously bent along his spinal column toward the direction of his progression. The horse should cross with his outside legs in front of his inside legs. The horse's center of gravity shifts to the side toward which he is bent and to which he moves. Because of these similarities, the rider's aids are placed in similar positions, however, with variations both in the strength of their application and in the patterning.

Combining Two-Track Movements

Because the horse is using both his skeleton and his musculature in similar ways, and because the rider aids all three exercises in a similar manner, the rider should develop a strategy of going from one to another of these movements.

Here are some strategies for teaching and practicing the half-pass, pirouette, and haunches-in, including some combinations of them.

With a young horse, you may start down center line and half-pass for a few steps. (See illustration on page 192.) When you lose control of the flexion or if he gets tired, go straight. Then repeat a few more steps, periodically going straight to reestablish control and help the horse to recover his balance. With more advanced horses, the straight steps help the rider to adjust his aids, correct his seat, pay attention to his inside leg staying in contact with the horse, and ensure that the haunches are neither trailing nor leading.

Performing this two-track exercise on the center line will appear as a haunches-in exercise, although the rider should be aware that he could consider the same a half-pass if he imagines the center line to be the diagonal of another, imaginary manege!

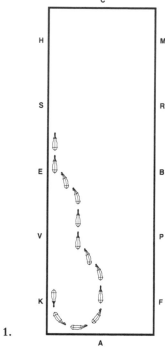

1.

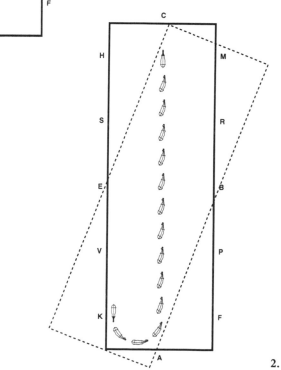

2.

TRAINING STRATEGIES FOR DRESSAGE RIDERS

Worth noting here, however, is the fact that the haunches-in and the half-pass are very similar but not identical. The horse should be bent slightly more during the haunches-in and therefore will cross with his legs less deeply than in the half-pass, where the crossing should be deeper but the bending less exaggerated.

Figure 3 shows that the training strategy of a half-pass across the diagonal can be viewed simultaneously as a haunches-in along the wall of another imaginary manege. Their similarity, however, is limited to patterning but not to leg work. In the half-pass the horse's legs must straddle, while in a haunches-in they merely cross.

Figure 4 shows the strategy of developing a good pirouette with the aid of the haunches-in. Pirouettes are often ruined by pulling the horse's head around and restraining his forward urge.

This exercise shown in figure 4 should only be done at the walk and not at the canter. During the canter pirouette, the horse should be collected in a schooled canter with a very light, elevated forehand. His turning should be incidental and easily controlled by the rider's seat and leg. The reins should not steer or pull. His forehand should merely be guided over an arc. In the canter an exercise of half-pass followed by half-pirouette followed by half-pass again can be used to engage the haunches.

Figure 6 shows the mirror exercise of the haunches-in, which is the haunches-out. It differs from the haunches-in only in the location of the closest wall. The haunches-out that you see in the drawing, when moved to the opposite wall, would be called haunches-in. Here we must note, however, that haunches-in is easier to perform because it begins with the bending of the horse that is already established in the corner preceding it. When a haunches-out is performed, the horse must first be counter-flexed, which requires more sophisticated control. When the horse moves on the center line with his haunches displaced, his forehand and haunches traveling on two separate tracks, we may either call the movement haunches-in or haunches-out depending on the hand on which the horse traveled preceding the exercise. For example, a horse traveling on the center line with the haunches to the left is performing a haunches-

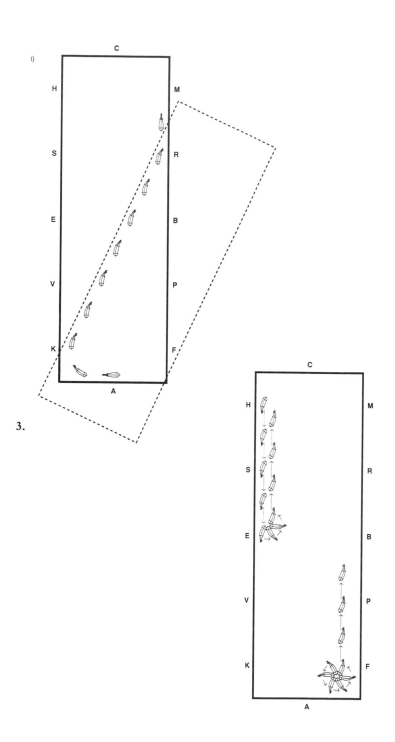

3.

4.

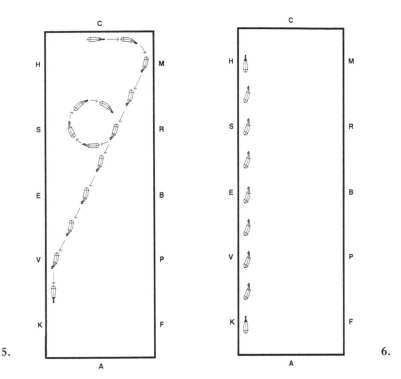

5.

6.

in if he was started from the left-hand side, as shown in figure 2, while the horse performing the identical movement approached from the right-hand side is performing a haunches-out.

When a young horse loses his bending and/or rhythm, he can be best reestablished by riding a circle after a few steps of half-pass as shown in figure 5 or haunches-in and then continuing with the two-track movement.

Exercises like those illustrated can be invented endlessly. The combination of patterns that help develop both the horse's understanding of what he ought to do and his physical ability to do it can be enhanced by patiently varying the patterns and combinations that build the half-pass, pirouette, and haunches-in.

In this sequence, Arthur Kottas-Heldenberg shows a canter pirouette to the right—absolutely remarkable for its precision of bending. The calm, collected, and precise turning of the horse is obvious. The bending of the joints of the hindquarters is exceptional and includes the most important element of sitting down on the haunches by the lumbar tucking of the pelvis forward and under. The croup is obviously lowered, the forehand liberated for the turning, and the lumbosacral joint obviously flexed. All the necessary ingredients of a superior pirouette are visually obvious.

One must observe that the rider is an integral part of the pirouette, enhancing and not disturbing it. With his deep and adhesive seat, the rider contributes to the image of the human torso sitting on equine legs. Notice how the incredibly relaxed and calm execution enhances engagement, precision, and balance. The horse should never be agitated, tense, disturbed, and thrown off balance to execute this magnificent feat, the highest possible collection in canter.   Photos: Charles Fuller.

Six

The Development of the Basic Gaits

The natural gaits include the walk, trot, canter, backing, and the halt. The halt is included in spite of its essence being immobility because it must show a willingness to move forward. The most prolonged training use is given to the trot. Based on the length of strides, there are the extended, medium, working, collected, and school trot, plus passage and piaffe.

Once the collected and medium trots have been established, the working trot becomes useful only during warmup periods.

All two-track movements should be ridden in a suitable level of collection. While the shoulder-in and shoulder-out increase the ability to perform a brilliant collected trot, the half-pass helps the development of a brilliant extended trot, by developing hip and stifle flexibility and freeing the shoulders. Development of collection, for most riders, is easiest in the trot, and it is by far the most difficult at the walk. The highest degree of collection in the different gaits is demonstrated at:

Collected walk—for walk.
Piaffe—for trot.
Pirouette—for canter.

Extensions in all three gaits are best developed by riding the extensions on a straight line, rather than through figures and turns. Extensions depend on even loading and striding legs used with maximum stretching.

When the natural walk of the horse is poor, in most cases his canter will also be poor. When purchasing a dressage prospect, the walk should be scrutinized most carefully, for the improvement of that gait is the most difficult and sometimes impossible. The trot is the gait most easily improved by schooling.

While there are periods of suspension in the canter and the trot, there is none in the walk. In both walk and canter, we ask for pirouettes, but we do not perform the same at the trot. The flying changes are unique to the canter and there are not analogous movements in the other two gaits. While in trot we may ride a piaffe, a movement lacking in ground-gaining advancement by the horse, we always gain ground and advance in the other two gaits. While we perform shoulder-in and shoulder-out at both walk and trot, we do not perform the movement in canter. However, one may ride a shoulder-fore in canter, which is an increase in the lateral bending of the cantering horse and invites his inside shoulder to track positioned slightly inward, in front of the inside hip. This canter exercise omits the crossing of the legs, but it does promote suppling, straightening, and liberation of the shoulders.

THE WALK, A NEGLECTED GAIT

Of the three basic gaits, the walk is the most difficult to improve. Therefore, when a rider selects a horse for gymnastic purposes, especially for dressage, he should take care to select one with a good natural walk. A horse with a good walk can be recognized as one moving forward with energetic marching strides, as if approaching something desirable. He should move with even four-beat rhythmic footfalls. He carries his weight with ease, lifting his legs up rather than dwelling on them. His hind legs print past the hoofprints left by the corresponding foreleg. Walking should be with a free extended shoulder reach. His rib cage will swing gently from side to side. His tail hangs relaxed, demonstrating the relaxation of his musculature, which is an important sign of the walk being effortless.

When free and at leisure, most horses move about slowly looking for forage, going from mouthful to mouthful, seldom on a straight line. Instead, they sidestep, turn, halt, and look about. Horses only walk keenly when approaching something of interest. Often, however, instead of walking, they take flight at the canter or trot when something disturbs their leisurely foraging.

For centuries, we have encouraged the development of a good walk by gently herding young horses toward grazing and watering places. Development of the natural gaits of a horse should take place during the first three years of its life, before the weight of saddle and rider are added. With insufficient movement during early upbringing, the horse might grow up to be a poor walker.

Riders may neglect improving the naturally undeveloped walk for various reasons. For some riders, the walk is a derogatory gait. This feeling may not be a conscious one. Yet, we realize that as novice riders, we all began riding the horse only at the walk, that being the slowest, smoothest, and therefore the safest gait. We may continue to associate the walk with these early equestrian experiences of insecurity, helplessness, stiffness, imbalance, discomfort, and fear.

Some skilled riders are simply bored with the walk. Yet, those with a thorough understanding of dressage and courage for artistic detail will find it intriguing and challenging. However, the majority of riders seem to value the trot as the primary gait for initial relaxation and will relegate the walk to periods of rest. Worse yet, riders resting their horses in walk will not demand enough impulsion but will allow a slow, meandering movement.

Most of us did not "fall in love" with the art of riding by being attracted to it by the walk. Exhilaration comes easier at the trot and canter because the horse moves faster and more energetically in those gaits. Had we desired to creep along at a slow pace, we could have saddled an ox.

At the walk, there is no period of suspension as in canter

and trot. This major distinction is the key to the difficulties encountered while attempting to improve the gait. The walk is potentially the slowest of the three basic gaits, thus exacerbating the rider's problem. The walk is earthbound; the beauty of the trot and canter depends both on the quality and duration of the suspension. We gymnasticize our horses to increase the strength and suppleness of their joints and muscles; our purpose is to enhance their ability to move with greater suspension. While we can ride our horse for improved flotation in suspension at the trot and canter, we are denied the same opportunity in the walk. Aids are based on changing currently existing balance and harmony. In the slow, earthbound walk, such aids become difficult. Because the horse never totally leaves the ground nor progresses with speed, he is quite capable of accommodating unbalanced situations with ease. Subtle changes in our aiding system may simply be ignored by the horse at the walk.

Improving the Walk

Two major dressage principles contribute to the improvement of the walk. The horse develops in his totality. While a broken-down piece of machinery may be repaired by fixing the malfunctioning part, a horse can never be improved by attempting to work on the faulty part alone. Therefore, appropriate gymnastic work at the trot and canter contributes remarkably to the development of the walk.

It is never the quantity but rather the quality of aids that improves the gait. Therefore, a sluggish walk will not be improved by vigorous kicking. Aids too strong for comfort or too rapid for the rhythm of the footfalls will fail to create improvement. The most effective aids are comfortably gentle, exquisitely coordinated with the horse's movements, and given when the hind legs leave the ground. No gait requires more "feel" than the walk!

The rider can improve the walk through correct aiding and also by logical gymnasticizing. The rider's legs should be adhesive but should not tightly pinch the horse's sides. To an observer, they should appear as if they were painted there with heels down to increase the strength of the calves by stretching without stiffening. Invisible pressures with these legs are always in rhythm and harmony with the horse's movement, coordinated with seat activities, and have proper strength without inhibiting measures. A deep knee position and well-elevated toes maintain quiet legs. With draped legs, the rider should insist on keeping his horse's spine parallel with the path of progression (while working on single track exercises). Often the walk fails to develop properly because the horse evades the rider's leg aids for straightening. Only well-attached legs can ensure that the horse does not step off the line of progression with one of his hind legs and that he progresses with equally long strides with both hind legs.

The rider should always be aware of the activities of the horse's hind legs, otherwise he cannot influence and control their activities. Only steadily adhesive legs can increase the feel of the seat in knowing where the horse's hind legs are and what they are doing. When the left hind leg is striding under the rider's weight, the rider's left leg is pushed out on the expanded left side of the horse's rib cage, while his right leg sinks in on the other, hollowed side of the rib cage. Simultaneously, on the horse's stretched side, the rider's seat bone is elevated, while on the contracted side, his seat bone sinks. Riders should train themselves to feel the horse's strides by closing their eyes periodically and calling out "right" and "left" to indicate the side on which the horse's hind leg is leaving the ground to stride under the center of gravity.

Both the direction and impulsive activity of the horse's hind legs can be influenced only when they are leaving the ground. A rider can redirect the left hind leg of the horse back to the straight or send it forward in a longer stride only when the left hind leg is leaving the ground. Should the rider fail to detect the instant of elevation or should his legs be too distant from the horse's side to give pressure at the required instant, the window of opportunity for improvement will be lost. Dangling legs, loosely banging, or kicking legs are meaningless annoyances that may disrupt the horse's rhythm. Even worse, they cannot synchronize with the horse's activities in his hindquarters and they can never be on time for aiding.

The walk is a gait without suspension. The horse has either two or three feet on the ground simultaneously. When the walk is performed with regularity, we should hear four distinct and evenly spaced footfalls. The order of footfalls will be as follows: right hind, right fore, left hind, left fore. The legs should lift off the ground and reach forward freely with generous, unhurried strides. The rhythm of the footfalls must remain the same in all modes of walk; only the length of the strides changes.

The *free walk* is volunteered by a balanced horse as his most comfortable walk under the rider's weight. The horse carries his rider with a stretched and elevated back. He strides energetically with comfortable, elastic, even strides. He is in lateral balance and therefore straight and neither hurried nor lazy, but looking purposeful.

The rider should not "drop" his horse into a free walk, but rather liberate him to it through stretching. The rider can perform a half-halt by momentarily strengthening all the aids. The rider concludes his half-halt by yielding his reins slightly while continuing to drive. Then the rider should invite his horse to "chew the reins out of his hands." The action should be gradual and continuous as the horse stretches his neck and head first forward, then downward. It is incorrect for the horse to abruptly yank the reins downward by hammering onto the bit or to lower and curl the neck without the forward stretch. However, when correctly stretched, the horse will lengthen his strides evenly to accommodate his longer frame.

Once stretched to the free walk, the horse should be encouraged to move straight. The rider's seat, legs, and hands guide him to do so. At the free walk, the reins should not be completely abandoned and held at the buckle. Rather, they should be stretched to the utmost but still held by the rider and lightly contacted by the horse in his new, stretched position. Thus, the reins remain a secret guiding instrument of alignment of the head and neck. The substantial weight of the head and neck should not be allowed to fall sideways; in that case, his body, which follows, will be compelled to meander after it in support of its weight.

The rider's legs not only maintain impulsion and encourage long strides, but they also guide the horse on a straight path, preventing him from deviating from it with his hindquarters.

The *ordinary walk* serves as a median of reference when comparing various modes of walk. At the ordinary walk, the horse must submit to and comply with the rider's aids. He must be longitudinally flexed in a shorter frame and taller posture than in the free walk. With his hind legs, he must stride past the hoofprints of his forelegs. An athletically suitable horse, moving at the ordinary walk, on the aids, striding correctly as described above, will cover a distance of 100 meters (330 feet) per minute. The ordinary walk can be monitored on a measured path with the aid of a stopwatch. The rider should memorize the "feel" of the walk when it is the required 330-feet-per-minute output and insist on performing it at that rate. All the aids are at the rider's disposal to regulate the walk until this goal is attained.

At the *working walk*, the horse "works" more from the haunches than if he were left without the influences of his rider at his ordinary walk. Most of this added "working" becomes visible at the hocks, which flex more than before. The strides made with the horse's hind legs should overstride the hoofprints left by his front legs.

The *medium walk* is more resolute and even longer (more ground gaining) in stride than the working walk. The "medium" gaits are educated gaits and therefore show amplification of the strides. The hind legs must overstride the footprints of the front legs. The front legs should reach longer than in the working walk. The medium walk is similar to and aspiring toward the extended walk. However, because the horse is not developed enough or asked to fully extend his walk, he retains a taller posture, shows more composition in his longitudinal flexion, yet reaches forward with great, ground-gaining strides.

At the *extended walk*, the horse is asked to maximize the length of his strides by reaching as freely forward as anatomically possible both with his forelegs and with his hind legs. While still maintaining longitudinal flexion, the horse moves with a longer, more stretched, lower-positioned neck than he does during a medium walk. The strides as well as the flexed body of the horse should stretch as long as physically possible.

At the *collected walk*, the horse strides with higher, and consequently shorter, steps than in the ordinary walk. As a result of this shorter, higher stepping, his frame is shortened and his carriage is taller. His hindquarters are engaged and his croup is lowered, thereby carrying less weight on the forehand and elevating the neck and head. The essence of a collected walk is in the high and energetic activity of the hind legs and not in the shortening of strides. Therefore, driving remains the most essential ingredient of its creation.

The rider must drive by frequently rebalancing through half-halts to teach the horse to elevate his steps rather than extend or hurry them. The rider should feel as if progressing uphill. The horse should round his lumbar back, tuck his pelvis forward, and lower his croup, thus lightening his forehand.

The aids must be in perfect synchronization with the horse's hind legs. The rider's legs must aid in harmony with the horse's strides. Then the feeling for the rider is as if his leg on the horse's hollowing side sinks into the rib cage. The rider's contacting leg should never part from the horse's swinging rib cage. The rider's body must be well stretched above the seat, including his neck, for the performance of half-halts. From the seat down, the rider should continue stretching the thighs, calves, and heels for synchronized leg aids.

Very often, untimely driving aids during the walk can create undesirable short and hurried steps. The reins must remain in contact with the bit. Yet, the feeling at the hands is a yielding of the reins, "pushing" them forward, encouraging the horse to stretch in order to keep in contact.

To summarize, the various modes of walk must be performed in identical rhythm, the footfalls remaining in the same even four-beat rhythm.

All modes of walk are defined relative to the ordinary walk. The free, collected, and extended walk represent varying degrees of assumption of more or less weight on the horse's hindquarters. The horse develops in his totality. All gymnastic exercises other than walk contribute to the improvement of the walk.

The gymnastic achievement of a horse is measured by the degree to which he can lengthen or shorten his strides while maintaining an even rhythm, in good impulsion, well balanced and always paralleling his spinal column with the path on which he moves. To be able to "round" and "stretch" a horse, making him an elastic accordion that never loses the rhythm of its tune, we must create an elastic horse interested in the aids.

Do not ignore the quality of the walk. Do not use it only for resting. Rest your horse in canter and trot, too. Yet, when resting him at the walk, insist on a free walk on loose reins. Use smooth aids that are synchronized with the horse's movements. Keep well-stretched legs perpetually molding to the horse's musculature in order to remain subtle, harmonious, and rhythmic in your aids.

As we create relatively collected or extended strides, as compared with those of the ordinary walk, the horse's longitudinal flexion becomes respectively shorter or longer. This precludes the rhythm from becoming slower or faster.

SCHOOLING THE TROT

The *ordinary trot* is the movement the horse voluntarily offers when his rider commences work with him. When a horse with suitable conformation is allowed to carry his rider in a comfortable trot, on light aids and in open country, he offers a so-called ordinary trot. That trot represents the horse's natural, unimproved movement under the rider's weight. The average horse covers about two hundred meters per minute at the ordinary trot.

The *working trot* differs from the ordinary trot, which is naturally offered by the green horse, in that it must show additional effort. This effort is in the form of improved impulsion. The horse should work more effectively with his haunches than voluntarily offered. A horse performing the working trot should perform in a "rounder motion," due to increased engagement of the joints in his hindquarters.

The working trot enables the horse to maintain his balance through the corners of a dressage arena and to remain balanced on larger arced lines, including circles. Due to the increased mobility of his joints, he will also be able to develop the muscles that foster increased bending. As a result, in addition to improved balance, the ability to bend laterally should also improve with the development of the working trot.

The working trot is asked for in lower-level dressage tests because the rider is expected to show a certain degree of improvement over the naturally offered, ordinary gaits. In the working trot the horse's hind hooves should stride forward enough to cover the hoofprints left on the ground by his forehands. The very readiness of a horse for testing must be demonstrated by these improvements in the gaits and in his balance and suppleness. Without this ability to work supply with his joints and muscles, the horse could not perform the geometric patterns of the test correctly. In addition, the patterns demand improved balance and suppleness.

The *medium trot* is a gait representing progress from the working trot toward the extended trot. While the working trot may still be highly individualized according to the horse's conformation and talent, the medium trot should comply with a more uniform standard of appearance. The medium trot is a result of schooling to improve the horse's gait and therefore should conform to more defined standards. Depending on conformation, horses will perform highly diversified working trots. They might all be working—i.e., engaging in the trot—yet look different in their effort, as the individual horses represent different breeds and different conformations. In the medium trot, however, the horse is expected to show lengthening of his strides, greater impulsion, and, as a result, an improved carriage. The tempo of the medium trot is greater than that of the working trot. The horse carries himself with his neck somewhat higher and yet with lengthened strides. His strides cadence higher off the ground. In the medium trot, he should show greater suspension than in the working trot, both by lengthening and by springing higher with his strides.

During the course of schooling a horse, the working trot is achieved much sooner than the medium trot. Care must be taken that the rhythm of the horse remains even in both. Both the working and medium trot benefit from frequent transitions from one to the other during schooling. Initially, posting the medium trot may be helpful to the horse's understanding that the length of his stride must increase. While sitting the trot, the rider can more easily keep the rhythm of his horse while working him toward improved impulsion.

Both the working trot and the medium trot are improvements over the voluntarily offered ordinary trot. The working trot is more individualized, according to breed and conformation, while the medium trot is more uniform in its execution. The working trot clearly demonstrates increased engagement of the joints, with resultant improvement of balance and facility for the execution of patterns requiring lateral bending. The medium trot is bolder than the working trot, showing both a longer and more suspended stride with a prouder carriage than the working trot.

A well-pronounced, expressive extended trot, alternating with a collected trot, can be the highlight of a dressage program.

During the *extended trot*, the horse reaches with his legs as far forward from the hips and shoulders as his conformation allows. The legs act as pendulums, suspended from the hips and shoulders, swinging freely forward while the suspension of the strides also increases, describing a generous, even floating movement.

The extended trot is full of impulsion. During it, the horse's hindquarters, acting as the engine, push him forward in rhythmic elasticity and with full force. This great power of locomotion is communicated to the outstretched forelegs by a relaxed and swinging back. Its importance lies in the full lengthening of the strides. In sharp contrast are the short and choppy strides with increased frequency of beats inherent in rushing.

In compliance with the horse's ground-gaining, powerful movement, the horse's body floats longitudinally through the air. His carriage becomes extremely steady and his front hoofs print where an imaginary line extending down the horse's forehead would pierce the ground. The horse's forehead and nose, in profile, may be stretched slightly forward in front of the perpendicular position. Under no circumstances should the profile point toward the chest, going behind the perpendicular (vertical) position.

When the horse is held too tight on the reins, he will be crowded and restrained in the front. In this condition, the horse cannot use his back to transfer the locomotion of the hindquarters through a swinging back to the forelegs. Consequently, the front feet will step on the ground behind the point indicated by them while in the air. The effect will be similar to goose-stepping.

When the horse goes behind the bit and his forehead is behind the perpendicular line to the ground, he is not moving forward but is resisting and evading engagement. His weight shifts to the forehand, and while his strides may become longer, they will also be more rapid and rushing. The horse can stretch his forelegs out only as far as the imaginary perpendicular line that extends from his face to the ground. If he is inhibited by the reins, he cannot accommodate the extended strides of the hind legs. Hence, extension will not occur.

Schooling the Extended Trot

In order to increase the tempo of the trot, the rider increases the drive with the legs, also increasing the pressure of his seat by rounding the small of the back, while contacting a steady, even rein, which yields as the horse's stride lengthens. Driving by the legs should be done with simultaneous pressure of both legs.

To increase the driving potency of the seat, the rider can increase the seat pressure by isometrically firming his abdominal muscles. Meanwhile, the lumbar back must continue to accommodate generously the ever-lengthening swing of the horse's back, which is caused by the lengthening strides.

The aids must be firm but calm and should be repeated until the horse steps with his hind legs forward, under his center of gravity with full power. It is crucial to keep a metronomically even two-beat rhythm. Should any violation of the clarity of the two-beat occur, the horse must be slowed to a shorter trot that is comfortable enough for him to recover his balance and rhythm.

The desire and willingness of the horse to go forward can be built best on long, straight lines, which if lacking in an outdoor space, can best be found on the diagonal of an arena. However, as the horse becomes willing to perform this powerful movement, extensions should be ridden on shorter, straight stretches. The horse, which is not yet able to carry himself and his rider naturally in the extended trot, may find the shorter periods of extensions easier at first.

As the horse increases his tempo by stretching into extensions, he will freely swing his legs from his hips and shoulders. At the beginning, this movement might result in the lowering of the neck and head position. It is not considered a fault and should not be corrected by tightening or disturbing the rein. As the horse matures in this movement, he should become capable of longer overstriding with his hind legs, increased engagement of his joints and muscles, and improved balance. With maturity of skills and increasing strength, the head and neck position will automatically come into its ideal place. A horse moving with impulsion and in balance will inevitably present the correct neck and head position. The motion should remain harmonious with unity in the timing of the diagonal pairs of legs touching the ground with precise synchronization.

Correcting Common Mistakes

When preparing for an extended trot, do not gather the horse into a tighter rein. Drive with steadily contacting legs and avoid banging on the horse's sides. If kicking legs seem necessary, it is a sure sign that the horse has not been prepared properly for the extended trot. By doing frequent transitions within the trot, we can improve the horse's forward urge. Lateral bending exercises will strengthen the horse's joints and muscles.

If the horse responds to the aids by extending with stiff, spread hind legs, he lacks sufficient strength and has stiff joints. Continue lateral bending exercises and longitudinal transitions for the demands of extensions.

If the horse moves with goose steps, with his forelegs stiffly flicking and showing the bottom of his hooves, then he is stiff in his back. The horse's back should be elevated and should swing to transmit the increased impulsion from haunches to forehand. We can strengthen the back muscles by cross-country riding with climbing, cavalletti work, and jumping from trot approaches. To limber up the strengthened back and to encourage swing, proceed with longitudinal transitions and try the extensions while posting the trot.

The horse may strike the canter when asked to extend the trot. When that happens, determine which one of the following three reasons may have caused the canter and correct it accordingly.

1. The horse strikes the canter as a result of exuberance and too much forward urge. In this case, drive the horse straight and forward in canter until he is calm and balanced. Then quietly take him back to a balanced trot and repeat the aids for the extended trot.

2. The horse strikes the canter because he is crooked. He may only canter with his hind legs and continue to trot in the front. He may fall on his shoulder as a result of losing his balance. In such a case, take the horse back to trot instantly but gently, straighten him, and ride him forward to a lesser degree of extended trot—one that could be performed on a slightly bending serpentine line.

3. The horse might strike the canter as a resistance to extension. He might overflex his neck or even go behind the bit. He might swish his tail or go above the bit. He canters to resist and evade the rider's driving legs and seat. In this case, continue to drive the horse forward at the canter until he elevates and stretches his back, lowers his neck, and hangs his head lower. When that is achieved, however long it may take, bring the horse back to the trot and repeat the aids for extension.

The greatest enemies of the extended trot are an inability to fully lengthen the strides and uneven loading of the hind legs. Riders must realize that the extended trot may not develop because of their own equitational shortcomings. Schooling the extended trot presumes that the rider is both skilled and sensitive. Riders must especially guard against extensive and unwarranted use of the spurs. The rider must have a balanced and supple seat and hands willing and able to yield generously, in coordination with the horse's movement.

Posting the Trot on the Correct Diagonal

The correct way to post the trot is by posting on the outside diagonal. The rider's seat rises when the horse's outside hind leg is anchored on the ground and his inside hind leg and outside foreleg are lifting and moving forward. The rider is reached by the saddle and thus becomes seated when the horse's inside hind leg impacts on the ground and his outside hind leg is suspended.

If the rider sits correctly while posting on the outside diagonal, he will feel the inside seat bone touch the saddle more firmly than the outside one. The reason is that the rider touches the surface of the saddle when the horse's inside hind leg touches the ground. At that time, the bulk of the rider and the bulk of the horse meet with each other for a moment. The rider's bulk is lowered, the horse's bulk is stabilized on the inside. The resultant feeling is a stronger pressure under the inside seat bone.

This feeling may be further exaggerated when trotting on an arc, whether it is through a simple corner or on a full circle. When a rider bends a horse laterally onto an arc, he not only uses his legs to do so, but also his torso. While bending a horse laterally, the rider's shoulders and hips parallel the position of the horse's shoulders and hips respectively. As the inside shoulder of the horse travels slightly behind the further-advanced outside shoulder, so must the rider's shoulders parallel that position with his inside shoulder slightly back. While the rider pivots his shoulders around the vertical axis of his spine, he should draw an imaginary horizontal line through his own shoulders that points exactly to the center of the circle. The rider's weight should be more on the inside seat bone when riding on a circle because his outside leg is kept back and his inside shoulder is back. The imaginary line through the rider's shoulders should point to the center of the circle like the spoke of a wheel points to the hub.

Changing the Posting Diagonal

Usually, we can change the posting diagonal in the center of the arena. However, changing the posting diagonal at X could disturb the balance of a horse performing an extended trot on the diagonal or center line: Therefore, during an extension, we can delay changing the posting diagonal to the end of the diagonal or line, until we collect at the opposite wall.

There are two reasons for this strategy: To change the posting diagonal at the beginning of an extended trot would upset the horse's balance even more than it would by changing at X. At the beginning of the diagonal, the horse's body needs to stretch to lengthen his stride. He must adjust to a new balance.

The rider should not add to the difficulty of this task by disturbing with his seat.

As the horse arrives at the end of the diagonal, however, he is once again collected to a more comfortable and familiar stride. For this reason, he will find a change in the rider's posting diagonal easy to accommodate without losing his balance or interrupting his rhythm. Actually, remaining seated for one stride in order to change the posting diagonal may contribute to a smooth transition to collection.

A trot that is difficult to sit is not necessarily a good, powerful one. Nor is a soft trot necessarily weak and inferior.

A rough trot, difficult to sit, is often a sign of stiffness. There are two kinds of stiffness. One is the result of unsupple joints and tense muscles. The other could be caused by an inarticulate, tense back, which prevents the soft transmission of energy from the haunches to the forehand. Another cause is hard or uneven footing!

If the rough trot is a result of stiff joints in the haunches and the forehand, then gymnasticizing will eventually eliminate it. However, if the rough trot is a result of a back problem, then it will improve commensurate with the rider's skills in sitting and performing half-halts correctly. Sometimes, conformation problems predispose a horse to have a rough trot. These include a short vertical pastern, short and steep (vertical) shoulders, and an extremely short and heavily muscled back combined with low withers. When conformation predisposes a horse to a rough trot, the horse can eventually become more supple with proper gymnastic work.

Riders should avoid buying a horse with a rough trot. If it is caused by conformation problems, the horse will not be easy to supple and will have a tendency to break down sooner than another horse with good conformation doing the same tasks. A horse with a rough trot is not only jarring to the rider but similarly jars himself, impacting the ground without resilience, causing damage to his own joints. After all, the means of riding should be therapeutic to the horse and should make him elastic for his own benefit. We ride to improve horses! A horse that is structurally handicapped cannot be improved efficiently for his own sake.

If the rough trot is due to stiffness of joints and muscles, the horse can be greatly improved.

In summary, try to find a young, green horse that has good conformation and natural elasticity. Such a horse will be easier to supple and more pleasurable to ride.

THE COUNTER CANTER

The counter canter is an exercise that helps perfect the horse's balance, strengthens his back muscles, especially those behind the saddle, and confirms utmost obedience to the rider's aids: thus, it beneficially affects the horse's skeleton, musculature, and mentality. It's worth noting that all three of these areas of improvement also are important for jumping horses.

In counter canter, the hind legs of the horse must continue to move toward the hoofprints of the forelegs, exactly as they do when cantering on the "true" lead. When performing the counter canter on a circle or arc, the hind legs must still continue to move toward the hoofprints of the front legs. The hind legs must track on the arc of the prescribed circle and under no circumstances deviate outward from that pattern. Nor should the forelegs drop off to the inside of the prescribed circular arc. In short, both fore and hind legs must stay on the arc of the circle.

Since the horse is to maintain a continuous but mild bend toward the lead, at the counter canter on the circle, his spine does not parallel the arc of the circle. Rather, he should be counter bent, albeit mildly, while maintaining his balance and remaining in collection—only a mild counter bending away from the circular arc of the path of travel is required. As the legs continue to move on the circular pattern, the horse's torso will bend equally but in the opposite direction. The horse, bent in the opposite direction from the arc described by the circle on the ground, should continue to move on the circle with both his hind and forelegs. If this were viewed from above, the horse's spine and the circle's arc would form an eye of a needle.

Frequently, mistakes occur that should be avoided: The horse might cross-canter or perform a flying change instead of obeying the counter canter on a circle. To avoid this, the aids should be sufficiently strong and correct. The outside leg stretched back, the inside leg in the perpendicular position, and both insisting on the maintenance of bending toward the lead. A lightly contacting outside rein should be steadily offered but never pulled. The inside rein should yield on every stride, as an extension of the rider's subtly pivoting torso. The rider's shoulders must parallel those of the horse's. The shoulder toward the lead should advance slightly ahead of the outside shoulder, promoting the weight distribution slightly more toward the inside seat bone. Here, of course, the "inside" continues to be the side on which the horse leads in the canter.

The horse may evade collection by deviating outward, with his haunches stepping off the circular track and not following with the inside hind leg toward the hoofprints of his inside foreleg. To avoid this error, make sure that the circular pattern is sufficiently large to accommodate the horse's development in collection. First, ride a true canter circle on the lead that is easier for the horse. Take note of his mild lateral bending, which should be continuous. Then change direction to an opposite circle, maintaining the same lead but taking care not to exaggerate the lateral bending, particularly at the neck.

The horse may lose his balance in counter canter because of a premature attempt to perform it on a tight pattern. If this happens, the horse will hurry and lean inward toward the center of the circle. In order to prevent a loss of balance, do not counter canter prematurely on a full circle. The first attempts must be made on a very large circle. If this position is correct, the rider's weight remains on the inside seat bone and in balance over the horse's center of gravity. The rider's spine must intercept the horse's spine perpendicularly and must not lean away from the horse either inward or outward.

The worst mistake is when the horse is allowed to bend incorrectly while counter cantering on an arc. For instance, a horse on a left lead moving on an arc to the right should continue to bend toward the left, where he leads the canter. If the horse were to change his bending to accommodate the right arc of the circle rather than continuing to bend left, he would merely be cantering on "the wrong lead." A canter performed with a bending away from the leading foreleg is a movement that produces no gymnastic benefits. Cantering "on the wrong lead" contributes to the breakdown rather than the improvement of the horse's balance, rhythm, collection, obedience, and strength.

While improving balance, collection, and submission, the counter canter is most beneficial for strengthening the muscles surrounding and supporting the horse's lumbar back. Both the counter canter and the rein-back develop these muscles well. These muscles are important for lowering the croup and increasing bending in the haunches. For instance, the counter canter, particularly on a circle, can develop athletic skills and strengths that will not develop easily with other exercises. The counter canter has no substitute. For this reason, it is an exercise of great value when correctly performed. An established counter canter is a prerequisite for starting to school flying changes.

Of course, the counter canter can be performed only by a horse that can move in a collected canter.

THE AIDING AND TIMING OF FLYING CHANGES

Both the horse and the rider should be ready for the correct execution of a flying change of lead at the canter. To be sure, horses will change leads on many occasions voluntarily, and often do so while jumping a course, during a polo game, or while working cattle under Western saddle. Often they do so improperly because they are "thrown over" to the other lead; that is, they change lead in desperation as they seek to reestablish their balance under a rider who upset it.

The purpose of dressage, however, demands that we do only that which enhances the horse's correct gymnastic development. Only a physically and mentally well-prepared horse will react to adequate aids and execute with ease a useful movement correctly. In dressage, we do not do things "*l'art pour l'art*," but instead we do gymnastically sound and valuable exercises to further the horse's development.

The rider is ready to perform the aids for a flying change when he has acquired a balanced and independent seat and, through supple lumbar following, a deep and elastic seat. Once he has done so, he can best demonstrate his achievement by riding an extended trot with a motionless torso, as if enthroned. He should be able to drive and follow the extended trot without lightening the weight in his seat as he elastically absorbs the horse's movement. He should maintain with ease a light and even contact with the reins, show steadily contacting yet relaxed legs, and a perpendicularly upright position.

The horse is ready for the flying change if he can maintain elasticity in performing the extended trot, half-passes with cadence at the trot, and collected canter. The horse should also demonstrate his maturity or readiness by smoothly performing transitions from the canter to halt and back to canter, as well as collected to extended and back to collected canter. While elasticity in the horse is detectable in many ways, I listed those movements and transitions that are most revealing or symptomatic of that condition of readiness.

The Six Phases of Canter Movement

The canter is comprised of six phases, the seventh being the resumption of the first phase belonging to the next canter bound. (See the following illustration for a better understanding of these phases.)

1. The outside hind leg starts the movement and remains on the ground while the other three legs are off the ground in suspension.
2. One phase later, the outside fore and the inside hind join the outside hind on the ground, leaving the inside foreleg suspended.
3. The inside hind and the outside fore remain on the ground as the outside hind leaves the ground and the inside fore approaches it.
4. The inside foreleg joins the inside hind and the outside fore on the ground.
5. The inside foreleg remains on the ground, while the other three legs are suspended.
6. All four legs leave the ground, suspending the entire horse in flight.

The sixth phase, when the horse is suspended in air with all four of his legs off the ground, is that moment when the horse has the option of coming down on either hind leg for the commencement of his next canter bound.

It is now up to the rider and his aids to determine whether his horse will commence the next movement on the original lead, again on the outside hind leg, or change lead, commencing the movement on what was the inside hind leg.

From the rider's point of view, only the last two phases, the fifth and sixth phases of the canter bound preceding the flying change, are of concern. He will have to prepare the change on the fifth phase and execute it on the sixth.

The rider must use diagonal aids during the canter; that is, his inside leg is positioned and is aiding differently from his outside leg. During the canter, as always, the rider's shoulders and hips must parallel those of the horse. Because the horse's inside shoulder and hip move slightly ahead of his outside shoulder and hip, the rider's inside shoulder and hip must also be slightly ahead of those on the outside.

The correct seat during the canter places the rider's inside shoulder and his inside elbow and hand slightly ahead of those on the outside. Because his inside hip also slightly leads over the outside, his corresponding seat bone, knee, and leg will lead slightly over the corresponding parts of his body on the outside.

The correct aids are related to the rider's slightly diagonal seat and to the harmony that the horse naturally offers during the canter. The outside hand is steady, offering a direct rein that determines the horse's length of stride. Because the outside rein acts as a rein of opposition to the outside hind leg, which begins the canter bound, it has the capacity to bring that hind leg down sooner or later (shorten or lengthen) after suspension. The inside hand should be generous, yielding to the head movement of the horse, encouraging rounder, more elastic movement with the horse's inside hind leg. It should encourage impulsion by its generosity.

The rider's outside leg should hold the horse's hindquarters steadily. The inside leg urges the horse forward with pushing pressure forward-and-down-stretched pressures. The rider's inside leg should be positioned just behind the girth, with the toe

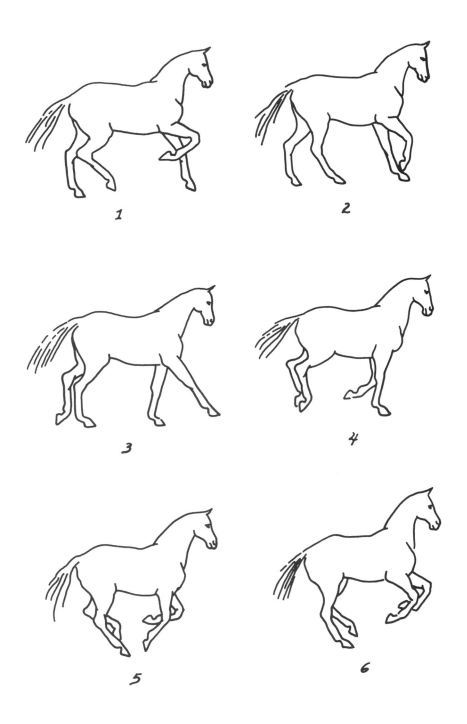

directly under or slightly behind the knee and the heel balanced under the rider's seat bone. It maintains both impulsion and the longitudinal inward positioning. The rider should synchronize the inside leg aid with the horse's lifting of the inside (leading) foreleg. The rider's outside leg, however, should aid when the horse is suspended over the inside foreleg.

The seat should feel as if it is anchored at the inside seat bone and leg, allowing the inside seat bone to float forward and down in the saddle as the inside shoulder pivots to drive, and with it, the inside hand yields. When felt by the rider, the resulting sensation is as if the horse is moving from the outside leg toward the inside knee.

The Flying Change of Canter

For aiding the flying change, we must be concerned only with phases five and six of the canter. In phase five, a rider can see the horse's outstretched foreleg on the ground slowly slant backward as his body travels over it. With this movement of the receding inside foreleg of the horse, the rider's inside (forward) leg must slowly recede. It travels backward on the horse's side into an "outside" leg position. As a result of the rider having changed his leg position to the opposite of what it was, his entire seat and hand position should change harmoniously.

In phase six, the horse is suspended above the ground and comes easily into harmony with the rider's new position. Without anchorage to the ground, the horse can rebend himself into a new lateral position. By the time his flight is concluded, he will exercise the option of touching down with the opposite hind leg on the ground. The flying change will have been performed!

Two words of caution: Before asking for a flying change, produce an impulsive, collected canter. As you change position, and with it aiding diagonals during phase five, you must do it harmoniously so that during phase six, you can once again clarify the new balance to the opposite side.

I disagree with any tendency to lighten the seat at the time of the flying change. Do not encourage an exuberant, leaping changeover. Neither hurry nor extend the canter strides before the change. On the contrary, make sure to stay deep in the saddle with a well-anchored seat, thigh, and knee contact, and in order to do so, stay very erect in the saddle. By bouncing forward, looking down, leaning to the side, or any other dislodging or "lightening" activities by the seat, the rider denies the horse the feeling of the rider having changed position and balance in the saddle. The seat is the most important contact area through which we communicate the change! Collect the horse more by a half-halt just prior to the change of lead. Keep your head high. As you change leg position, the new outside leg should move with friction along the horse's side without leaving it. By kicking backward, you will aid in the wrong rhythm.

The Flying Change on Every Stride

The flying canter changes done every stride are also called "*a tempo*" changes. There has been some knowledgeable discussion in the past about the flying changes on every stride not being a natural movement, and that they should not be included in dressage, which is committed to the development of the natural gaits of the horse. Horses, however, will do flying changes on every stride voluntarily and without a rider. It is natural and it is done at the canter.

The primary difficulty of that movement, as far as the horse is concerned, is its great demand for perfect coordination and balance. The flying change on every stride may not be the most salient demonstration of suppleness, collection, or bending. Yet, it is certainly the finest exercise for the demonstration of impeccable coordination.

Flying changes of lead on every stride demand from the horse perfect balance, suppleness, and collection, but only as a means to the end. He must use these components to perform acts extremely fast and in perfect harmony. The horse has not only to change the use of his leg order in a split second while floating in momentary suspension, but must also change his center of gravity with split-second accuracy in order to remain straight throughout the exercise—an incredible athletic feat, especially under the foreign weight of the rider. This exercise, naturally, presumes perfect balance from the rider as well.

Let us suppose that the rider's balance and coordination are perfect, his timing and rhythm are accurate to the split second, and the problem of making mistakes remains with the horse. Let us suppose that we have a "perfect rider" and a horse that knows the flying changes on every stride, but he makes mistakes in tests.

With such a horse, repeat the exercise often, but with only a few strides of tempi changes alternating with periods spent cantering on the same lead. Repeatedly resume the tempi changes for four to six strides. Do this both on straight lines and also on a large 20-meter circle. Frequent repetition improves attention and coordination best. A movement whose very essence is coordination suggests improvement through repetition.

If the horse becomes confused during this movement, some riders make the mistake of punishing him. They either halt abruptly, or punish the mouth, or spank him. When utmost concentration from the horse is called for in order to create perfectly synchronized coordination, any punishment is unreasonable and will create adverse effects. The horse will become tense, inattentive, worst of all, mistrustful of his rider, and will rush from anticipated punishment.

SQUARING THE HALT

There could be a number of reasons for a horse not squaring his halt. The corrections are varied according to the cause.

The horse may make poor halts if he is inattentive and develops careless habits. In that case, you should increase the horse's attentiveness by driving him more keenly forward. You should not "pull up to a halt," but rather use half-halts terminating in a halt. If a halt is not square, touch the horse with the leg, and if not responding, the whip on the same side where the hind leg was left behind. Repeat gently whenever necessary, until the horse halts square in a balanced position.

If the horse halts out of balance because the rider interfered through the reins, the remedy will have to be different. The horse understands a rein of opposition and will naturally tend to respond to the rider's pulling by halting with the leg left behind on the side of the pulling rein. He will think that the rider wanted the hind leg positioned slightly behind. If the hind leg were to stay behind due to relative weakness in its development, the remedy involves strengthening it. Like horses, humans support their weight on a stronger leg while standing and rest the other.

For the weak, tardy hind leg, try these strengthening exercies:

- Shoulder-in toward the weaker hind leg.
- Half-passes toward the stronger hind leg.
- Canter departs to the lead on the side of the stronger hind leg.
- Halt-to-trot transitions on a circle ridden to the side of the weak hind leg.
- Spiraling in and out on a circle bent toward the weak hind leg.
- Try the halts when riding on the rail or when proceeding on a circle on the weak hand. In this exercise, precede the halt by two strides at shoulder-in, then straighten and halt.

Using a combination of these solutions may be the most effective. In summary, ride strengthening exercises, then prepare a halt from two steps of shoulder-in. Yield the rein to the horse, particularly on the weak side, just as the halt is performed. Over-indulgent riders who pester their horse at the halt with an imaginary need for "squaring" them often achieve the opposite of their purpose: they dislodge a square horse into an unbalanced second halt and in doing so destroy his immobility as well.

TEACHING THE REIN-BACK

Look for willing and joyful submission while backing, the high lifting of the diagonal pairs of legs, and an eagerness for forward progression. All this coupled with fine collection and lowering of the croup without resistance give the rider the pleasure of good rein-back. The horse performing this movement correctly will lift his legs well off the ground.

The purpose of a rein-back is to demonstrate the horse's

willing submission to the rider's forward will and to gymnasticize him in utmost collection. This movement helps in schooling the horse to lower his croup by rounding his lumbar back,
which in turn pushes his pelvis forward and farther under from
the lumbosacral joint. The horse should not "back away" from
the rider's aids in a rush, or show timid reluctance. He should
not avoid the increased articulation of his joints by stepping
sideways and backing crookedly.

The correct rein-back is manifest in a relaxed horse, steadily
on the bit, moving backward with even diagonal strides and in
good balance. He should move with impulsion, using the joints
of his hindquarters well for the greater assumption of weight.
His croup should have been necessarily lowered to achieve this.
He ought to assume a more compact posture because of the
keenness of the flexion of his joints and a supple yet strong use
of his muscles. The beauty of the rein-back lies with the expression of a forward urge in the horse, a desire and readiness to
resume forward progression in any gait commanded by the rider.
All beauty in riding rests with the horse's desire to move forward, and during a rein-back and also at the halt, we can show
off this thorough obedience. During both the halt and the rein-
back, the horse should not be asked to abandon his forward
urge, his readiness to move on.

The correct aids for the rein-back should prepare the horse
physically and mentally before he is asked to perform. In order
to perform a good rein-back, the horse must halt correctly. The
hands assume a position of passive resistance to prevent stepping
forward. Do not pull back, however, if the first aids do not get
a prompt response. Shift the pressure of your seat from the back
of the buttocks toward the crotch and thighs, slightly taking
some weight off the back of the saddle. This "opens the gates"
to backward progression. However, do not tilt the torso forward, ahead of the perpendicular.

Stretch both legs downward and ever so slightly backward
and aid with them identically and simultaneously. The instant
the horse lifts his legs to move backward, the aids described
above must change to yield to confirm and verify for the horse
that he responded correctly.

The hands should relax. The impression is that the stress

on the rein stops feeling like a stretched rubber band and has given way to its normal, relaxed position, yet not dropped slack or dangling. The driving pressure with the legs remain unaltered. The lumbar back muscles relax with the relaxation of the fists. The legs should not lose contact with the horse's sides. Aiding and yielding should interchange in a manner imperceptible to an observer. Forward yielding hands should give the horse freedom from inhibition.

Make all aids parallel aids; that is, influence identically on both sides of the horse. Since the horse is required to remain straight and to use himself identically on both sides, it is logical that we create the movement by aiding likewise. Reserve diagonal aiding for the occasions when the horse is evading by stepping sideways. Do not overflex the wrists and curve the fists inward or downward. Nor should you push the fists outward, hollowing the wrists. The wrist position should remain straight during both the passive resisting and forward yielding activities. The wrists should be positioned so that the top of the hand forms a straight line in continuation with the lower arm and forming one plane with it.

Aids, as always, should remain inconspicuous. The rider should look and feel tranquil.

Reining back is very important gymnastic exercise for the horse. Gymnastically and athletically, a rein-back has these important properties: It will tax, and therefore strengthen and supple, all the joints in the horse's hindquarters. It will strengthen the musculature in the lumbar back and in the hindquarters. Some muscles develop efficiently only through slow motion. In human terms, the gymnastic strengthening value of push-ups increases as the speed of the exercise decreases. The rein-back shifts the horse's center of gravity backward, toward the haunches. Therefore, it is an eminent promoter of collection.

Let us analyze the rider's actions that produce a good rein-back.

Preparation. The horse should be halted foursquare in perfect balance. He should be relaxed but attentive. He must be longitudinally flexed. By placing both legs slightly back, the rider should lighten his seat bones.

Aiding. The rider should straighten his back and firm his

elbow position to effect passive resistance to thwart any attempt by the horse to pull the rider's hands forward. All horse-initiated stress on the reins should "pull the rider down" into the horse's spine, deepening, rather than lightening, the adhesiveness of the rider's seat. The rider should "close the gate" to forward progression. This is done as the elbows are anchored by perpendicular upper arms and straight shoulders. This provides the necessary passive resistance in the reins that prevents the horse from walking forward, yet prevents the rider from pulling back. The legs drive simultaneously as if for a "forward walk."

Yielding. As soon as the horse begins to lift his legs, the rider should relax his musculature. The lumbar back, the legs, and the buttocks should relax to terminate the passive resistance, replacing it with yielding reins. As a consequence, the rider's seat should fill the saddle, and that concludes the backward progression. Then, forward driving with the legs sends the horse ahead rather than backward because he senses the yielding of hands and the forward urge from the seat.

Following. With diminishing isometric tension in his musculature, the rider travels with the horse's movement in an erect, perfectly balanced position, making the beginning of the communication sequence once again possible.

The above description resembles a recipe, but I caution my readers to regard these "ingredients" as guides to feelings. It is essential to understand that: (1) there is a logical sequence to the communications and (2) it never includes pulling on the reins.

Inevitably, a green horse will attempt to evade. The usual reasons for this include that he has difficulty understanding the rider's new aids (wishes) and that the new task is physically taxing for him. As soon as the horse evades, by becoming crooked or coming above the bit, the rider should either halt or begin walking forward to reestablish longitudinal flexion and straightness before attempting to repeat the exercise.

When you teach a young horse to rein-back, ask him to do only one step at a time. After each step, relax the reins completely and pet him, praising his performance. This strategy will not only make him understand and like what you want of him, but will also ensure that he cannot evade easily and move incorrectly. Eventually and gradually, you can piece a sequence of steps together.

Seven

Schooling for Gymnastic Improvement

Riding must first be understood, then it can be practiced correctly. That is, *there is no successful riding without academic knowledge of its goals and the various means of attaining them. It is not the quantity, but the quality, of daily work that produces success.* Good riding strategies are based on scholarly knowledge of the physique and nature of the horse, the correct, tried, and proven ways of getting the best results from him, and reasonable, well-planned goals.

Riding goals fall into three basic categories:

1. Long-term goals are the most general. In essence, they include the aspirations of developing the horse's natural abilities to their ultimate extent and of specializing him in the areas that give us pleasure, that is, in cross-country, jumping, or dressage, after a proper foundation in the rudiments of all three.
2. Intermediate goals are often guided by competition goals and are designed to meet deadlines. Various exercises will be evaluated on show dates. These goals give us time limits and serve as motivation for achievement within certain time periods.

3. Daily goals address the major gymnastic needs by regular repetition of tasks, which develop the desired results. While these should be knowledgeably planned, the rider must remain flexible enough to be able to adjust these goals according to the very needs of each moment of each schooling session. This implies quickness in responding to the needs of the horse and inventiveness in responding to his needs appropriately.

Artists and human athletes work in a similar manner, and in their activities, we can find parallels with riding goals. A painter will have an overall goal of depicting certain things on canvas. He may paint for commissioning patrons or for exhibitions that press him with deadlines. But as daily work continues, he finds himself constantly adjusting to the needs of each particular canvas and subject matter. When he begins, he has a general idea of what to paint and how to do it. Yet, as he goes along, he alters his composition, color scheme, and texture in order to eventually achieve the desired results. Discovery of the correct means may happen along the way.

Riders are often victims of our cultural dictates. These include our notion that any change is progress. Some of us believe that true progress can best be depicted on a graphic line that proceeds onward and upward.

Preoccupation with change is contrary to sound riding goals. Not all that is new is progress. That notion may serve the purposes of technological innovation and commerce. However, adding new movements and figures just to keep busy in daily work may result in a stiff horse with a false superstructure. Hurrying training, making shortcuts, introducing artificial aids, may all be technologically ambitious. But riding is not a technology and the horse is not a machine. Efficiency, speed in traveling and in solving problems, may be highly valued in our age. But none of these values is applicable to horsemanship. Should a rider be misled by popular values, the long-term, general goal of producing a supple horse that performs according to his natural abilities will have been lost.

True progress will take place only when something better replaces the status quo, that is, when there is athletic improvement rather than just change taking place in the horse. Therefore, I suggest we consider an Eastern (instead of our technologically minded Western) view of progress. The Eastern view of progression (particularly Hindu) can be depicted as a stretched-out soft coil of spring, viewed in profile as consecutive circles that loop through one another.

With this image in mind, we can visualize riding strategies that involve constantly revisiting the places where the rider and his horse have been before. When schooling goes wrong, the rider should take the horse back to simpler tasks he can perform gymnastically correctly and continue development of new efforts only after his natural gaits and proper posture have been regained. Most important in classical training is that we maintain the natural beauty of the horse and improve only on his natural tendencies. We must accomplish that only by kind methods and in the horse's own time. He is, after all, a living creature who has earned our love and respect over centuries of loyal service.

As the rider pursues the classical teachings of riding, he must have the patience and humility to change plans when the horse indicates that he cannot cope with an excessive rate of schooling. When we change schooling plans, we keep in mind that the horse begs for simplification, not complexity.

In daily work, the rider must keep in mind that we should be first and foremost a listening device, and when the horse signals stress, we simplify tasks by revisiting the simpler known ways, by pursuing the familiar, and by reviewing the foundations. Repetition reinforces learning and habituates development. This training method will yield true progress!

While observing the workings of nature, which we are a part of, biologists discovered a long time ago that the development of the individual microscopically repeats the development of the species. The human embryo and fetus pass through developmental stages that recapitulate in brief the evolutionary development of the human species from the one-celled organism through aquatic, amphibian, and terrestrial creatures to the shape and complexity of a human adult.

In riding, daily work on any level must consist of a recapitulation of the total progress we hope to have achieved with the horse to date. Therefore, regardless of his current gymnastic accomplishments, the horse will have to be started each day at the most basic level of achievement, starting with relaxation, and briefly progressed through a review of the more sophisticated achievements, such as balance, rhythm, elasticity, suppleness, impulsion, collection, engagement, and cadence. Repetition of the developmental phases in daily work will produce a cumulative effect on the horse's athletic development by accelerating it. Progress is made from embryonic beginnings to fully sophisticated accomplishments. Each developmental concept, such as relaxation or cadence, has a minimal, feeble beginning that, with knowledgeable care, develops progressively in time to its full sophistication.

Gymnastic Progress of the Horse

STAGES IN TRAINING	THE MANIFESTATIONS OF TRAINING GOALS DEVELOPMENTAL SOPHISTICATION OF GYMNASTIC CONCEPTS		
	HOW THE HORSE'S DEVELOPMENT IS MANIFESTED		
	BODY	GAITS	ATTITUDE
Beginning	Relaxed	Balanced	Attentive to rider
Campaign	Loose muscles	Rhythmic	Stretched forward/down
Diversified	Supple joints	Impulsive	Flexing haunches/bascule
Advanced	Elastic front to back Movement blanketing liquid horse	Cadenced Gaits amplified Engaged	Collected Most of weight borne in haunches

This system, repeated daily, consists of the following conceptual, qualitative elements:

Relaxation is indispensable to any further achievement. It must be both physical and mental. With a green horse, this goal must become the rider's consuming task for the entire riding period. As the horse shows an absence of tension, transmits the propelling energy originating in his haunches through a relaxed musculature, his impact on the ground will soften and the rider will need to spend less and less time and effort on relaxation. He will be free to go on to more complex and sophisticated goals. Without relaxation, the horse cannot render himself attentive to the rider's aids, accept the bid, and listen to correct guidance concerning his haunches. Without mental relaxation and trust in the rider, the horse cannot achieve substantial physical relaxation.

Balance can only be achieved when the horse has a relaxed musculature and when he carries the rider with a swinging, articulating back that is stretched and elevated. A balanced horse will be able to keep identical strides through straight and bent paths and will make transitions that are distinct, with demarcation, yet without impure steps. Longitudinal balance is completely dependent on regularity and evenness of rhythm. Lateral balance, in addition to the above-mentioned needs, depends on the perfection in the evenness of the horse's lateral (spinal) bending.

Rhythm is born of the composite success of relaxation and balance at work. The horse moves with absolutely even rhythmic strides in all three gaits both on straight and curved patterns and remains fully attentive to the rider's guidance of lateral bending. His gaits will improve in purity and gain expression. The clarity of rhythm is indispensable to correct gymnasticizing of a horse because his evasions to the rider's aids can only be by changing rhythm or becoming crooked. The rider cannot be careful enough as a guardian of rhythm. He should be able to adjust it immediately upon the horse's changing it. Both slowing and speeding are equally detrimental evasions to the rider's aids. Horses that are allowed to use rhythm changes for evasions will lack impulsion and engagement.

Elasticity occurs when the horse can stretch and contract various muscles in his body. Consequently, he can move his joints with greater articulation. As a result, depending on his development, he can show proficiency in stretching or contracting his body, thereby also lengthening or elevating his strides. Thus, he can show modulation in his gaits and perform more extended and more collected movements. An elastic horse shows extension and collection without altering the rhythm of his strides.

Impulsion is controlled energy. Impulsion is the correct propellant energy emitted from the haunches. It is expressed by flexibility of the joints, causing increased articulation, particularly rotation. Impulsion depends on the equal and proper utilization of flexion in all the joints, rather than one joint overworking to save efforts in others. A horse in correct impulsion will not appear hasty. Rushing is the enemy of impulsion. To be sure, impulsion is born of the horse's natural instinct for flight. Swift movement is the instinctive potential for impulsion. Yet only when that instinct is tamed, controlled, and educated will impulsion occur. Impulsion is manifested by the horse's ability to increase the activity in his joints, yet decrease his tempo. It is realized by slower, yet more articulate, flexibility and rotation in the joints. Born of the horse's instinct to flight, impulsion is the sophisticated, gradual controlling of the flight instinct into brilliant, yet majestically slow, activity. Instead of headlong speeding ahead with stiff, rapid, small strides, the horse achieves a schooled way of moving by economy of speed in a gracefully coordinated carriage. Thus, the horse's natural tendency to run, to move with joy and alertness, are tamed gradually and by careful, gentle control. Impulsion must be based on the preceding developmental stages.

Suppleness is three-dimensional: longitudinal, vertical, and lateral. A horse properly connected from the haunches to the bit is longitudinally supple. This must include the feeling of muscular "liquidity" that allows the horse's impaction on the ground to blanket him softly, dispersing any stress, trauma, or shock to his system. Longitudinal flexion must be in self-carriage, terminating on a contact with the bit so light that the rider feels only the combined, actual weight of the reins and bit hanging in the horse's mouth. There should never be a feeling of connection with weight exceeding that of the equipment. The horse must remain moving on his four legs, rather than being pushed into and "nailed onto" the "fifth leg" of the bit. Vertical suppleness is commensurate with the horse's ability to flex his strengthened joints so as to press his pelvis forward, lower his croup, and increase the vertical, lifting articulation in his joints. When vertically supple, the horse will not only lift his limbs higher with increased flexion at the joints, but also will sink softly down on them when contacting the ground. The importance of this distinguishing characteristic of the horse softly sinking on supple, strong joints at the time he is impacting the ground is the crowning effect of vertical suppling. The softness of the vertically supple horse's movement allows the rider to sit on motion so soft and elastic that his perceptions of the horse's haunches can be exquisitely accurate. The lateral suppleness of the horse is based on his spinal alignment being even and exactly parallel with the pattern of his progression. The horse's ability to bend evenly ensures that his hind legs can continue moving in the direction of the forehand on the corresponding side. When a horse evades lateral bending by pushing out or cutting in with his shoulder, or by skidding out or curling inward with his haunches, he refuses to stride correctly forward. The correctly bent horse, however, is moving with his "shock absorbers." Lateral suppleness is very important because that is the primary source for the horse absorbing the shocks from ground contact when moving on an arc. Without bending, nature's shock absorber, the horse will be traumatized by his impact on the ground and gradually be damaged. Riding skills should emphasize the skills for bending the horse, because riders who cannot bend the horse's spine also cannot straighten it. Longitudinal, vertical, and lateral suppling are totally interdependent. It is inconceivable to develop one beyond the others. They interdepend even regarding the extent to which they develop. Riders, therefore, must see to it that the horse is always correctly aligned, between all aids, in self-carriage and with maximum lifting functions of his joints. Suppleness allows a feline movement of utter softness, as if floating over rather than hammering into the ground.

Collection is based on impulsion. It is the horse's ability to shift his center of gravity more toward his haunches. Collection refers to an increased assumption of weight by the haunches. It is not a shortening of the neck by a pulling rider. Increased weight assumption in the haunches develops from increased articulation of the joints, including the lumbosacral joint, which is pushed downward by the horse's lumbar back muscles. That causes the important tilting of the horse's pelvis more forward and under. The result of true collection, by definition, includes the lightening of the forehand. This is manifested not only by the obvious grace with which the forearms can float from liberated shoulders, but also by the absence of leaning on the shoul-

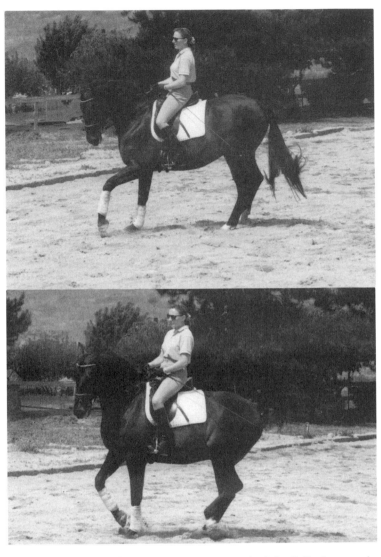

Elizabeth Ball schools a canter pirouette to the left. Collection must be achieved, of course, without pulling on the reins. Canter pirouettes are born of the correct collected canter. Suspended and bounding, the canter must "sit down," and the center of gravity ought to shift toward the haunches. Once the horse is correctly collected in the canter, the turning in the pirouette is almost incidental and just done to show that all is available from the haunches. The lowering of croup and the resulting "uphill" look from croup to poll are well demonstrated. Photo: Richard Williams.

ders, allowing the horse to bounce higher at the withers. A collected horse's movement feels and looks as if he is progressing both upward and forward.

USE OF AIDS IN COLLECTION

The horse should be brought into collection without pulling on the reins. Collection is a shifting of the balance toward the haunches produced by isometric contractions in the rider. Round the lower back and lift the crotch off the saddle with the abdominal muscles. Press the shoulder blades together and straighten the back. With the upper arms and elbows, fuse the actions of the reins to those of the seat. Close the thighs, thereby making the seat bones float forward. Then lighten the inside rein to yield the contact. Such transitions to collection can be understood easily by the horse through repetition and practice. When the transition to collection is performed, the horse should feel "uphill," as if you could raise him slightly with your spine.

Engagement is born of all the earlier developmental stages. It depends especially on the sophistication of cadenced collection. An engaged horse is noted for his ability to amplify his natural gaits and maximize his performance of all school figures and exercises that reveal his gymnastic accomplishments. By the skills of collection and the strength inherent in remaining anchored over the haunches, the horse will, when engaged, maximize the performance of all his exercises. Furthermore, he will be able to prolong and sustain his maximum performance with optimal lightness in the forehand and, therefore, appear grand in his carriage. He will sustain longitudinal posture and lateral bending equally effortlessly and for prolonged periods of time without loosing cadence. He will carry his rider with grace.

Cadence illuminates the accomplishments born of impulsion and collection. A well-cadenced horse adds artistic elegance to effortlessness by progressing with maximum suspension created by minimum touchdown on the ground. A well-cadenced horse is so accomplished athletically that he uses his native talents with utmost economy and educated appropriateness. With the least expenditure of energy, yet the greatest application of control over his own body, he moves with brilliance. Just as music is made of sounds alternating with silences, so is the horse's movement composed of periods of contact with the ground and those of suspension in flight over the ground. A cadenced horse will produce movement with minimum touchdown, resulting in maximum flotation. In music, this is analogous to the percussion of brief sounds alternating with longer silences.

WHAT WE WANT	HOW IT MANIFESTS ITSELF
Relaxation	• Longitudinal bending (on the bit).
	• Acceptance of driving aids (stepping under rather than speeding up, or lengthening rather than hurrying).
Balance	• Lateral bending (with continuous spinal flexion and without speeding up or slowing down).
	• Transitions from gait to gait (without impurities or uneven footfalls).
Rhythm	• Lengthening and shortening strides (the base of the horse) without losing flexion (relaxation and stretching of muscles while skeletal balance changes).
Impulsion	• Controlled energy, manifested in slower but more suspended action; more fluent, continuous, and round action; supple use of joints owing to elastic musculature.
Engagement	• Cadence: effortless flight (suspension); minimum energy produces maximum suspension because the haunches carry maximum weight, liberating the forehand.

The confluence of all the developmental phases is the suppleness of the horse. This, of course, is the ultimate goal of good horsemanship. For suppleness is the greatest good that serves the beloved horse's well-being. Suppleness, indeed, liberates the horse from the burden of his rider, who is now perceived as a harmonious partner to their composite structure and their unified pool of energies. The supple horse surrenders his energy to his rider, and thus permits his rider full access to his haunches and full control of his entire being. The supple horse responds to his rider's imperceptible aids and gives these aids permission to travel unhindered from haunches to muzzle. The utter permeability of the horse gives the rider a feeling of moving through liquid as all tensions melt away in the horse. So it transpires that with suppleness, the omega of riding accomplishments, we once again arrive at its alpha. The journey completed, the schooling fulfilled, we find the horse utterly relaxed. The absence of all tension, the ideal that we sought at the beginning, becomes a permanent and pervasive condition.

RELAXATION

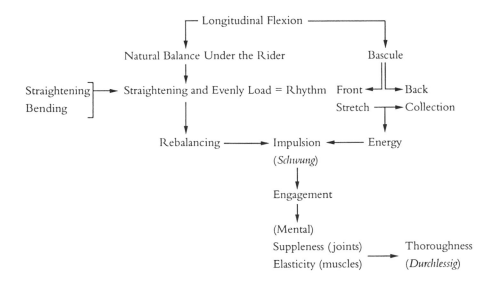

TRANSITIONS FROM WORKING CANTER TO WORKING TROT

Correct ground work is indispensable for later advanced work. Therefore, working fluent, balanced, elastic, calm, and obedient transitions from working canter to working trot is part of the foundation training. The horse can perform these transitions with relative ease. For the rider, the most important concept to understand is that every transition must be prepared. Preparation

The author riding a canter half-pass to the left, photographed to show the back of horse and rider in the mirror of the manege. This is another example of a deep, adhesive seat, a straight back and tall posture, and upper arms steadied to become part of the torso's "cabinetry" for proper seat influences. The legs are adhesively draped along the horse's sides but do not show tension by turning out toes and drawing heels up.   Photo: Richard Williams.

through half-halts enables the horse to respond calmly to the transitional aids.

Here are some guidelines offered with the customary word of caution not to regard them as recipes. Invest all schooling of a horse with feelings. Understand the tasks intellectually and then feel for their proper physical application when riding.

Start by schooling until a supple, bounding, round, and suspended canter is felt. The rhythm must stay even, and canter strides should be long enough for the horse to relax.

During the canter, the rider's inside leg, seat bone, and shoulder are positioned slightly ahead of those on his outside. If a rider sits correctly, he simply parallels with his own body the position of the horse's body. If the reins are connected cor-

The author riding trot and canter to show a deep, adhesive seat, draped legs, deep heels, and the pleasure of being balanced and in harmony with a horse. These pictures were taken while warming up and limbering a horse prior to schooling.   Photo: Richard Williams.

rectly to the torso, the inside fist leads ever so slightly ahead of the outside, stabilizing one, because the shoulder position naturally causes that to happen, provided the hands remain extensions of the seat.

Prepare the transition to trot by half-halting the horse. Essentially, this means increase all the aids that are already in use. The half-halt should always result in improved balance. Create more engagement from the haunches and as the energy increases, invite the horse's forehand to slow down. This creates collection, a shorter posture for the horse with higher strides, yet in the original rhythm. When the horse's attention and collection have readied him for a transition, the aids may be applied. The most important effects of half-halts are better balance through collection, mental readiness to receive instruction, and slower forward impetus of the body's mass. As the horse's mass is collecting, it should increase its suspension upward. In the meantime, care must be taken that the half-halts are soft and that inhibition of forward progression is avoided. The half-halts must be repeated on a green horse often and sometimes for a prolonged period of time. They should softly "run through" the horse in order not to stiffen him in the process!

Downward transition aids must be coordinated and executed simultaneously at all contact areas. The rider's legs return to a parallel position on the horse's sides. Draped around the horse, the rider's legs deliver a different rhythm to suggest that of the trot.

The rider's inside shoulder should pivot back to a square position, parallel with that of the outside one. This movement of slight rotation at the shoulder also brings the seat bone back to its position parallel to those of the horse's at the trot. As soon as the horse makes his first trot step, your entire aiding system must yield to produce the sensation of harmonious satisfaction. It is essential that the rider confirm the horse's correct response by yielding all pressure of instruction. Changing from aiding for a change to aiding for maintenance confirms to the horse at that instant that he understood his rider. Most important of all is the instant yielding of the reins. On a green horse, a rider may lengthen the reins to the buckle as a reward to dramatize his pleasure with his horse's response.

Often, the first few steps of the trot show rushing. The horse may be running because a lot of weight has fallen onto his forehand. At first, allow this to happen. If the rider has aided correctly and the horse still rushes in the trot, it is a sign that he is not yet sophisticated in balancing himself. His center of gravity is still shifting in spite of the rider's efforts, simply because the horse is physically not strong enough yet. He lacks the skills to manipulate his center of gravity. Do not punish the horse for rushing. With the repetition of the exercise and other gymnastic efforts, he will eventually be able to maintain his balance despite the radical changes that naturally occur when a trot follows the canter. As always, when a horse falls out of balance, resume half-halting.

The rider should soon realize that the balancing process in the transitions might take five minutes initially but will soon be resolved in seconds. However, this dividend will be forthcoming only if a rider has the patience to teach the transitions without causing tension or resistance in the horse.

DIMINISH THE CIRCLE WITHOUT LOSING BALANCE AND IMPULSION

In a dressage arena, ride a 20-meter diameter circle, the width of the arena. Make the center of the arena (letter X) the center of your circle. Make sure that the horse is bent evenly throughout the length of his body. It helps a novice rider in establishing this proper circle to place a cone on the ground at X to define the center of the circle. The only two points at which the legs pass the rail are at the letters E and B. Establish the other two points on the circle where the circle intercepts the center line of the dressage arena and place two cavalletti ground poles tangent to the circle on the ground at these spots. After you have established this measured circle and can ride it with a correctly bent horse in good impulsion, start to spiral inward gradually. By spiraling inward, arrive at a smaller circle, ideally of 10 meters in diameter, and with appropriately increased bending in the horse. Maintain good impulsion. Then spiral out gradually until riding on the original 20-meter circle again. The inward spiraling should

Elizabeth Ball is viewed from slightly above to help depict the beautiful bending of the horse on small circles. Straight shoulders, tall posture, giving hands, correctly positioned legs. This fine equitation somehow makes a circle a gymnastically important, body-building exercise rather than just a line returning to its point of origin. Photo: Richard Williams.

only continue as long as you can ride without losing balance or impulsion. Eventually, the horse will be able to spiral tighter, to an even smaller circle. Of course, the ultimate goal is to ride a circle called the "volte," about eight feet in diameter. However, before the horse reaches that stage, time will be needed to develop the necessary skills and strength.

Always ride the horse on all circular lines, including circles and spirals, by using diagonal aids. The inside leg must be aiding for impulsion and hang perpendicularly under the rider's seat bones to define the place around which the horse is to bend. The outside leg should be placed slightly farther back, in the "canter position," to prevent the hindquarters from skidding out.

Do not lean inward, like a motorcycle rider traveling on a curve. Obviously, as the spiraling continues inward toward smaller circles, the bending aids of the rider must be intensifed accordingly. The line connecting the rider's outside shoulder with his inside one, if continued in the imagination, should always describe the radius of the circle. In other words, the inside shoulder should pivot back enough behind the outside one to point toward the circle's center. As the circle is gradually squeezed smaller, this pivoting position must increase. On the spiral, the horse should be moving inward gradually. The outside leg provides continuous pressure, suggesting displacement inward, in addition to creating bending. However, when enlarging the spiral and moving the horse outward to reestablish the original circle, the inside leg should displace the horse outward as if giving the aid for a shoulder-in. When riding the spiral, there is always more weight on the inside seat bone of the rider, as the natural consequence of the outside leg's back and down position.

Spiraling would become meaningless if the rider were to "cut in" to make the circle smaller. That might happen if the hands of the rider are used for steering. Therefore, the spiraling exercise should be performed with legs and seat only. Any irregularity in the shape of the circle indicates that the rider's balance is wrong or that the aids were changed abruptly. Also, a stiff horse will just "fall" inward with an unbent torso, rather than bending and spiraling properly on a continuously curved pattern.

Practicing this exercise will develop the physical suppleness of the horse. Eventually, the volte will no longer be the goal, but one of the many circles you can perform, without strain or loss of balance.

Eight

Insubordination of Horses to Riders

The Thoroughbred is an excellent horse. Having been bred to excel at speed, the breed developed into potentially fine sports horses, for running is what nature designed horses to do best. Therefore, the fastest-running breed cannot be anything but a terrific natural example of an efficient horse. Yet, for dressage purposes, the Thoroughbred has often proven to be a difficult prospect. Even those horses that are without physical weaknesses, damage, or injury may fail to excel in dressage because of their temperament.

Thoroughbreds are sensitive by nature. In addition, difficulties could arise as a result of their early and often taxing training schedule. The young horse, often facing tasks more strenuous than he is mature enough to bear with comfort, soon develops fear, mistrust, and apprehension of the rider who induces his discomfort. To relax a horse with a past full of negative experiences is indeed a challenge.

With a high-strung horse, relaxation will come most easily at the walk. Many riders warm up their horses at the trot. They might even trot on a loose rein, which, for some reason, is believed to induce relaxation in horses. Often the result is a madly rushing horse, usually falling on its forehand, trying to find its balance, remaining stiff both longitudinally and laterally. This so-called "relaxation, limbering, warming-up" effort on a loose rein, however, promotes tension, stiffening, rushing, and an ever-diminishing chance to come into harmony with the rider. A great deal of schooling can be achieved by trotting. However, the trot must come after the horse has been relaxed at the walk.

Relaxation can be easier to achieve at the walk. It is the slowest gait and is the only one without a period of suspension, allowing the horse to adjust to the foreign weight of the rider. Being the smoothest gait, it allows the rider to sit in harmonious balance and apply a minimum of aids.

At first, the rider should walk his horse around the work area in both directions on a long rein, allowing the horse to move any way he desires, to stretch all his muscles and to realize that he is trusted by the rider who does not encumber, limit, or adjust his movements in any way. After having walked the horse freely around, contact should be sought gradually and gently. Contacting the horse should begin with the lower legs, continue with the thighs and the driving seat, and terminate by the gathering of the reins into a light contact only after all other contact areas have found their positions and feeling.

The horse on contact is also one in control. He can be asked to follow the rail of the arena more exactly or be ridden on large circles. He can be expected to flex longitudinally and when necessary bend laterally. Gradually, the horse has a chance to accept the rider's control, then his commands, all without tension. If tensions were to arise, the horse would be allowed to stretch out, again with the aids relinquished. A rider must either terminate demands (however simple they may be) or return to earlier, more simple stages of training when tension arises. Chances are, however, that the horse will react favorably to this patient, quiet, and comfortable beginning.

Once the horse is quietly on the aids, flexing longitudinally and bending laterally on arcs and circles, suppling work may be added. I cannot emphasize enough the value of the walk in calming a horse. The walk is the most difficult gait to develop and improve; it is also the one during which important muscle development and the suppling of joints may take place. However, riders must be warned that the walk is the most fragile gait. It can most easily be destroyed, its purity lost. Too short a rein contact, extended periods of walking on contact, can contribute to loss of overstriding hind legs and the purity of the clear four-beat gait.

A patient limbering and relaxing introductory session at the walk will ready horses, especially the mistrusting and nervous ones, for the faster suspended gaits of trot and canter. The trot on a relaxed horse should be a balanced trot with flexion. The trot should also show a certain degree of elasticity, depending on the level of its development. With athletic development the trot should become slower, more balanced, and therefore more engaged.

MOUTH PROBLEMS

Horses not properly introduced to the bit may resent it. If the situation is not improved, the horse might develop a mouth problem (such as opening the mouth or grinding the teeth) that will hinder him in dressage achievements. There may be two major reasons for the horse's resentment of the bit. First, improper equipment or equipment adjustment may cause him discomfort. The rider should use the gentlest bit possible. Ideally, a simple-jointed snaffle should be used. It should be as thick as possible for the individual horse's mouth size. This is the gentlest kind of bit.

A second cause of resentment might be that the rider uses his hands improperly, thereby causing discomfort. Pulling on the reins causes the horse to evade the pain by opening his mouth. The opening of the mouth is often accompanied by pulling against the rider's grip with a stiff neck and a high, lifted head. Such an inversion of his neck, using the lower neck muscles in resistance against the contact, is caused by the horse's instinctive claustrophobia. His reaction to the confinement of a pulling rider is to pull even harder on the reins in order to escape from the sense of confinement. The horse may also shake his head periodically or tilt it sideways, raising one side of his mouth higher than the other and lowering his ear on the opposite side. Evasions against contacting the bit or pivoting the head at the poll, are severe and are sure signs that the rider is causing discomfort with his hands.

Contact with the bit should be made by the horse, not by the rider. The rider should merely feel the weight of the bit and reins in his soft, closed hands. When the horse has accepted the weight of the bit, the rider should accept his soft contact with it by holding the reins steadily and with hands motionless. At this stage, the rein should be frequently lengthened and recontacted only for brief intervals. No mechanical means will correct a suspicious horse's tense mouth. Tightening nosebands, including flash nosebands, or other mechanical attempts to deal with problems caused by bad hands will just cause horses to develop even more anxiety toward the bit. No force should be used to correct a mouth problem. For centuries, a lot of good

Arthur Kottas-Heldenberg has the hands that could ride horses on a silk cord without breaking it. He demonstrates how to pick up the reins to contact the horse. Correct contact often depends on the correct assumption of it. Mastery of this skill has a great deal to do with developing a master's hands. Note that contacting the horse starts with the legs, addressing the horse's attention and activating the hindquarters. This is followed by the rider isometrically firming the torso, permitting the seat to function as a transformer of energies. The final act is the assimilation of the reins.

The upper photograph shows the free walk on a loose rein, with the rider establishing the leg and seat contact that must precede the assumption of the rein contact. The lower photograph shows already-contacted reins, with the rider making sure that the strides are not inhibited or the horse's posture stiffened by them. Hence, the rider's hands reassure the horse of his freedom yet connect the downward adhesiveness of the seat to the bridle enough to invite flexion. The contact is completed because the hocks are connected to the muzzle through a "liquid" body and uninhibited strides.

Nowhere in these photographs does one see pulling or inhibition or confinement of the horse. The mastery of contact is to manage it with forward yielding and softness. As here, the rider's hands should offer an imaginary, tender silk cord for a trusting horse to seek to contact. The rider contacts with legs and seat. He merely offers his hands for the horse to contact!

Photos: Charles Fuller.

training was done without, or with generously loosened, simple cavesson nosebands. The way to quiet, closed mouths was always an educated rider's hand expressing knowledge of horsemanship and goodwill toward his partner.

Some riders complain that the horse opens his mouth whenever contacted by the bit and when more collection is asked for. This complaint suggests that the rider asked for collection through the reins, that he pulled or tightened the reins, hoping that the horse would collect his strides. This cannot be done. Collection is never a result of a shortened neck, nor has it ever been developed by a pulling rider. Like everything that is gymnastically valid, collection proceeds from the haunches toward the bit by the horse seeking it. The horse collects only when he assumes more weight on his haunches. Collection develops by the actions of the rider's legs, abdomen, and back, and not by pulling hands! Collection of the gaits always develops from the hindquarters. It cannot occur as long as the horse shows resistance anywhere in his body, including his mouth. The more a horse is pushed against a pulled bit, the more he is "nailed onto the bit," the more he will bid his entire musculature against that intolerable confinement. A horse tensing all his muscles to brace against confining hands cannot relax them and will not be supple. His haunches will not be free to propel and carry, which is their twin function. Instead, the haunches will push to brace stiffly against "the wall" built by the rider's hand.

The horse may also grind his teeth as a sign of anxiety or fatigue. A horse that surrenders his haunches to his rider's disposal does not grind his teeth. When the horse relaxes, the rider's hands should become gentle and confirm to the horse that he can trust these gentle hands. Whenever increasing contact with the horse's mouth, the rider should increase his driving aids. He must send the horse's hind legs toward the bit. If the horse responds to the rider's driving aids by rushing, he must perform gentle, repeated, and gradual half-halts. Therefore, the reins should be held short enough to connect the rider's torso (weight) and back muscles directly to the horse's mouth. Yet, the reins should not be held too short and force the horse to carry in his mouth part of the weight of his rider's arms and hands. Thus, when the half-halts are performed, the horse will feel a coordinated aid that involves the rider's entire body: the legs attached and draped in order to drive, the torso upright and perpendicular to increase the weight on the hindquarters and to stabilize a passive contact with the reins. The shoulder blades should be pressed flat into a straight back with the shoulder joints, folded back and down. The rib cage and the abdomen must be ahead of the upper arms and the elbows. This position allows for the simultaneous driving of the hindquarters while inviting the fore-hand to slow down. Done gently and with utmost coordination, these aids allow the horse to shorten his body and flex his muscles correctly, without pain or disharmony and in a relaxed manner. These aids must be dynamic and constantly, rhythmically yield-ing, perpetually in coordination with the horse's muscular move-ments of stretching alternating with contracting. The aids may also alternate with periods of passivity or relaxation!

THE HORSE LEANING ON HIS RIDER'S HANDS

First of all, the rider must identify the cause of the problem, because the horse's leaning on the rider's hands is merely a symp-tom, and depending on the cause of the problem, the remedies may vary.

Let me hypothesize that the horse is heavy on the hands because of insufficient and incorrect use of his hindquarters. If the horse is leaning on the rider's hands evenly, he is likely to push the composite weight of himself and the rider forward, rather than lifting it off the ground, therefore progressing in space without flotation or periods of suspension. If this is the cause of the problem, then slowing down the horse's progression by half-halting and urging the hindquarters to step closer to his forehand with stronger legs is, indeed, a useful correction. The rider should communicate to the horse that he must slow down the tempo of his mass in order to allow his hindquarters to carry rather than push it. The result will be a shorter horse, in a posture of taller flexion, capable of striding under a more compacted mass, with its center of gravity shifted farther back.

If, however, the horse leans heavier on to one of the reins rather than the other, then in addition to the above-suggested slowing down of the traveling mass, another remedy needs to be employed. Contacting heavier on one of the reins is caused by the horse using his hind legs on the heavy side with a shorter, stiffer motion. Such a horse will move either unevenly or "unlevel."

Unlevel strides can be eliminated by several different efforts.

In case the horse steps shorter with one hind leg, yet tracks properly in the direction of the corresponding foreleg, he will make longer strides, but will cross slightly with the opposite hind leg. This will push the horse's shoulder toward the shorter-stepping side, resulting in heavier leaning on the rein seeking his rider's support on that side. To improve the situation, the rider should yield rhythmically on the heavily contacted rein at the very moment when the longer-striding opposite hind leg is lifting off the ground. Meanwhile, the lighter rein should be held in contact continuously to support (direct rein) the lighter-contacting side and should serve as a point of reference toward which the heavier rein is yielded. The lightly contacted side must be held in steady contact offered by the rider to encourage the horse to develop muscular stretching toward it. Whenever a problem in the hindquarters forces a horse to seek heavier contact with one rein, part of the corrections is to include an insistence on seeking his contact with the other rein, which he has abandoned. The driving should intensify on the heavier-contacting side of the horse.

Another reason for one-sided pulling may be that the horse is not tracking toward the corresponding foreleg on the side opposite from the heavier rein. He may indeed be tracking outside the path of the corresponding forehand, thus moving with haunches displaced slightly outward. This would cause the horse to lean heavily on the opposite shoulder (falling on the shoulder), making the rein feel heavy there, too. If this is the cause of the problem, then the rider must yield on the heavy rein forward identically to the above-suggested method, but instead of driving the troubled hind leg forward, the rider ought to push it inward to encourage alignment with the track.

Beyond these specific methods that correct the use of the horse's hind legs, certain other exercises are valuable. A horse that somehow moves incorrectly with one or both of his hind legs has a physical reason for doing so. Basically, the reasons for such shortcomings are: (1) weak joints, (2) weak muscles, (3) stiff joints, and (4) stiff muscles. Therefore, exercises that strengthen the joints, develop muscles, or supple both are in order.

The following gymnastic exercises may be helpful:

If the horse is heavy on both reins evenly and is supple enough, the rider can do rein-back exercises on more advanced horses to encourage coordination, the shortening of the body, and the carrying of more weight on the hindquarters. Ride frequent transitions between trot and canter, riding twice as many trot steps as canter strides (for example, twenty trot and ten canter). You may reduce the number of each gradually as the horse learns to shift his center of gravity backward, which is manifested in the lightening of the rein contact. Canter-to-trot transition work also increases mobility in the horse's back muscles and is particularly effective in relaxing the horse's lumbar back.

If the horse is heavier on one rein only, there can be two causes, as mentioned above. Perform frequent canter departures from the walk on the lead where the rein is contacted heavier by the horse. Ride the extended trot, and turn onto the diagonal from that side where the rein is lighter. Also ride serpentines at the trot. More sophisticated corrections may include the shoulder-in and circles to the side where the rein is heavier, half-pass toward the side where the rein is heavier, haunches-in to the side where the rein is heavier, canter departures from the walk on the lead on which the rein is lighter.

Again, riding cannot be done according to a recipe book. It is not a technology. Far from it, riding must be schooling that never becomes mechanical drilling. The exercises suggested are not recipes, instead their particular value is in strengthening and suppling those joints and/or muscles that need improvement. Remember that when a rider does something on one hand, he must, within a reasonable period of time, repeat the same exercise on the other hand. The suggested exercises should assume, for the time being, a predominant role, but they are not to be an exclusive diet. In short, the rider could emphasize these exercises until improvement occurs, but for every two of them, he should ride one "mirror image" on the alternative rein. As soon as the problem noticeably diminishes, exercises should be done in pairs, "mirror images," to keep the improvement confirmed and stablilized. Because each problem is unique and changes its nature even from moment to moment as a result of the horse's reactions, riding will always be dependent on expert coaching. In some cases, for example, with horses that have different needs for muscle and different needs for joint development, exercises might always have to be done in pairs.

GENERAL ADVICE ON PUNISHMENT

Punishment is seldom needed and should be seldom employed. When punishment is indispensable, it should be as mild as possible for the attainment of a needed correction. It should be instant when a misdeed warrants it. Delayed punishment is not understood, is confusing, and can damage the horse's trust in his rider. Punishment should always be commensurate to the seriousness of the horse's evasion or disobedience, yet never be cruel. Never punish when angry, irritated, impatient, stressed, or revengeful. Only punish when the horse actually needs it, rather than when you think he "deserves" it.

Punish instantly when evasion or disobedience occurs. The horse must learn to associate punishment with the deed that provoked it. If you do not succeed in punishing instantly, do not do so at all, for the horse cannot understand and assimilate belated punishment. Such belated punishment leads to confusion and loss of confidence and trust on his part.

Punishment should be limited to one effective act. It should never be a prolonged act of annoyance or sustained for an extended period of time. Make peace with the horse as soon as possible. Be quick to follow even the mildest scolding with ample rewards. Brevity of punishment is the very essence of its effectiveness. Help the horse overcome the feeling of discord by requesting something easily performed by him and then use the opportunity to reward him for doing something well.

Punish only in ways that do not result in loss of control over the horse. Avoid punishing by any rough handling of the horse's mouth. A rider can destroy the horse's confidence and trust easily with punishment that is too frequently meted out or too severe. Good riders can punish with a smiling face and reward with a frowning one.

Different Modes of Punishment

Punishment by omission is based on denial of rewards. Repetition of aids when an exercise is not done properly on the first request denies the horse confirmation by the rider relaxing, harmonizing, and yielding. Rewarding begins with the slightest relaxation of demands, which is why every time we gain the horse's performance of what we aided for, we should confirm our pleasure by the cessation of aids. There are aids to initiate a change and aids to maintain the status quo. The latter is really a phase of rewarding.

Punishment by ommission also means denial of rewards such as petting, stroking, resting the horse on a long rein, giving sugar, or unsaddling.

Punishment by commission is based on actively causing the horse displeasure and is the more dramatically effective of the two. It may mean stronger, more forceful aids, demanding instant forward motion in an extended gait, or a light application of the whip. Punishment may include halting for a prolonged period of time. This is particularly effective with advanced horses. It frustrates their will to move with pleasure. The rider is in a strong position of control on an immobilized horse. The halt is most suitable to communicate to the horse the need for submission to the rider's will.

Punishment should always be done with empathy for the horse's level of development and the particular deed that provoked it. Young, inattentive, playful, happy horses should not be punished for periodic, mild frolicking. An advanced dressage horse, however, should not be allowed the same liberties. Before punishing at all, always quickly determine whether the mishap was not actually induced by the rider. Never punish the horse for your mistakes. Much wrong is caused, even provoked, by the rider.

Nine

Clinics, Competitions, and Judging

PARTICIPATING IN CLINICS

Every instructor has preferences as to the appearance, equipment, and preparedness of students. I can only speak about mine, while trusting that they correspond to some of the expectations of fellow instructors. Expectations may vary somewhat, depending on the frequency of instruction for a particular pupil. An instructor may have pupils seen only once a year or much more frequently.

The horse should be in continuous training and athletically prepared for a dressage clinic. He should be strong enough to take an hour of gymnastic work, although intense work limited to exercises in a manege should last only thirty minutes. Good muscle tone and good cardiovascular functions result from regular training and correct feeding. A horse regularly schooled should also have a prolonged attention span and the ability to concentrate on his rider. Horses benefit immensely by frequent rest periods, which must not be long and may even be limited to one minute. Resting periods are more for the horse's mind than for his body, unless, of course, he is in strenuous training for cross-country work. Resting for a minute is the most effective reward and it also allows the horse to realign his body and work as his own "chiropractor" with a loose neck. Resting could be as frequent as every six minutes for young, weak, or nervous horses. Even the most educated and willing horse needs a rest period after every fifteen minutes of work.

The rider should also be athletically conditioned. Sick, injured, or weak riders have low physical and mental tolerance for learning. They should not participate in clinic lessons. Unfit riders cannot be given proper education and athletic guidance through a clinic format. Unfit riders should not take lessons because their learning abilities are impaired.

Ideally, riders with an independent, balanced seat benefit most from an occasional clinic. I believe that the seat and aids of riders need serious attention. Few riders have been started correctly, and therefore equitation becomes the most important part of a clinic. During a clinic, an instructor must teach the horse using the skills of his rider. Daily instruction or supervision, however, may still be the best for riders who need to learn an independent, balanced seat and riding theory in a thorough manner. Poor riding habits are much harder to correct than giving good riding skills and habits to beginning riders. Bad riding, habituated during many years, is well learned. Unlearning it is a monumental task, all the more so because the bad habits feel "normal" and good to the rider who habituates them.

The horse's equipment should include a dressage saddle, well-adjusted headgear and the proper bit for the level of the horse's schooling needs. (Regulations concerning equipment for competition are found in the rule books of national and international regulatory organizations.) Many riders come to lessons with unevenly adjusted stirrup leathers. They are accustomed to riding in uneven stirrups in order to compensate for a crooked seat that shows in a collapsed hip. Or they did not notice that over time, one leather stretched. Stirrup leathers should be checked and measured weekly. All tack should be clean.

The rider's equipment and attire should approximate, as closely as possible, that used in competition. Competition attire is standardized because in it riding can be done well. In it, the rider can also be accurately observed. By all means, do wear clothing that reveals the position of the torso and the use of the back. Wear leather riding boots for correct feeling and effective aids. Gloves are indispensable in any weather as protection for the rider's hands and as instruments for "generalizing" the feeling on the reins.

Carry a riding whip. Both the rider and the horse have two equally important sides. Therefore, carrying two whips might be a great asset with lazy horses. Changing the whip from side to side could be very disturbing to the horse, destroying continuity of the contact and regularity of rhythm, unless skillfully done by an educated rider. Correctly changing the whip skillfully from hand to hand should hardly be noticeable to the horse. Basic training should be schooled without spurs. Prior to the horse's ability to collect, spurs are useless because their function is occasional and "percussionary," to enhance cadence or to increase engagement. In any case, spurs are instruments for refinement and should not be worn by riders who cannot keep their heels away from the horse's sides and who cannot ride with draped, effectively driving calves. Sensitivity to mild leg aids is paramount in dressage riding and, even on phlegmatic horses, can best be developed with the help of reinforcement of the leg aids by the whip. Spurs are useful when collection and cadencing work commence. They are instruments of sensitivity, similar to the double bridle. However, their use should slightly precede the use of the full bridle.

At the beginning of a lesson, the rider should walk up to the instructor and halt there. They could exchange greetings and the instructor could ask the student about essential information concerning the horse and the rider's experiences. While the instructor inspects the equipment and adjusts it if necessary, the rider should offer a short and relevant report on the horse. This should include the horse's age, training background, current schooling plans, and particular problems or strengths in performance. After the equipment has been inspected and, if needed, adjusted, the lesson proper may begin. An instructor should adjust the rider's skeletal position while still at the halt. This is the time to sculpt the rider's torso and leg position.

SUGGESTIONS FOR RIDING DRESSAGE TESTS

Let us make use of a musical analogy. Playing the piano with great skill is not enough for a great performance. Special performance skills must be added before success is achieved. Just as a great concert pianist does not need a score but plays by heart, so any great dressage rider rides his test from memory. Having a ringside prompter may be necessary when competing on several horses and with each one in different tests. Practice makes perfect. The rider who has the test called because he is not fully familiar with it will perform as poorly as would a pianist who is searching for the notes in a musical score while playing a concert. Only a well-practiced test will show brilliance. There is a myth about not riding tests frequently in practice, because the horse might learn and anticipate the patterns. No horse turned loose in the dressage arena will perform any test from memory. The horse cannot analyze and will not learn tests by heart! International riders might perform the Grand Prix test on the same horse for a decade, yet the horse will not spoil the test by anticipation. Every dressage test ought to be a logical composition unfolding a sequence of gymnastic exercises that allows the rider to show how well his horse is developed mentally and physically. As a composition, the test has fluency and beauty inherent in it through logic and balance. Dressage tests must be performed in their totality, not in bits and pieces or as patchwork. Riders should perform each test as an organic whole, like a concert pianist, who does not play notes or measures, but rather the whole musical composition that is beautiful only in its entirety.

Uneven standards in musical performances are not satisfactory. When some parts are played harshly and others with poetic expression, it shows either a lack of understanding of the piece or a lack of skill in unfolding it correctly. Riding a dressage test often owes its greatest beauty to consistency. Once the horse and rider's temperament develop a distinct style, perform in that style consistently.

Practicing the parts of a dressage test is as necessary to the rider as it is for a pianist to rehearse certain passages of a composition. However, that activity should be limited to practice sessions. Ride the entire test often. It will establish a mood and it will reveal any shortcomings. Repeat exercises for schooling purposes only if they are weak.

Whether competing or schooling the horse, do not ride merely the test patterns, instead, always ride your horse! You should know the test so well, have ridden it so often and polished it in such detail that you should not really need to note the letters of the manege. You should instead know the composition of the ride, "forgetting" the letters that initially aided in memorizing it.

Riding tests belong to the "examination" rather than to the "diagnostic" or "athletic development" phases of riding. Some horses enter the arena tense and showing major faults. Worse than the horse's shortcomings could be the rider's acceptance of them. Immediate attempts should be made to change these shortcomings. Although improving and correcting a horse may not be easy during a competition, sometimes just seconds of correctly influencing the horse can reestablish lost rapport and win the horse's attention and cooperation.

ADVANCING IN COMPETITION

Ideally, the rider should compete on a level where his horse can perform the exercises effortlessly. This, then, presumes that the horse's athletic and mental development are accomplished for the performance of the test.

Riders should not enter their horses in tests where they can expect less than a 50 percent score. However, should they receive scores of 60 percent or higher consistently, they can interpret that as encouragement to progress to the next higher level.

Riders should understand that in dressage, one does not compete only against other riders for a ranking among those showing on a given day. In this art form, one competes also against oneself. Improvement should be interpreted in terms of percentage scores and not merely in terms of placement. In other words, it is important to know the difference between a first place with a low score and a poor ranking in a class, yet with a high score. Despite winning with a low score, the rider should realize that there are severe shortcomings in the horse's development. These should prevent the rider from advancing to the next competition level and make him want to dedicate more time to consolidating gains on the current level.

Ironically, sometimes riders score higher on a more advanced test than on a lower-level test the same day. The reason for this may be that the horse actually improved on the higher-level test by having been warmed up in the earlier, lower-level test. Also, some horses show their best gymnastic achievements on tests that challenge them better. Other horses work best when they are fresh. Under no circumstances should horses be fatigued before showing them. If a rider believes that only exhaustion will calm his horse enough to be manageable during a show, the entire training is proven to have been wrong.

Many riders show their horses on two consecutive levels in the same show. The lower level, presumably, is the more accomplished, more polished achievement. The higher level is the one on which the horse is "breaking ice." This is good competition strategy. Educated dressage riders are aware that their horses should be doing gymnastic exercises more advanced and even different from ones shown during competition.

Riders may enter shows and ride tests even if they feel insecure about having attained a show-worthy level of development. Riders may use competitions as instructional opportunities. They ought to compete in order to be evaluated by an expert and seek his comments to facilitate further improvement.

THE FREESTYLE TEST

The Freestyle may be the king of dressage competitions provided the correct gymnasticizing of horses is not compromised. Judging it should be a pleasure. The element of novelty, the ingenuity manifested in composition, the thrill of the unexpected, all contribute to that feeling of evaluating something that is now "world premiered." The Freestyle Test lets the rider emerge not only as a performing artist, but also as a composer/creator of art as well. Watching a brilliant Freestyle Test may give us a thrill similar to what audiences must have felt when Rachmaninoff played his own piano compositions in concert. Perhaps even more so, for often a Freestyle Test is seen for the first time, while Rachmaninoff's works may have been heard before his performing them.

Riders earn scores by the propriety and ingenuity of their composition on the one hand and the level of technical perfection of performance on the other. The propriety of the Freestyle Test demands that the rider display all the gaits and movements appropriate to the level of development required by a standard test.

The ingenuity of the Freestyle Test depends on the rider's artistic creativity, sense of proportion, and thorough knowledge of how to display his particular horse to his best advantage.

Composing a Freestyle Test

The test should appear fluent in composition and in movement. Movements should flow easily from one to another and offer a sense of gymnastic logic: progressing from simpler toward the more complex. Part of fluency is a vigorous beginning and crescendo ending, not unlike symphonies, which usually begin with lively, attractive passages and have an impressive finale.

When composing an impressive beginning to a musical freestyle, keep in mind that a rider ought to top the entrance by a magnificent ending. For instance, in a Grand Prix Freestyle Test, entering with a passage would leave diminished choices for an ending.

Here are some examples for building from simple to complex exercises:

In patterns, larger patterns such as large circles to smaller ones. Commonly used, familiar patterns are easier, such as riding on the center line, as opposed to riding on less frequently used patterns such as a quarter line. Or riding a serpentine limited in size to only one-half of the arena is more difficult to ride than one from wall to wall. While using new patterns can add interest and novelty to the test, making transitions at rarely used or not designated points (letters) can cause confusion and detract from the value of the design.

Transitions should also become more complex as the Freestyle progresses. In an old version of the Grand Prix test, there used to be complex and sophisticated transitions in the movement number 34: down center line at collected canter to halt at L. Followed by a rein-back of four steps, and then proceed directly in passage! A rider should provide such transitional feats later rather than at the beginning of a Freestyle Test.

Gaits can also be shown from simple to complex. Obviously, a working or medium gait is simpler than an extended or collected trot. Also, exercises at the walk are simpler than those at the canter. Think particularly of the pirouette.

The symmetry of the patterns is important. Not only is a symmetrical test aesthetically more beautiful, but also riding logic expects it. After all, the horse has two equally important sides that should be evenly gymnasticized. However, even the symmetry of a test's design can progress from simpler to more complex expressions of symmetry. When the symmetry is simple, then an exercise performed on one rein is immediately repeated on the other rein. The figure eight is an example of this. An intricately sequenced pattern can include symmetry by several transitions repeated and its mirror image on the other rein delayed. A balanced test design gives an equitable distribution of effort to display all three basic gaits.

A rider may show more at his best gaits and much less at the weaker ones. He can do that without compromising the balance of the test by showing weaker gaits in a more novel pattern and at unexpected locations. Show the slow walk on short patterns. Show bold gaits on longer lines and for longer duration. This is gymnastically logical and also gives the impression of a bold, forward-thinking performance.

A Freestyle Test is artistic when it is logical rather than ambitiously confusing. When composing one, scrutinize it as to its fluency, complexity, symmetry, and balance. Ride it, to feel the performance quality, and have the courage to alter it when needed. Freestyle Tests should reflect perfect riding logic and the best performance of a given horse. Musical accompaniment is very important. Therefore, its quality and appropriateness strongly influence the rewards it may earn in the scoring.

Todd Bryan, riding the stallion Equitanius to a near-perfect halt. This picture captures the moment that judges hope for: an excellent performance that could be rewarded with a score of 10. This is a balanced halt—with the poll proudly the highest point of the horse—straight, relaxed, attentive. Immobility is the essence of the halt. It goes beyond just standing; it requires the total absence of motion. The rider's salute is exemplary, including such details as an eye contact with the judge.

This elegant picture proclaims that in classical equitation that which is correct is, by definition, also beautiful. It also reaffirms the importance of the halt as "a movement." At the halt, movement is latent but present, in the willingness of the horse to assume immobility in perfect balance and to move off in perfect balance at the rider's will. Furthermore, such a rider appears like a king on his throne. The classical seat, from seat bones upward, is identical to the posture of a person standing at attention. Photo: Susan Sexton.

THE SALUTE

A proper salute is very important. It is the first major impression the judge has of the rider and it is also a personal contact between competitor and judge. The salute has a traditional and specific form that is elegant and at the same time not disturbing to the horse or his balance during the halt. It is a formal greeting derived from long-standing traditions. It expresses respect toward the horse, the judge, and, most of all, to the art of riding.

The Correct Way to Salute

The salutes at both the beginning and end of the test should be performed identically.

1. Settle the horse into a balanced (foursquare) halt. As you ride the center line facing the judge (including the transition), establish eye contact with the judge. Do not appear anxious about the horse or preoccupied with your transition. Halting as still as a monument, put all reins into your left hand. Be careful not to shorten a set of reins on one side, since that will bend the horse's neck and head to that side during the salute. The horse *must* remain straight.
2. A woman drops her right arm straight down. The arm should be relaxed and the fingers should be relaxed and natural, not outstretched and tense. A man should reach for his hat and hold it somewhat in front of his right ear.
3. A woman bows her head in a relaxed, continuous motion. She does not drop her head down abruptly. She *will* have to lose eye contact with the judge. A man lifts his hat *without* losing eye contact with the judge.
4. A woman will sustain a bowed head somewhat longer to correspond to the time it takes for the man to lift his hat.
5. A woman must maintain her salute with bowed head without anxiety or tenseness. A man drops his arm straight down, holding his hat with its top facing outside and with the lining facing the horse's side. No tension should be visible in the arm. The hat should be close to the horse and not visible to the judge at this point.

Demonstrated by Elizabeth Searle.   Photo: Kerry Schroeder.

6. A woman reestablishes eye contact with the judge and separates the reins into the hands. A man replaces his hat firmly, with a minimum of fuss, so as not to lose it during the ride.
7. Depart from the halt.

Common Faults and Mistakes

1. A too-fast or hyperactive salute that upsets the horse's balance and projects an attitude of ignoring the judge rather than honoring him.
2. For men, a lack of continuous eye contact with the judge while riding down the center line and during the salute. We greet someone by looking into his eyes, and the same procedure is used here since the salute is essentially a silent greeting. Eye contact while riding on the center line is essential to riding a straight track. We go in the direction we look; the horse follows our unconscious body attitudes. Therefore, you cannot ride on a straight track from A to C (the judge) unless you *look* toward that point. Men should *never* lose eye contact with the judge during the entire proceedings. Do not tilt the head.
3. Women bending from the hips or waist to salute. Only the head salutes. Otherwise, the seat contact will be lighter, which could upset the horse's balance and possibly make him step back. Theatrical, sweeping arm gestures are both unbecoming and humorous.
4. Men stretching their saluting arm to the side. This should not be done, since it may collapse their hip, frighten the horse, or upset his balance. Showing the inside of the hat in the begging position is also inappropriate.

THE ROLE OF THE JUDGE

A good judge is knowledgeable and good judging is a by-product of expertise. Both expertise and skills in judging should improve with practice. Both theoretical and practical knowledge are needed for expertise. In dressage, as in many other performance sports, the evaluators have mostly been competitors themselves and their scholarship about horsemanship is indispensable. Reading, conversation among experts, attending forums and seminars about judging, observing various riders training and showing are some of the ingredients that sharpen judging skills. Training horses, riding in competition, and teaching are probably the most valuable preparatory assets for good judging.

A judge is not a scoring machine. His expert opinions are sought not just on his score sheets. He may be asked questions before, during and after shows. The foremost duty of a dressage judge should be to promote the classical tradition and gymnastic standards of horsemanship. He is primarily an educator of riders. He educates with his score sheets both by scoring and commenting. He rewards all tendencies that are correct while punishing wrong developments and compromised efforts. Judges, more than any other equestrians, are responsible for the upholding and maintaining of the classical riding tradition. They influence and guide with their opinions and views the coaches, trainers, and riders. Most riders hope to succeed. They know that they can only succeed with a judge's approval. Therefore, if judges approve correct horsemanship and gymnastic development in the horse, they will, more than anyone else, further the cause of classical equitatian. Scoring should not be altered to accommodate special situations. Even in areas where dressage is new and riders are novices, the same standards of judging must prevail as elsewhere. Otherwise, the curious situation may occur that the rider gained his highest test score percentage when he was a novice and as he became more accomplished, his scores gradually diminished. Scores are not just numbers: they represent a fast, efficient code-language for communicating how closely the rider approximates the ideals of classical equitation and training development. The words for the conceptual equivalents to the scores can be found in national and FEI rule books.

Judging involves the interaction of three activities:

Knowledge of the rules of dressage competitions and of the goals of gymnastic exercises in the athletic development of the horse and its appropriate developmental stages.

Skills to observe accurately what actually happens; to

quickly decide on the hierarchy of importance of all that was observed; to make an instant value judgment and record by a numerical score that expresses the merits of each exercise based on the hierarchy of importance.

Insight into the natural and sequential development of the horse; sensitivity to the conditions under which the horse is shown; empathy with the rider and the horse, as it may be relevant in their pursuit of an ideal achievement.

Neither appropriately thorough knowledge of dressage nor insight can be developed easily to the level of expertise. Only those who are familiar with the classical principles of dressage and who implicitly trust them can be expected to be uncompromising in upholding the correct principles of equitation and standards for the horse's development. Both theoretical and practical knowledge are needed to support the commitment that maintains and promotes the classical standards of dressage.

Scoring is a by-product of expertise. It must reflect only what is observed at the moment, rather than memory of what one may have known or heard about the rider and the horse. Observation must be keen in order to avoid judging by recollection of what went on the moment before. A judge often has reasons to follow a score of 3 with that of an 8 if memory is not involved.

Whatever is perceived will need evaluation in terms of the hierarchy of its importance in the horse's development. The score must represent a knowledge of what is more and what is less important in each movement. Knowing that the movements of each test were designed to demonstrate certain specific achievements by the horse, the judge must look for the proof that those standards have been attained. As movements flow with "connecting tissue," the essence of what is shown is often introduced through an "overture," which must not be overemphasized.

A judge must make a quick decision about both the score and the succinct comment appropriate for guiding the rider. In order to do that, the judge has to retain in his memory what he has observed, relative to all the other rides observed in the same class, and must measure equally well its value in terms of absolutes and ideals. Ideals should be clearly in the judge's mind like transparencies superimposed over the actual ride. For each test, the "transparency" reflects an appropriately different ideal by which the horse's performance is compared and contrasted.

The most important judging activity is the perception of the horse's activity relative to the uncorrupted vision of the classical standards or requirements. Only when the perception of what is taking place is correct can the knowledge of the required classical principles be put to use to evaluate the activities observed.

To know the essence of each movement in a test is indispensable for accurate evaluation. In a sequence of activities, the judge must know the most important features, as distinct from the modifiers, and in scoring must weigh the important elements more heavily than the modifying features. In observing both the purity of the gaits and the demarcation of transitions, the following hierarchy of values should prevail.

Relaxation is a prerequisite to all other components of the correct performance of a horse. Without mental and physical relaxation, only the horse's legs move; with relaxation, the horse renders himself into an athletically suitable position so that his entirety is involved in the motion. Total body involvement in the motion allows for athletic development. A horse that only moves with his legs, due to tension, is not gymnastically involved. A relaxed horse is easy to recognize by its longitudinal flexion toward the bit. A horse not flexed in his length is neither relaxed nor stepping through his whole body.

Balance may develop once the horse is relaxed. It is revealed most accurately during transitions. When in balance, the horse must appear as a harmonious unit. His neck should not be artificially shortened or set higher than the loose back muscles would allow as correct and uninhibited. Thus, depending on the level of development in the horse, the balance is different at various stages. A balanced horse is not overdeveloped in one area at the expense of another. Transitions performed by a balanced horse look smooth, without loss of rhythm. The last step of the original gait and the first step of the next gait should be as clear, pure, and harmonious as all others in the respective gaits are expected to be. A balanced horse will also move in exact rhythm and pure gait when changing from straight to bent patterns, such as from the long wall to a corner, without speeding up or slowing down.

Rhythm develops as a consequence of consolidated balance. The sophisticated rider perfects the horse's balance by monitoring and controlling his rhythm. The mastery of rhythm is best revealed by the added sophistication of lengthening and collecting the stride without losing the purity of the gait and the evenness of the rhythm. When the horse no longer rushes to extend or slows when collected, rhythm is a proven accomplishment.

Impulsion is controlled energy that increases the articulation of joints and allows for efficiency of movement that results in longer periods of time in suspension and decreased periods of time touching the ground. In the walk, where there is no suspension period, the relative quality and time that the horse's limbs travel above the ground (roundness, elevation, reach) reveal the degree of impulsion. Impulsion is certainly based on the horse's natural forward zest and enthusiasm. Yet, a fast, running horse that moves stiffly and close to the ground is working with speed rather than impulsion. Impulsion presumes the kind of muscular and joint development that allows the horse to carry the rider slowly, yet with powerful lift. Impulsion causes effortless locomotion that looks smooth and suspension–oriented by the round and large strides that are synonymous with it. Amplification, rather than haste in the gaits, is the proof of impulsion. It cannot develop without relaxation, balance, and rhythm.

Engagement develops gradually as the last stage of sophistication in the horse's gymnastic development. Therefore, it is introduced gradually. Engagement is revealed by the horse's ability to carry more weight with his haunches, that is, collection, thereby lightening the forehand and making all movements, both extended and collected, look equally effortless. As a result, all movements have an excessively cadenced look. That is, immaculate longitudinal flexion and lateral bend, perfect balance and rhythm, buoyant impulsion, are all united to cause the horse to spring off the ground by lifting rather than pushing. Engagement enables the horse to perform with the lightness of a dancer and the efficiency of a gymnast.

Suppleness is the perpetual verification of the correct achievement of all the other elements described above. Only when supple can a horse display the other building blocks of his gymnastic achievements.

The natural hierarchy of the development explained above should be appropriately weighed by the judge who evaluates the horse. An educated judge knows which of these stages is emphasized in each level of testing. He should also know through which movements each of the developmental stages are best revealed. Therefore, correctly grading the movements becomes easy and decisive. The judge should punish more severely the lack of development prerequisite to advancing than the shortcomings more appropriate to higher developmental stages. For instance, if relaxation is missing, even a First Level horse is deemed insufficiently accomplished. When it is missing from the performance of a Grand Prix horse, punishment by lowering the scores should be increased. Conversely, as a First Level horse is not expected to show collection, therefore, the lack of it must go unpunished.

Undivided attention and observation cannot be overemphasized. For the rider, those few minutes in the arena are the most important minutes, for which months or even years were spent in preparation. A judge cannot afford to be tired, bored, or uninterested in any of the horses or any of the rides! Only when the judge observes everything can a correct, meaningful score be given.

Appropriate commenting on score sheets is important. Contestants, if they are mature sports people, will come to a show to be evaluated and guided rather than just to try to win.

Comments should be concise, succinctly phrased, but relevant in addressing the most important issues in each movement. Use of standardized, classical terminology that refers appropriately to the gymnastic meaning of the movements performed is indispensable. Often, because of the lack of time and space and because of their instructional value, negative comments are appropriate. They need not be stated in derogatory terms. When the score is low and major improvement is desirable, it should be pointed out to the rider. Negative comments can be stated in a helpful manner, if possible in full sentences rather than just with single words or phrases.

Judging should punish the more severe mistakes, those difficult and time-consuming to correct rather than those that are easily correctable.

Dressage is concerned with the horse as a gymnast. All that contributes to gymnastic ideals should be rewarded and developments hindering them should be punished. The goal of gymnasticizing is to straighten the horse and ride it forward with evenly loading and well-engaged hind legs, so that the horse can carry his rider with maximum efficiency painlessly. That can only be achieved by a relaxed, balanced, rhythmic, impulsive, and engaged horse. Allow the horse to develop gradually and systematically by improving his natural abilities and allow him to look beautiful naturally. Nothing substitutes for the knowledge of the classical standards of equitation. Perceiving them and knowing how to rate them in their relative values for the horse's natural development is at the heart of judging. All judges should be experts who coincidentally adjudicate.

Ten

Equipment for Dressage

If saddles were not extremely important for increasing the rider's effectiveness and the horse's comfort, we would still be riding bareback. Horsemen recognized centuries ago, however, that saddles are necessary. The importance of riding in a suitable saddle cannot be emphasized enough. The best rider on the finest horse can lose much of his effectiveness as a master of the art because of a bad saddle.

CHOOSING A SADDLE

The fundamental purpose of a saddle is to allow effective communication of the rider's bodily attitudes to the horse, while ensuring the maximum comfort for the horse. A saddle is meant to facilitate unity and harmony between the two vastly different body structures of the rider and the horse. Therefore, a good saddle's topline must approximate a negative mold of the rider's bottom line, while the shape of the saddle's bottom line should be a negative mold of the horse's topline at the relevant part of his back.

An ideal saddle would be either custom-made or customized and adjusted to the shape of the rider sitting on its top side and to the shape of the horse on its under side. Saddlemakers can study a horse, measure him, and even make molds of his back. They can measure the rider accurately and inquire about the riding purposes for which the saddle will be used. Based on this information, they can create a near-ideal saddle for a particular pair.

The bottom of the saddle, generally, should distribute the rider's weight on the horse's back over as large an area as possible. Therefore, a saddle that is constructed on the principle of an old-fashioned rocking chair, pressing on and pivoting over the horse's back on a small area, will be very uncomfortable for the horse. Rather, the opposite should be sought: a saddle that rests evenly on either side of the horse's spinal column over long, parallel, and equal contact areas. Under no circumstances should the saddle press against the bones of the horse, that is, the saddle's bottom stuffing (cushioning) should be ample enough to provide a deep channel that arches high above the horse's spinal column and withers.

A person standing and spreading his legs will create the shape of an upside-down Y. When sitting in a saddle, the rider's seat bones should be widespread and evenly placed on either side of the saddle's center line. Thus, it is good to have a saddle that will allow the deep drop of the knees resulting from comfortably resting thighs.

In my opinion, a rider could use a dressage saddle that fits for riding any young horse whose specialization has not been determined. Initially, his training will be on the flat, involving gymnastic exercises analogous to foundation dressage work. Moreover, a dressage saddle will develop the rider's seat most appropriately. Naturally, competitors will always benefit from a dressage saddle. However, even those who school jumpers need to work on the flat, and the dressage saddle is still the most appropriate equipment for that. For jumping over obstacles, of course, a specialized jumping saddle is indispensable.

Staying in close contact with the horse is essential to good riding. Therefore, saddle pads should be as thin as possible and shaped to fit the saddle. Overhanging saddle pads are unsightly and inappropriate, and thick ones are neither necessary nor elegant. A good saddle, suitably fitted and softly padded, can sit on a horse's back without a saddle cloth. Saddle cloths may be useful to protect the saddle from horse sweat, which causes leather and stitching to deteriorate. They can also protect the horse's skin from chemicals used to treat the leather. When a saddle pad is used, however, the rider should pull it up into the channel of the saddle so that it does not touch the spine or press down on the withers of the horse. Such pressure, however mild, will cause profound discomfort and pain. Equipment should support the belief that dressage represents elegance through simplicity of equipment. It is the quality of the horse's and the rider's work that should be awe-inspiring, not their flamboyant tack.

POSITIONING THE SADDLE

The position of the saddle on the horse's back should always be firm and at the right place. There is only one place where the saddle stabilizes on any particular horse. The saddle should not travel forward or backward while the rider works.

When placing the saddle, you should start from the withers and slide the saddle back on contact with the horse's back with a short, firm push. Stop the sliding when the saddle settles just behind the withers. The horse's back, depending on its shape, receives the saddle at the correct location, because sliding it farther back would be made difficult by friction. Pushing the saddle back from the withers with a short downward pressure helps to find the area by "feel." The horse's back widens and a saddle pushed too far back will not mold into the horse but sit above his ribs and leave cavities over the shoulders.

After the saddle has been correctly placed, it should be cinched up very gradually and gently. You should tighten the girth three times. Before mounting, the girth should be done up securely enough to prevent the saddle from sliding sideways toward the rider's weight. After a few steps of walking on a long rein, you should tighten the slack in the girth again. Finally, after about ten minutes of riding at the trot, complete the tightening process. With a tight girth, the saddle will not slide back or forward, or tilt from side to side. Riding with a loose girth is dangerous and also painful to the horse. The girth should be pulled as snug as possible! It does not hurt the horse. However, any looseness will bruise and hurt the horse's back muscles and make him sore.

Saddles should fit both horse and rider. However, if a compromise is needed, the comfort of the horse must be placed ahead of the rider's. A rider can accommodate many more different kinds of saddles, even highly specialized ones. Because the horse's back and shoulders cannot tolerate a great variety in shape and size, he ought to be carefully accommodated.

The rider should have ample room in the saddle to carry out the variety of tasks that his daily work demands of him. There should be enough room for him to perform a rising trot and to drive with his seat in an extended canter. If the saddle is too tight and denies horizontal pelvic thrust to the rider, it will "imprison" his pelvis and diminish the effectiveness of his seat influences.

A saddle might slide because the rider does not sit in it correctly. Some riders also make the mistake of "riding the saddle" by shoving it with their hips and lower back. They might "scoop" the saddle with their abdomen, lifting with it in a gyrating motion. Some misinformed riders nudge the saddle forward on every stride, especially at the walk, which makes the horse's back tense. None of these actions with the pelvis that attempting to ride the saddle instead of the horse are correct!

Sometimes, special supplementary equipment many be needed to stabilize the saddle on a horse that has unusual comformational features. These may include a breastplate to prevent sliding back, or a crouper, which is a leather loop going under the horse's tail, to prevent sliding forward.

STIRRUPS

Offset stirrup irons are inappropriate for dressage! Their construction mechanically prevents the correct position of the rider's leg, stiffens the ankle, and prevents the use of the pushing aids. For many riders, the most difficult area to relax while riding is the ankle. The offset stirrup, instead of contributing to relaxation, forces the rider to immobilize his ankle, and so, instead of contributing to a correctly hanging leg position, it makes the rider a prisoner locked into one set position by his stirrup irons.

Stiffness anywhere in a rider will spread from the stiff area and eventually affect most of the rider's body. That is why suppleness in the ankle is particularly important.

The primary purpose of the rider's leg aids is to create impulsion (forward locomotion, energy) and secondarily to create and maintain proper bending. In essence, all riding depends on the appropriate use of the legs because all gymnastic progress is based on the control of the horse's hindquarters. Therefore, the correct position and effective use of the rider's legs are greatly important, which is why offset stirrups are inappropriate.

Use a heavy stirrup iron for better feel, as well as for the occasion when you may lose contact with it. A heavy stirrup soon comes to rest at a vertical hanging position and therefore will be easier to regain. The rider's foot should rest on the stirrup so as to touch the outside edge of the iron with the outside rim of the boot. The stirrup is a resting place for the foot and not an area for gripping or support. There is no need to press down onto the stirrups in order to remain in contact with them. Supplely rotating ankles, belonging to hanging and draped legs, will always accommodate the gentle swinging of the stirrups. Correctly placed and supple legs will not be ejected by the stirrup's jarring. Instead, such legs will move the irons in harmony and rhythm with the horse's motion. The more foot length available by contacting the stirrup close to the toes, the easier it is to push the heel down behind a flexible ankle. The lowering of the heels is a result of lifting the toes upward and stretching the calf muscles. Keep the toes turned inward and nearly parallel to the horse's side with the help of supple ankles. Without this position, the calves cannot stretch and drape along the horse's barrel for the soft, perpetual contact that is necessary for driving in rhythm and controlling the haunches.

Initially, adjust the stirrups short enough to encourage the stretching of the thigh and calf muscles. As these muscles stretch, a deep seat and longer leg position will earn the incremental lengthening of the stirrup leather. One earns longer stirrup leathers gradually by stretching the limbs while retaining their correct angularity and positions at the ankles, knees, and hips. Do not arbitrarily lengthen the stirrup leathers to seek the appearance of a deep seat without actually possessing deeply stretched calves and thighs. More than two hundred years ago the stirrups were shortened on the advice of de la Guérinière because he realized that riding improves by a perpetual contact with the horse's sides. The shorter stirrup enables the rider to keep his legs folded and draped around the horse's rounded rib cage. Shorter than necessary stirrups initially may assist in stretching the rider's leg muscles and eventually enable him to earn the much-coveted long stirrup leathers. Looking at the old engravings predating de la Guérinière's teachings, we can observe that riders' legs were not in contact with their horses' sides. Contact, in fact, is denied by having too long a stirrup leather, which causes the legs to dangle forward and away from the horse's sides.

The rider's legs act, move, accompany, harmonize, and aid differently in the three different gaits. Yet, in all three gaits, their activities and their effectiveness depend upon supple ankles, well-stretched thighs keeping the knees in a deep position, and well-stretched calves keeping the heels in a deep position. Without such leg position, there can be no effective control over the horse's haunches.

BITS

Bits serve the primary purpose of allowing the horse to feel the termination point of his kinetic energy, which develops from the haunches and transmits through longitudinal flexion toward the bit. The horse should only feel the combined weight of the bit and the reins. The rider's seat influences are transmitted to the bit by the unity of his torso with his upper arms and elbows. The rider should only hold the reins and not his horse. The horse must seek a gentle contact with the bit because through it, he can sense his rider's thoughts. The rider does not "take the contact," the horse does. The rider's intentions are transmitted from the seat to the bridle only when the reins are held lightly.

When the horse flexes toward the bit correctly, he changes

the position of his neck and hangs his head loosely from his poll. This physical position, when coupled with mental relaxation, and pleasure, produces saliva by activating the digestive salivary glands at the base of the horse's tongue. Thus, horses have a wet mouth when they contact the bit correctly.

The most gentle and therefore the most appropriate bit is a simple jointed snaffle. It should be correctly measured to fit the horse's mouth and should not hang out of its corners too far. It should be as thick as the horse's mouth structure will allow. The slimmer the metal of the bit, the stronger its effect. Outfitting the horse with a gentle bit requires the thickest possible mouthpiece. A bit with only one joint in the center is recommended.

ARTIFICIAL CONTROLLING DEVICES

In classical horsemanship, there is no need for artificial devices for training. Indeed, classical horsemanship advocates the systematic, gradual, natural, and kindly development of the horse. That, of course, presumes that knowledge and time liberate riders from any need for artificial devices. The tradition of classical horsemanship is based on the belief that we cannot shape any horse, only influence his energies. When the horse's energies are correctly utilized, they produce the most efficient and at once the most elegant posture and carriage. A horse shapes himself, and what results is determined by whatever his energies allow him to create. He cannot look better than his energies allow him to look. No amount of artificial mechanical devices can effectively shape the horse's body. By tying him up and forcing him into a shape with straps, he will refuse to stay in that shape when released from his holding devices. As soon as the shackles are dismantled, the horse snaps back to the shape, posture, carriage, and looks he had before his torment began. Except that by shackling, confirming, and shaping a horse, he will bid himself against his confinement. His genetic instincts are claustrophobic. The perpetual muscular stress against confining equipment will create monstrous muscles that will make the horse look and resist worse than ever before. Therefore, artificial shaping devices are not only painful to the horse, but also utterly counterproductive, not to mention inhumane.

Those acquainted with the classical school of thinking on equitation know that all devices have been tried and fail to do any good. What is surprising is that there is seemingly endless supply of riders uninformed about the trials and errors of the past. They continue to try to use these unworthy devices even after generations of riders before them have failed to succeed by applying them. The classical heritage promotes the rather comforting and accepted notion that horses can develop all of their athletic talents without artifice. Horses become beautifully shaped and elegant in posture voluntarily simply as a result of being schooled correctly.

When knowledge ceases, force commences. Where ideas are lacking, compulsion takes their place.

Drawreins, tie-downs, and martingales have no place in dressage. These tools affect the front of the horse, his neck, his shoulders, and head, without doing anything beneficial to the hindquarters. Furthermore, these tools affect the horse only temporarily, for the duration of their use. In fact, they inhibit the correct use and therefore the correct development of the hindquarters. The horse's front should act in a desirable way as a result of correct engagement of the hindquarters. By manipulating the neck into a false flexion, or by restricting its range of movement, the rider works in vain on the form and ignores the athletic content.

Sidereins, properly and generously adjusted, however, are useful at times and therefore have a legitimate place in dressage discussion. A rider may use sidereins both when the horse is being worked from the ground (lungeing and long reining) or when he is working under a rider.

When the horse is worked from the ground, being lunged or driven on long reins, he should always be equipped with the sidereins. Like all tools, sidereins are beneficial only when properly applied, that is, properly adjusted. The horse should stand relaxed with an extended neck and head when the sidereins are adjusted, and when the horse is in this position, the sidereins should just barely (gently) offer contact. Sidereins should never, under any circumstances, be tightly adjusted and cause any inhibition of the horse's ability to use his entire musculature freely. Sidereins should not inhibit the free use of the limbs either.

At the horse's head, the sidereins may be attached to the ring of the cavesson or to the rings of the snaffle, depending on which is used. On the horse's body, the buckled end may be attached to the lower rings on the surcingle or to the girth of a saddle. When attached to a girth, they function best when placed just below the saddle's skirt where the girth emerges visibly from the saddle.

Sidereins should always be adjusted evenly. They should be of equal length and equal material on both sides, regardless of the fact that the horse is moving on a circle while being lunged. To shorten the inside siderein while lungeing encourages the horse to track away from the line of the circle with the outside hind leg and remain straight in the body, bending only in the neck. It would also inhibit the liberty of engagement of the inside hind leg. Because the sidereins should always be generously adjusted, the equal length of the reins will not encourage the horse to counter bend. If the sidereins are adjusted to a generous length at the halt, they should remain soft for the walk and actually hang at the trot and canter, during which the horse naturally shortens his neck. The purpose of the sidereins is to offer more weight to the bit and for the horse to feel the termination point of his longitudinal flexion better.

The sidereins inspire the horse's acceptance of a generous frame supporting his stretching neck and flexed position. They also help with the alignment of the horse's spine and develop the feeling of how the actions of the hind legs influence the behavior of the bit.

Drawreins, tie-downs, and martingales encourage false neck and head positions that are incorrect and deny any possibility of development and engagement of the hindquarters.

THE FULL BRIDLE

The use of the full bridle must be earned by the horse and deserved by his rider. An instrument of refinement, its use signals delicacy and tact in communication.

The full bridle is comprised of a curb bit and a bridoon and therefore it is often called a double bridle. The width of both mouthpieces should be identical and fit the width of the horse's mouth exactly. Otherwise, the equipment will lose its effectiveness and will cause problems by being uncomfortable for the horse. The thicker the mouthpiece, the less severity, therefore, for horses with sensitive mouths, thicker mouthpieces are recommended. The curb bit has an arched elevation in its structure, the port, which accommodates the horse's tongue. In order to prevent painful pressure, the port should be suitably large to accommodate the tongue. A port with an exaggerated high arch can hurt the horse's palate and is more severe than a port with a lower arch. Care should be taken to select a bit with a sufficient but not oversized port.

The severity of the effects of the bit are determined by the thinness of the curb bit and the bridoon, the height of the port, the proportions of the upper and lower parts of the cheekpiece, the length of the shank, and the length of the curb chain. The longer the cheekpiece, the more severe its effect. The longer the proportionate size of the lower part of the shank is to the upper part, the more severe is its effect. The tighter the curb chain is fitted, the more severe is its effect. Adjustment of these pieces of equipment should be planned carefully according to the horse's needs, keeping in mind that the lightest possible effect

The double bridle.

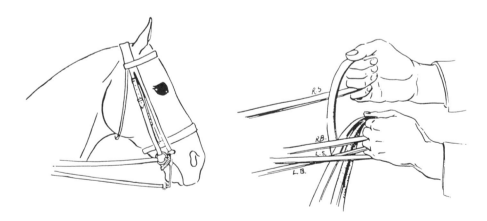

on a particular horse is the most desirable and remains a great witness to the rider's skills.

The curb chain, fitted into the chin groove under the horse's jaw, should be adjusted so as to have a lesser effect (pain induction) than the bit in the mouth. The thinner and smaller the chain links, the more severe their effects become. For sensitive horses, a large-linked chain flatly lying into the chin groove and adjusted with some looseness is most appropriate. The curb chain must always lie flat against the horse's chin and its links should be carefully turned until flattened. The last link should be hooked on to the left hook so that the point of that receiving hook is turned away from the horse's lips. The full bridle, consisting of the above-described pieces of equipment plus headstall (curb bit with port, snaffle, cheekpieces with leverage and curb chain), is capable of very severe action on the horse's mouth. It is an instrument of refinement, not of powerful restraint.

Again, the full bridle must be earned by both the horse and rider. The horse must become so developed physically and mentally that beyond relaxation and balance, he shows elasticity and suppleness and consequently is able to move with proper engagement of the hindquarters. The horse should be able to perform truly collected and extended gaits in order to demonstrate his readiness for this instrument of sensitive refinement.

The rider should not just be a craftsman capable of riding a well-trained horse. Instead, he should be accomplished enough to have developed his own horse to the level of proper collection and extension. He should be able to work the horse with leg and seat aids, needing his hands merely as a sensitive termination point of his communications. His hands must be able to maintain a forward feel and remain unrestrictive. The rider's hands should be those of a giver, not those of a miser. A rider's hands should reflect ever so mildly only the actions of his seat, rather than being separate instruments with a "mind of their own." Riding a horse with a full bridle should be a declaration that the rider no longer needs hand influences and that his horse is totally obedient to the influences of this seat and legs.

About six months prior to using the full bridle, the rider should begin to work with spurs. As the development of the horse must always proceed from his hindquarters toward his mouth, rather than the other way around, the horse's impulsion must be secured, strengthened, and improved by the spurs prior to the curbing effect. Only when the horse's increased impulsion is developed to a higher level in about six months will he be ready for the full bridle.

If the full bridle causes the horse to overflex, open his mouth, move with a "broken neck" (bent at the third vertebra instead of at the poll), lose impulsion, or throw his head, its use is proved premature. Even when the full bridle is offered at the right time and used with great refinement, the horse should continue to work mostly in the simple jointed snaffle. The frequency of returning to the simple snaffle should be determined by the reactions of the horse to the full bridle. At the beginning of its use, the full bridle should seldom be put on the horse. Even within the same schooling session, the horse should be started on the snaffle and during a resting period reequipped with the full bridle. As he becomes more accustomed to it, the frequency of the use of the bridle can increase.

The full bridle should serve the purpose of enhancing the horse's development in his haunches. It should enable him to increase both the locomotive and the carrying functions of the haunches. Only the rider can sense when the full bridle stops enhancing and starts diminishing its benefits to the horse. If the horse reacts to it as if it were restricting the flow of impulsion and engagement, the rider must revert to the use of the simple snaffle bridle. Initially, more days in a week should be spent working in the snaffle than in the bridle. Gradually the length of time the horse spends in the full bridle can be increased both as to its use during a lesson and as to the number of days it is used during a week.

The double bridle refines communication to its utmost sensitivity at the horse's mouth. It also creates a steadying effect that cannot be achieved with the jointed snaffle bit. The snaffle bit can affect the horse's mouth more strongly on one side than the other because of the joint in the middle. This function may be useful in a less developed horse. However, on a more advanced horse, an even effect of the bit in the mouth is indispensable for the steady development of movements. By the time the horse has earned the double bridle, he should be straight and

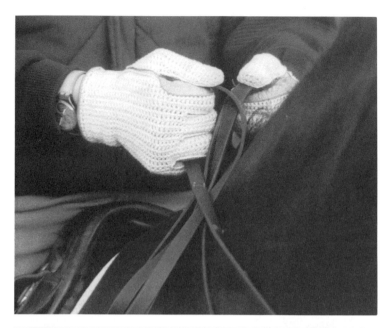

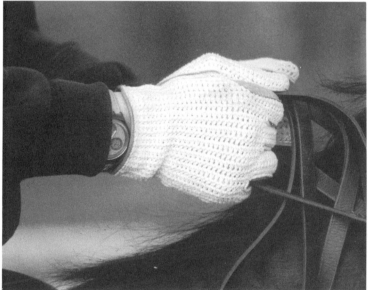

Arthur Kottas-Heldenberg shows in these photographs and in those that follow how to hold the reins properly. Here he demonstrates the traditional way of holding only the bridoon with the right hand and all other reins in the left hand. Photos: Charles Fuller.

TRAINING STRATEGIES FOR DRESSAGE RIDERS

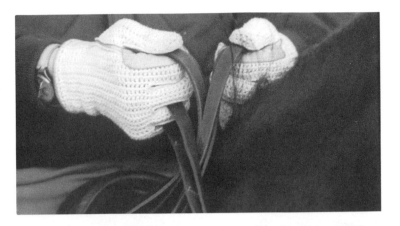

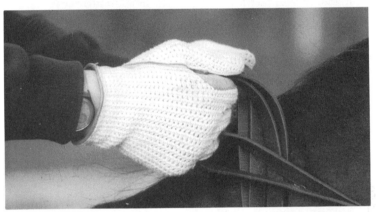

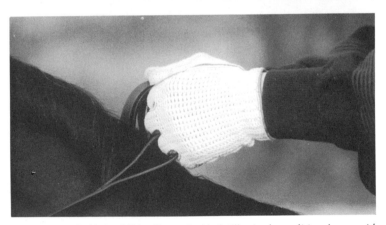

*How to hold the full bridle, or double bridle, in the traditional way with
neither set of reins going outside the little finger.* Photos: Charles Fuller.

not in need of uneven uses of the bit. The full bridle offers stability that will enhance self-carriage, consistent posture, and promote the dynamics of engagement.

The four reins of the full bridle, two emitting from the bridoon and two from the curb bit, may be held in two different ways. One either distributes them so as to hold two reins in each hand, each holding one of the bridoon and one of the curb, of course. They are held in the same manner as the regular snaffle bit reins, except the curb bit reins are added on each side. Or a rider may hold three reins in the left hand and only one in the right.

In the latter case, the left bridoon (snaffle) and both curb bit reins are held by the rider in his left hand, while the remaining right bridoon (snaffle) rein is held alone in the right hand. This three-in-one distribution of reins is the more traditional but currently less practiced mode of holding rein contact.

The advantage of the three-in-one position is that of increased steadiness of contact with the curb bit, which is more severe in its effects. This makes the double bridle's use keener, since the dual purpose of this equipment is to achieve sensitive contact and a steadying effect. Both values increase when both bridle reins are held in one hand. Then is there no chance to saw, even inadvertently, with the reins.

Holding the four reins equally distributed, two in one hand, two in the other, is an imitation of the simple snaffle contact position and offers no advantages to the art of riding other than easier adjustment for the rider, who is used to an even distribution of contact. Although it may add aesthetically to the image of symmetry, from a riding point of view—that is, the horse's developmental needs—this commonly used position is inferior.

In the full bridle, the rider should continue to contact his horse primarily on the snaffle bit and merely lightly contact with the reins of the curb. Initially, only the snaffle should be contacted and the two reins connecting to the curb bit should hang loose until the horse gets used to their weight, size, and presence. Since the rider should continue using the snaffle part of this equipment, it is more beneficial to separate the reins in the traditional three-in-one position. The curb in one hand will provide increased sensitivity and steadying, even contact.

The alternative method of holding the bridoon's rein outside the little finger permits more modulation, as the contact can increase when the rider's wrist position creates a slight thumbs-forward and downward tilt.

Photo: Charles Fuller.

The full bridle is not a powerful new brake to confine a pulling, runaway horse. In fact, the full bridle is the rider's declaration that his horse has reached the development of being ridden without the hands. He responds to the legs and seat. The full bridle increases the weight of the equipment in the horse's mouth, offering a clearer, more stable termination point to the greatly enhanced engagement in his haunches. When riding with the double bridle, the reins may no longer be used for either guidance or lateral bending of the horse. These functions must now come only from the rider's legs and seat. The horse should move on any pattern and bend in either direction without the reins influencing him.

The abuses of the full bridle can be many. An ignorant rider may use it to control his horse through pain, or to artificially shape the horse's neck. A knowledgeable rider, however, will always remember that the areas of the horse visible to the rider

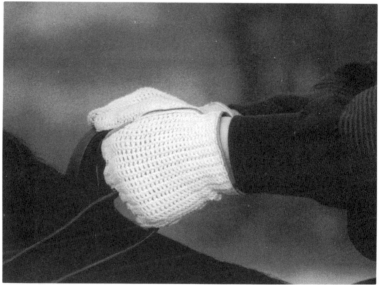

Here the reins are entering the rider's fist in the widest possible way. This method reduces the latitude of influencing and makes the rein contact on the curb the most generalized and mildest of the three ways reins can enter the rider's hands when holding two in each hand.   Photos: Charles Fuller.

in the saddle are not responsible for his athletic development. His hindquarters are not visible. Good riders ride by feel rather than by sight. They should know that the horse's neck and head position are merely symptomatic of the activities of the hind-quarters (locomotion) and the back (communication). They must never use the full bridle, an instrument of sensitivity, insensitively so as to inflict pain on the horse. The full bridle should not break but rather enhance locomotion.

EQUIPMENT IN GENERAL

All equipment should be safe and painless to both horse and rider. Safe and painless equipment depends on its appropriateness and quality. Equipment should be correctly sized, placed, and adjusted. All equipment should be well maintained and looked over often to check its durability and condition.

Beyond suitability and propriety of equipment, rider safety also depends on knowing the horse and dealing with him knowledgeably and lovingly. Rudeness, brutality, and carelessness can become dangerous for the rider. The horse is a placid, phlegmatic, grazing animal. Yet, he has genetically coded instincts for his defense and survival. He uses his defenses instinctively and indiscriminately. Nature provides no time for its creatures to think things over and make decisions based on careful analysis. The kick, the flight, the spin, the strike, the nip, and the bite, all come with the horse and belong in his survival kit. He can mete them all out to his rider without any feeling of malice. The horse cannot change his instincts, which do not include looking after the rider's needs and welfare. The rider must remain alert, circumspect, cautious, and exercise all precautions to avoid injuries and even death.

Epilogue

The ideas in this book now come full circle. In a gesture of recapitulation, I will offer a brief, schematic outline of what I believe horsemanship is all about.

The goal of all riding should be the prolongation of the horse's useful life. Because that depends on more than just good physical care and knowledgeable training, it is rooted in and based on a sincere love for the horse. Not just a specific horse, but a love for all of them.

The duties of riders include the will to develop each horse's nature-given potential to the fullest. Heredity determines the horse's potential for development and performance. But it is the environment, produced and controlled by the rider, that brings the horse's inherited talents to fruition.

The acceptable training methods are based on a commitment that the horse be trained:

1. Lovingly, with his well-being kept foremost in his trainer's mind.
2. Knowledgeably, recognizing that horsemanship is a vast and multifaceted science and is based on scholarship.

3. Gradually, because the horse is a living organism and a unique individual that can develop only at his own rate. The horse is the clock, and he provides the calendar of progress. All measurements of time are useless.

4. Naturally and therapeutically, based on logic that compels the rider to utilize the horse's natural assets. His nature must not be destroyed, rather it should be enhanced, recognizing that anything based on artifice and pretense is destructive and ugly, while the unfolding of the horse's nature produces good for him and beauty for us.

5. Systematically and by repetition and review, allowing the cumulative effects of daily work to reinforce learning. The consistent repetition of useful exercises in the correct manner accelerates progress according to geometric, rather than arithmetic, proportions.

There are two qualitatively different sets of goals:

1. To reestablish the horse's natural balance under the foreign weight of the rider and his equipment. This seemingly simple goal must be pursued every minute while riding and for the duration of the horse's entire athletic career.

2. To unfold the horse's athletic potential and to develop him athletically beyond those limits to which he would voluntarily perform. By human intelligence, insight, and artistry, to add to the horse's motion brilliance through skill and strength. Based on rider-given efficiency and brilliance of motion, the horse will have an educated mind and fully developed body that, if left to his own will and devices, he would not have otherwise achieved. The rider elevates the horse, a creature of nature, to become a monument to art.

The suitable training methods that lead to the achievements of the corresponding goals mentioned above are as follows:

1. Diversification of activities develop a variety of skills and provide the horse with the necessary strength to carry the rider's weight effortlessly in balance. The greater the variety of the tasks, the more interesting and challenging they will

be to the horse. While keeping him alert and contented, the variety of tasks will advance the horse's athletic powers and efficiency. An all-round equine athlete should be developed, with strengthened muscles, suppled joints, stronger ligaments, and hardy bones. The horse's athletic improvement depends also on improving his cardiovascular system.

Work strategies are based on knowing how:

1. Bending creates straightness.
2. Collection facilitates extension and vice versa.
3. Two-track movements supple and strengthen the joints and make the balance more sophisticated.
4. Stretching and contracting the horse's topline elasticizes his muscles.
5. All the school figures we ride must help us diagnose needs, further gymnastic progress, or verify athletic achievements.

The nature of daily work should be:

1. Restorative of balance and rhythm.
2. Therapeutic in straightening spinal alignment and allowing the even loading of the two hind legs, resulting in greater strength.
3. Athletic in the ability to amplify the natural gaits, due to improvements in impulsion, suppleness, elasticity, and engagement.

There is no neutrality in riding! Whatever is done by the rider, whatever he provokes his horse to do, he will learn. The horse cannot discern "right from wrong" because he was never given our standards for doing so. He knows no statistics. He lives and remembers whatever he experiences. His guideline is his ability to distinguish between pain and pleasure. Practice makes master. He masters all we deem "wrong" with the same ease and élan that he masters all things we discern as "right." Therefore, riders ought to do everything they can to produce only desirable actions, memories, and feelings in their horses.

Life in the saddle should include a readiness for the opportunities riding presents. Seize the moment and take what the horse offers if it has any merit. Take chances to give the horse opportunities to dare try a new experience. Know the basic nature, the momentary mood, and the potential anxieties of your horse while in his company.

THE MANY MEANINGS OF ENGAGEMENT

PHYSICAL

Doing something better than it was done before.

Prolonging improved locomotion and self-carriage.

Performing well the most definitive portions of each exercise in progression.

Willing assumption of weight over the haunches: collection.

Surrendering to the will of the rider by:
1. Promptly doing whatever is requested.
2. Carrying him on an elevated and supplely articulating back.
3. Yielding to him the energies of the haunches.

MENTAL

Paying attention to the rider rather than to the diversions of the environment, resulting in discerning the rider's wishes.

Confirming the rider's will by sustaining the activities he prompted.

Discerning the important elements of the action required.

A RECAPITULATION OF THE HORSE'S GYMNASTIC DEVELOPMENT

STAGE	THE HORSE'S BODY	THE HORSE'S GAITS	THE HORSE'S ATTITUDE
Beginning	Relaxed, longitudinal flexion; ability to transmit in full bascule, to carry energies of haunches toward muzzle and terminate it there.	Pure, and return to natural balance horse had without rider.	Relaxed, lacking tension; attentive to the rider; in a dreamlike state, leaving his pasture mentality behind; not acting upon instinct but surrendering his existence to his rider.
Campaign	Loose muscles; increased ability to stretch and contract the muscles; improved lateral ability to bend.	Reflect rhythmic clarity; strengthened demarcation.	Stretch forward and downward, pouring tea from teapot; downward and forward; raise back and stretch neck deeper as rider commands.
Diversified	Improved flexibility of joints.	First impulsion: activity without speed. Increased activity, flexibility, and articulation of joints.	Show beginning of flexing of haunches; rounding of lumbar back; lowering of croup; tilting of pelvis forward; willingness to cover ground with hind legs more toward the muzzle.
Advanced	Gives more elasticity, not just back to front, but from front to back; should allow rein effect of bit to softly travel back and accumulate in haunches.	Cadence; improved suspension; carries rider—carry means lift: progress with lifting action, not just forward action.	Collects and voluntarily begins to shift center of gravity toward haunches instead of tilting to the forehand and running.

A RECAPITULATION OF THE HORSE'S
GYMNASTIC DEVELOPMENT

STAGE	THE HORSE'S BODY	THE HORSE'S GAITS	THE HORSE'S ATTITUDE
Results	The body in all movements is liquid and his entire movement blankets his body.	Fully engaged; shows amplified and maximized action—bigger than he would normally do in pasture.	Bears most of weight on haunches; all the time maintains voluntarily the lumbar thrust; focuses on the rider; has precision on delivering when asked; delivers maximum action without being prompted: He can and he wants to.

Index

References in italics denote photograph or illustration